Praise for *The Dating Divide*

"The authors analyze the data that have been 'hiding in plain sight' to show how the search for love and intimacy is racialized. This asks us to ask ourselves, Is the 'taste' for a homogeneous racial match in itself racist?"

Pepper Schwartz, Professor of Sociology, University of Washington

"Does your race affect whether you get messages on a dating site? Using data from a major dating site, the authors of *The Dating Divide* reveal the sad truth that whether you're white, black, Asian, or Latino/a trumps almost everything else. But the effect of race depends on whether you're a man or woman and whether you're gay or straight. This is the definitive intersectional analysis."

Paula England, Professor of Sociology, New York University

"Online dating offered the potential to dismantle racial boundaries by democratizing courtship. Not only has it failed to deliver, but it has created a unique form of digital-sexual racism marked by white privilege, anti-Blackness, and gendered tropes. These categorical preferences and biases are reconstructed through and within online dating sites under the veil of individual preferences. Based on analyses of millions of dating profiles and in-depth interviews, the authors masterfully show that despite the increasing racial and ethnic diversity of dating pools, dating apartheid remains in place."

Jennifer Lee, Professor of Sociology, Columbia University

"Online dating opens doors for people to meet across racial groups. This groundbreaking study nevertheless uncovers a manifestation of digital-sexual racism in American intimate life, based on data from millions of users on a dating website, along with in-depth interviews of seventy-seven online daters. For understanding race in America, this thought-provoking book is a must-read."

Zhenchao Qian, Professor of Sociology, Brown University

The Dating Divide

The Dating Divide

RACE AND DESIRE IN THE ERA
OF ONLINE ROMANCE

Celeste Vaughan Curington,
Jennifer H. Lundquist, and
Ken-Hou Lin

UNIVERSITY OF CALIFORNIA PRESS

University of California Press
Oakland, California

© 2021 by Celeste Vaughan Curington, Jennifer H. Lundquist, and
Ken-Hou Lin

Library of Congress Cataloging-in-Publication Data

Names: Curington, Celeste Vaughan, 1988– author. | Lundquist, Jennifer
    H., author. | Lin, Ken-Hou, author.
Title: The dating divide : race and desire in the era of online romance /
    Celeste Vaughan Curington, Jennifer H. Lundquist, and Ken-Hou Lin.
Description: Oakland, California : University of California Press, [2021] |
    Includes bibliographical references and index.
Identifiers: LCCN 2020033282 (print) | LCCN 2020033283 (ebook) |
    ISBN 9780520293441 (hardback) | ISBN 9780520293458
    (paperback) | ISBN 9780520966703 (ebook)
Subjects: LCSH: Online dating. | Racism.
Classification: LCC HQ801.82 .C87 2021 (print) | LCC HQ801.82 (ebook) |
    DDC 306.730285—dc23
LC record available at https://lccn.loc.gov/2020033282
LC ebook record available at https://lccn.loc.gov/2020033283

Manufactured in the United States of America

29 28 27 26 25 24 23 22 21
10 9 8 7 6 5 4 3 2 1

Contents

List of Tables and Figures   vii

Introduction: Dear Tinder, Guess Who's Coming
to Dinner   1

1. Where Hate Trumps Love: The Birth and Legacy
   of Antimiscegenation in the United States   24

2. From the Back Porch to the Computer Screen:
   The Rise of Choice in Courtship   45

3. New Rules? Gendered Online Engagement   69

4. A Privilege Endures: Dating While White in the
   Era of Online Dating   82

5. The Unique Disadvantage: Dating While Black   114

6. The Asian Experience: Resistance and Complicity   144

7. "Hey, You're Latin. Do You Like to Dance?":
   The Privilege and Disadvantage of Latino/a Daters   168

8. Postracial Multiracialism: A Challenge to the
   White Racial Frame?   191

Conclusion: Abolishing the Dating Divide   214

Acknowledgments   229
Appendix: Data and Methods   231
Interviews   241
Notes   245
Bibliography   267
Index   297

Tables and Figures

TABLES

A.1. *Descriptive Statistics from Online-Dating Website, Men and Women*   234

A.2. *Interview Participant Demographic Characteristics*   238

FIGURES

I.1.   *Disapproval of Intermarriage between Whites and Non-Whites*   6

I.2.   *Observed versus Random Interracial and Interethnic Marriage Rates*   7

I.3.   *Percentage Intermarried by Race and Sex in the United States*   10

3.1.   *Gender Composition by Race of Users on Online-Dating Platform*   71

4.1.   *Non-White Daters' Relative Likelihood of Messaging White versus Same-Race Men*   84

4.2.   *White Daters' Relative Likelihood of Messaging White versus Minority Men*   85

4.3.   *Non-White Daters' Relative Likelihood of Messaging White versus Same-Race Women*   98

4.4.   *White Daters' Relative Likelihood of Messaging White versus Minority Women*   99

4.5.   *Proportion Strongly Preferring Someone of Their Own Racial Background*   102

4.6.   *White Women's Relative Likelihood of Responding to Minority versus White Men*   102

4.7.   *White Men's Relative Likelihood of Sending to Minority versus White Women*   105

4.8.   *White Men's Relative Likelihood of Sending to Women by Race and Body Type*   107

4.9.   *White Men's Relative Likelihood of Sending to Women by Race and Height*   108

4.10.   *White Women's Relative Likelihood of Responding to Men by Race and Body Type*   109

4.11.   *White Women's Relative Likelihood of Responding to Men by Race and Height*   110

4.12.   *White Women's Relative Likelihood of Responding to Men by Race and Education*   111

4.13.   *White Men's Relative Likelihood of Sending to Women by Race and Education*   112

5.1.   *Black and White Daters' Website-Based Attractiveness by Sexual Orientation, Gender, and Race*   117

5.2.   *Non-Black Daters' Relative Likelihood of Messaging Black versus Same-Race Women*   121

5.3.   *Non-Black Daters' Relative Likelihood of Messaging Black versus Same-Race Men*   122

5.4.   *Black Men's Relative Likelihood of Sending to Non-Black versus Black Women*   131

5.5.   *Black Women's Relative Likelihood of Responding to Non-Black versus Black Men*   131

5.6.   *Gay Black Daters' Relative Likelihood of Messaging Non-Black versus Black Daters*   132

5.7.   *Proportion Strongly Preferring Someone of Their Own Racial Background*   135

6.1. *Non-Asian Daters' Relative Likelihood of Messaging Asian versus Same-Race Men* 155

6.2. *Asian Daters' Relative Likelihood of Messaging Non-Asian versus Asian Men* 156

6.3. *Non-Asian Daters' Relative Likelihood of Messaging Asian versus Same-Race Women* 162

6.4. *Asian Daters' Relative Likelihood of Messaging Non-Asian versus Asian Women* 163

7.1. *Latino/a and White Daters' Website-Based Attractiveness by Sexual Orientation, Gender, and Race* 175

7.2. *Non-Latino/a Daters' Relative Likelihood of Messaging Latino versus Same-Race Men* 176

7.3. *Latino Men's Relative Likelihood of Sending to Non-Latina versus Latina Women* 178

7.4. *Latina Women's Relative Likelihood of Responding to Non-Latino versus Latino Men* 178

7.5. *Gay Latino/a Daters' Likelihood of Messaging Non-Latino/a versus Latino/a Daters* 179

8.1. *White Daters' Relative Likelihood of Messaging Multiracial Daters versus Single Race Daters* 199

8.2. *Asian Daters' Relative Likelihood of Messaging White or Asian-White Daters versus Asian Daters* 200

8.3. *Latino/a Daters' Relative Likelihood of Messaging White or Latino/a-White Daters versus Latino/a Daters* 201

8.4. *Black Daters' Relative Likelihood of Messaging White or Black-White Daters versus Black Daters* 202

Introduction

DEAR TINDER, GUESS WHO'S COMING TO DINNER

Quotidian racism in the American tradition might be
dependent upon economic and political relations, but it
escapes our notice when such relations turn their attention
to the procreative possibilities of our erotic lives.

Sharon Holland, 2014

In the 1967 movie *Guess Who's Coming to Dinner,* a White woman brings
home her Black fiancé to meet her unsuspecting but liberal-minded parents.[1] Released just fifty years after the Ku Klux Klan–idealizing film *Birth
of a Nation* and just six months after antimiscegenation laws were struck
down by the Supreme Court decision in *Loving v. Virginia,* the movie was
as radically provocative as it was acclaimed. Fast forward fifty years, and
we must ask, Is the topic of interracial dating noteworthy anymore?

At least in popular culture, interracial relationships feature across a
multitude of celebrity romances, from Serena Williams and Alexis
Ohanian to Prince Harry and Meghan Markle, and they are no longer rare
in popular television shows and films. A remake of *Guess Who's Coming to
Dinner* was released more recently, to little notice or acclaim (note to
Hollywood producers: when Sidney Poitier's character is played by Ashton
Kutcher, you know you've lost some political edge). Yet, beyond Hollywood,
interracial unions remain rare in the United States. When they do occur,
they are far from universally accepted, often evoking deeply fissured
debates around gender, race, and sexuality. We decided to write this book
because we wanted to understand why.

To social scientists the internet—and the social commentary it fosters—can open a window into what people are really thinking. Amid easy (if incomplete) anonymity and low consequences, people often reveal their innermost, atavistic thoughts and beliefs, especially in moments when they are emotionally charged or under the influence of substances.[2] Thus, the internet provides a powerful lens through which we might see how ordinary people think about sensitive issues such as race, gender, and sex. Their commentaries and comments show us how many people are still scandalized by interracial relations.

Among recent controversies we can point to a 2013 Cheerios commercial in which General Mills featured what appeared to be an interracial family enjoying their breakfast cereal. It was removed from YouTube because so many viewers were enraged by the depiction—and so many racial slurs punctuated the user comments below the video.[3] Another advertising kerfuffle arose around an Old Navy sale promotion in 2016. This spot's biracial family prompted a similar barrage of bigoted responses on Twitter, with the #LoveWins hashtag arising as a sort of counterprotest.[4] These spontaneous expressions of internet racism are not isolated examples but symptoms of a long-simmering problem.[5] The rise or, more accurately, rearticulation of racist and xenophobic fear in this country has emerged, in part, in backlash to the BlackLivesMatter movement and in support of the "Make America Great Again" era of political and personal expression. Racial fear and antipathy and the desire to police strict ethnoracial boundaries are not relics of the past but apparently indelible features of U.S. life.

Intimate life often falls outside the realm of public attention because it is seen as a private affair and it seems, on its face, unremarkable. Indeed, intimate relations are the one remaining area of race relations that, while having received particularly intense scrutiny and regulation in the past, have become obscured from the public. In this book we look at the way race, gender, and desire come together in shaping people's private life in a society that has yet to fully acknowledge or remedy systemic racial oppression.

Much of our research takes advantage of the specific platform of online dating, drawing anonymized data from millions of online interactions to observe how U.S. Americans react to others of different races when their actions are not under the watch of their friends and families. In combination with a separate sample of seventy-seven in-depth interviews with daters of various racial backgrounds and a multitude of archival and secondary sources, we show that interracial relations are not nearly as harmonious in twenty-first-century U.S. life as Hollywood might paint them. At the same time, our research also points to something optimistic: the unprecedented access online dating offers people to find partners different from themselves holds tremendous potential for change in a society that is otherwise still racially segregated.

Online dating has created one of the few remaining public arenas in U.S. society in which it is common to openly express racial preferences—and exclusions. Many daters we interviewed described such preferences as simple matters of attraction, something natural and uncontrollable that, presumably, falls outside the realm of racial prejudice. As one White dater insisted, "Just because you wouldn't want to date someone doesn't mean you're going to culturally oppress them."

But narratives about personal choice have long since obscured prejudice, fear, and desires for segregation. They elide the deep, pervasive impact of historical antimiscegenation sanctions and overstate the equality of contemporary society. They glide past the deep fissures of racial marginalization reflected in and encouraged by centuries of legislation and social practice. Despite what we may tell ourselves, mate preference is never completely personal, nor is racial taste in romantic partners inconsequential. Racial dating preferences may *feel* as though they are natural and vary according to personal taste, but these preferences, in fact, have predictable, systematic patterns that reflect the shameful roots of racism in the United States. main idea

This book connects the evolution of online dating today to the invention of dating in the early twentieth century—a new form of courtship that diminishes familial and state control over intimate choice. This and the growing emphasis of individualism together paved the way for present-day acceptance of racial discrimination in dating. As a form of courtship, dating originated just as the U.S. racial categories we know today were being solidified and regulated through laws and everyday practice. Ironically, this meant that the birth of individual preference and the modern notion of romance were deeply imprinted with racialized desire and calculus. We interrogate the presumption that such preferences are indeed personal and benign, revealing them as the product of exclusionary social constructs that interlock courtship, race, gender, and sexuality.

While we situate the popularity of online dating within the evolution of racialized patterns of courtship, we also find that racial discrimination online has formed a distinct manifestation of racism. Even though deeply rooted in the past, the new form of racism interacts with fast-evolving technologies in ways that produce experiences and consequences distinct from traditional racism. We build from Patricia Hill Collins's concept of "new racism," which operates heavily with the propagation of harmful ideas and images of people of color within the mass media and through the politics of the post–civil rights era.[6] We also draw from Sonu Bedi's work on digitized "private racism," defined as racialized injustice that transpires in the private sphere of the internet, and Ruja Benjamin's work on the New Jim Code, or "the employment of new technologies that reflect and reproduce existing inequities but that are promoted and perceived as more objective or progressive than the discriminatory systems of a previous era."[7] We argue that the contemporary context of neoliberalism, consumerism, *and* the rise of new digital technologies give rise to a unique form of digital-sexual racism—one that disguises enduring racial discrimination in intimate life as nothing more than idiosyncratic individual preference. These "individual preferences," in the meantime, massively and systematically segregate cyberspace, reinforce categorical thinking, and police digital self-presentation, all without the need of in-person avoidance and confrontation.

In fact, even though online dating has the potential to democratize courtship, it has, so far, failed the promise. We illustrate how racial divisions are in fact reproduced through and within the cyberspace context of online dating. Just like how antimiscegenation laws codified racial categories throughout much of the nineteenth and twentieth centuries, twenty-first-century online-dating apps and websites maintain the divide with "ethnic" categories and filtering mechanisms. The seemingly immense opportunity of these platforms demands an efficient search method that comes with constant categorization of people based on markers (skin color, eye shape, hair texture) that are tied to social categories of ascribed difference (race, gender, etc.) As argued by Brandon Robinson, this new racism allows users to filter or ignore entire groups of people on the basis of those markers, yet it remains invisible from the public eye.[8] At the same time, the anonymity fosters aggressive forms of sexual racism that rarely occur in face-to-face courtship markets. We call this "digital-sexual racism," a distinct form of new racism mediated through the impersonal and anonymous context of online dating.

While new technology promises their users greater personal freedom, we argue that the promise is laden with racism and sexism that generate systemic exclusion and alienation. The neoliberal language of individual choice is part and parcel of current digital technologies that have become so deeply ingrained in our lives that they amplify, reinforce, and rationalize oppressive social relations.[9]

Our analysis makes clear that race is the most important predictor of how White daters select whom to date. More often than not, White daters ignore the overtures of racial and ethnic minority daters with (conventionally) more desirable education background, height, and body type, while being responsive to those without similar qualities but are White. Some racial and ethnic minority daters develop strategies to navigate this racially hostile dating world, while at other times they themselves internalize and reproduce this pervasive digital-sexual racism. These findings suggest that, as online-dating technologies increasingly replace local, in-person markets of romantic interaction, daters use these private tools free from social sanction to even more efficiently apartheidize their dating experiences.

WHAT IS THE CURRENT STATE OF INTERRACIAL INTIMATE UNIONS?

U.S. Americans have altered their public stance dramatically on interracial marriage since the midtwentieth century. In 1958, the first time Gallop ran an opinion poll that asked U.S. Americans whether they approved of marriage between Whites and non-Whites, 96 percent of respondents voiced disapproval. By 2013 that portion was only 13 percent (see figure I.1 for trends over time). Strikingly, Black Americans have always been far more supportive of interracial marriages than Whites. The gap, to be sure, has narrowed significantly, but the overall difference is still substantial. In the late 1960s about half as many Black Americans as

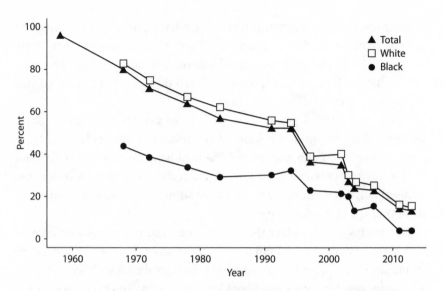

Figure I.1. Disapproval of Intermarriage between Whites and Non-Whites. In 1969 Gallop began separating survey responses by race identity. *Source:* Calculated by authors using Gallop polling data accessed from Jones and Saad, "Gallup Poll Social Series."

Whites disapproved of interracial marriage (at 44 percent compared to 83 percent). Today, although both populations have become far more open, Whites are still nearly four times more likely than Blacks to voice disapproval for interracial marriage (at 15 percent compared to 4 percent).

No other social opinion in the history of the U.S. Gallop Survey has reversed so completely over time. In just five decades the vast majority of U.S. Americans went from disapproving to approving of interracial marriage. Some of this shift reflects generational change. The disapproval trends shown in figure I.1 would be all but nonexistent if we limited surveys to gathering only the opinions of young adults, given that younger generations tend to voice more progressive views toward race. The only other comparable shift in public opinion relates to gay rights, but that lags far behind a level that might be called near-universal support.

Another barometer for testing attitudes about interracial marriage is the extent to which groups participate in the practice.[10] The intimate act of marriage between two people from different groups provides an indicator of social distance, and social scientists have argued that an increasing

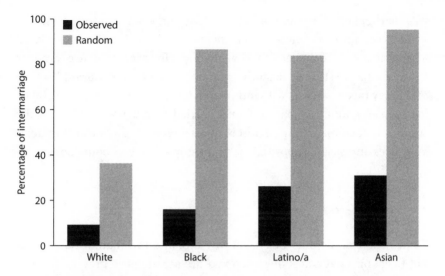

Figure 1.2. Observed versus Random Interracial and Interethnic Marriage Rates.
Source: Calculated by authors using data from U.S. Census Bureau, *Decennial Census Datasets;* and Taylor, Passel, and Wang, *Marrying Out.*

prevalence of marriage between racial and ethnic groups over time suggests fading prejudice.[11] Moreover, intermarriage itself drives further racial integration, interrupting channels of resource and wealth acquisition that have been historically concentrated among White families.

Despite the sea change in public opinion, actual intermarriage rates are low. Only 6.3 percent of current U.S. marriages are interracial.[12] If we include Latinos/as as a distinct group in these measures, intermarriage rates would still tally up to only 17 percent of current unions.[13] Figure I.2 compares actual intermarriage to the rates we would expect if marriages happened at random across the population. Comparing the observed bars to the random bars, we see that, across every racial and ethnic group, the actual intermarriage rates are three to five times lower than what they could be. These numbers point to a large and ongoing racial divide in marriage partners.

A number of studies have also indicated that cohabiting and dating partnerships are more likely than marriages to be interracial.[14] Indeed, while intermarriage continues to be a meaningful indicator of race relations, changes in U.S. society have made marriage less central than it once was, particularly for young adults in their early- and midtwenties. The wider acceptance of nonmarital partnership and cohabitation has delayed and even begun to replace marital unions. However, evidence suggests these unions are still significantly separated by racial boundaries. Because of the way race intersects with intimacy in virtually all contexts, cohabitating couples, nonmarital partners, and married couples are all subject to the scrutiny that animates our interest in racial preference and racial hierarchy. Why does our racial "happy talk" seem to stop at the bedroom door?[15]

PREJUDICE? OR LACK OF EXPOSURE TO OTHERS?

Some people argue that the reason why U.S. interracial unions are rare is not racial bias but a lack of social exposure across racial groups. There is no question that residential segregation continues to be a defining feature of U.S. society, despite legislation from the civil rights era onward.[16] In addition to leading to a pernicious concentration of disadvantage, segregation severely limits cross-racial exposure in everyday life. Beyond the neighborhood, segregation patterns spill out across school districts, churches, and employment settings. As a result, the U.S. population is diverse, but most people are in only infrequent contact with people from other racial backgrounds. The contact that exists is rarely meaningful. This is particularly true of Blacks and Whites, both of whom are more segregated from each other than they are from any other group.[17]

Racial segregation and the consequent lack of exposure is more profound than simple spatial impediment. Lack of familiarity can lead people to develop problematic perceptions of those who are socially distant—in this case, people from racial groups other than their own. Unfamiliarity may exaggerate any difference—from religious traditions to tastes in music, for example—such that it seems like a clear indicator of romantic incompatibility. Worse, separation reinforces stereotypes and fuels racist antagonism.[18] As a result, racial bias and racial segregation are not independent reasons behind the rarity of interracial unions—they are mutually reinforcing causes of ongoing separation.

In the United States explicit racial prejudice among Whites has certainly declined. However, Whites' growing commitment to racial equality does not mean they don't still harbor implicit biases that favor Whites over other groups.[19] In the long run, U.S. Americans may have become more tolerant of difference in theory, but tolerance—and the rhetoric of tolerance—may have little bearing on choosing intimate partners.

Race also operates intersectionally, or in ways structured by combinations of statuses, like race *and* gender *and* sexuality. This intersectionality is perhaps nowhere as clear as within intermarriage. Black men are twice as likely as Black women to marry outside of their racial group, but it is the reverse among Asian women, who are more than twice as likely as Asian men to marry non-Asians. These trends contradict what some theories would predict, given that Black women and Asian men, on average, have higher levels of education. Thus, the gender differences are unlikely to be explained by individual characteristics. Most likely, as argued by gendered racial formation theory, they reflect pathologized notions of desirability and ideals of masculinity and femininity.[20]

Throughout U.S. history the White racial frame has cast Whiteness as the virtuous baseline—and all other races as inferior deviations.[21] Combined with gender norms, the White frame has produced an intersectional hierarchy of desirability. The most typical of these are images that associate passive femininity with Asians and hypermasculinity with Blacks. Played out intersectionally, this leads to emasculated, negative images of Asian men and compliant, sexually alluring images of Asian women. The same frame produces images of Black men as dangerously virile and Black women as unfeminine and overly dominant.[22] Despite the apparent contrasts in how these associations play out for different groups, make no mistake: they are all forms of dehumanization. The mosaic of controlling images that perpetuate harmful stereotypes may be driving some of the outmarriage trends seen in figure 1.3.[23] They are certainly firmly embedded in the legacies of the United States' racial history and contribute to the intersectional asymmetry of inclusion.

These harmful stereotypes further serve to justify racial inequality because they obscure the structural arrangements that lead to unequal concentrations of power; that is, stereotypes emphasize individual and group flaws as the ultimate explanation for differential opportunities and outcomes. The results of racist structures are, in turn, utilized to justify unequal treatment and otherwise reinforce White advantage.

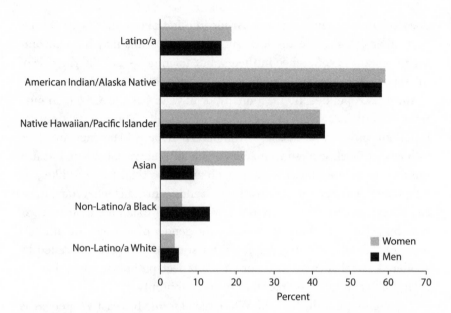

Figure 1.3. Percentage Intermarried by Race and Sex in the United States. Source: R. Kreider, "Married Couple Households."

As Patricia Hill Collins asserts, all of these "controlling images" concern, first and foremost, sexuality. But it is clear that narratives of sexual deviance create, solidify, and justify many other racial distinctions. Joane Nagel argues that such sexualization of outgroups is a ubiquitous, universal feature of power in the role of interethnic relations—that is, alleging the sexual depravity of "others" versus the moral innocence of "us" is a central construct of White racial hegemony.[24] Written histories of colonialism and conquest, for example, often include graphic depictions of the sexual depravity of subaltern groups encountered during the "civilizing" process. In the Americas early colonists detailed the problematic and lewd sexual practices observed among indigenous people, which later served to justify warfare and extermination policies.[25] African sexuality was similarly depicted by Europeans and later U.S. Americans, likewise helping to legitimate enslavement.[26]

While the White gaze remains dominant today, it is also true that marginalized groups—even if they internalize some of the oppressors' cultural ideologies—often develop alternative hierarchies of desirability that resist White beauty standards. This resistance to White or closer-to-White beauty standards was frequently mentioned by the minority daters we interviewed, and it, too, is critical to understanding how race influences dating preferences.

Moreover, although gendered racial hierarchy produces animus within and across racial groups, we find that the behavioral difference between men and women is much smaller than popular stereotypes suggest. For example, despite the fact that Black men and Asian women outmarry more often than their same-race counterparts, the vast majority of Black and Asian Americans still seek unions within their own racial groups. This book examines how all racial groups make sense of these dynamics by interrogating the social construction of racial preference in dating. We elucidate how dating decisions and ideologies are nested within relations of power.

THE LONG LEGACY OF HISTORICAL ANTIMISCEGENATION LAWS

As the United States diversifies, some scholars have called on their peers to move beyond the Black-White binary focus on racial oppression, prejudice, and race relations. Juan Perea influentially argued that race scholars often problematically ignore racial groups other than White and Black and that, when they do acknowledge these groups, it is only briefly and only because they feel required to designate where a given group falls in the middle ground of the Black-White axis.[27]

In this book we push past the binary to analyze intimate relations among Blacks, Asians, Latinos, Whites, and multiracial daters. Still, we also subscribe theoretically to the Afro-pessimist perspective that, as Jared Sexton put it, highlights the "specificity of anti-blackness" under White supremacy.[28] Particularly in the United States, the Black-White monolithic remains a principal racial dialectic that undergirds White supremacy.[29]

To understand where racial partner preferences come from, we must first delve into the history of the U.S. racial divide in intimate life. This is an uneasy task in a country that has yet to fully come to terms with its own history of racial violence and exclusion. Specifically, we must begin with the peculiar relic and weapon of anti-Blackness that marks our history of intimate racial boundaries: antimiscegenation laws.

Antimiscegenation laws in North America date back to well before the founding of the republic. Some were enacted as early as the seventeenth century. At its core miscegenation policies were explicitly intended to prohibit Black-White unions. But they were also used, albeit more haphazardly, to police the marriages of Whites with non-Black racial outgroups. In the midnineteenth century, the majority of the population of several southern states were Black.[30] When slavery was abolished, White southerners feared a demographic "White genocide" threat, a moral panic that might rather be forgotten by the White majority today but thrives among the White nationalist alt-right.[31]

Antimiscegenation laws, which proliferated such that they became key to Jim Crow after the Civil War and Reconstruction, became weapons in a war to maintain the social and political privilege of Whites. They all but ensured a postslavery racial caste system. Between 1874 and 1913 the number of states passing antimiscegenation laws nearly doubled.[32] Such laws perpetuated and reinvented anti-Blackness in response to a brief, post–Civil War rise in Black political, economic, and social power, especially in the U.S. South. Indeed, Jim Crow policies were so effective in preventing Black-White racial integration that the architects of the Third Reich in Germany and the apartheid regime in South Africa would draw inspiration from the United States in constructing their own antiassimilation laws and policies.[33]

In 1967 the Supreme Court decision in *Loving v. Virginia* determined that all state antimiscegenation laws and laws criminalizing interracial sex were unconstitutional. However, many of these laws remained on the books until recently. The last two state-level antimiscegenation laws were not overturned until 1998 (South Carolina) and 2000 (Alabama). Even where antimiscegenation policy and the racial ideologies that it perpetuated were no longer legally enforced, the ideologies of racial separation had become accepted ways of life. Their legacy is now self-enforcing, perpetuating the centrality of race in intimacy and family formation. Throughout this book we will marshal extensive data to discuss the evolution and consequence of this history, well into the present era.

RACIAL CHOICE NARRATIVES AS SEXUAL RACISM

One intriguing, and telling, aspect of the online-dating industry is that it is one of the only venues left in modern-day U.S. society where it remains acceptable to articulate racial preferences. In education, employment, housing, and lending, racial preferences have been recognized as not only legally but also *morally* wrong. Yet racial categories are explicitly and unapologetically part of the selection process of dating websites. Many of the most popular dating sites ask users to specify their racial preferences in their profiles and codify them with partner searches filtered by race. We challenge readers to name another public venue in which it is socially acceptable—or legal—to ask individuals to indicate whether they prefer some races over others.[34] In any other public context, we believe, the open expression of racial preference would be condemned, boycotted, and even prosecuted as unlawful discrimination.

The use of racial preference on dating sites points to several complicated but critical issues underlying the formation of race itself. We cannot talk about race in the dating context without having a conversation about racialization—that is, the social construction of race through which we attach meaning to racial categories that carry economic, political, and social consequences. It is an oxymoron to describe racial preferences as individual because race is by definition a social construct, a manufactured distinction generated through the regulation of intimate life.

For centuries the state has taken keen interest in encouraging and policing marriage by racial status. The individual choice stories we tell about mate preferences today are connected to the legacy of antimiscegenation laws and racially segregated social practices and go beyond Black-White binaries to affect the dating choices we see among all racial groups. It has not been so long—no more than a generation—since intermarriage laws were on the books, and so intermarriage norms remain on our minds.

Attempts to resist a critical examination of racial preferences, such as narratives about chemistry or homophily, take existing racial boundaries for granted and rationalize them as natural. They fail to recognize that the preferences for similarity, as well as for difference, have a social basis. Individuals we interviewed talk about it openly, saying, for example, "I'm just not *into* Asians," in much the same way they might talk about their dietary or music preferences. But, of course, it's a false equivalence: one's preferences for White partners are not so innocent as preferences for anchovies or avocados.

During our research for this book, we asked a group of predominantly White college students their opinion of people being able to filter their searches by race on dating apps and websites. A full 64 percent of them had no problem with it at all. Commonly, we heard that racialized sexual attraction is effable and uncontrollable: "If you know you are only attracted to one specific race or look, then that's that. It's not something we can control," said one respondent. Others believed that racial preference was merely idiosyncratic, on par with physical preferences: "I prefer people with blue or green eyes. That doesn't mean I'm generally prejudiced against dark-eyed people. I have brown eyes myself," we heard. Many people we interviewed were clearly invested in the idea that personal choice in intimate partners is above critique or judgment, even when that choice means a rejection of entire racial categories. One gay White man who excluded Black and Asian profiles from his dating-site searches rhetorically asked us, "Does the fact that I'm also not into women make me a sexist?"

Certainly, some people, particularly racial and ethnic minority daters, saw stating racial preferences as a form of racism. Others accepted the existence of racial preference with an air of inevitability, indicating that what bothered them more was the normalization inherent in such assertions. For example, a Latina woman told us she thought it was okay to have the preference, but it was not okay to check a box and filter potential dates by race. "If it's a subconscious thing, it's less problematic than if you verbalize it and make a conscious decision. Like, 'I'm only gonna look at White guys.'" These sentiments contain undercurrents of modern, color-blind racism, where racialized sentiment is considered impolite, but implicit racial biases are granted tacit allowance.[35]

Does this mean that daters who are more attracted to some races over others *are racist?* Many would disagree with such a claim, countering that partner choice is a question of individual desire, not a matter of prejudice or racial superiority. To be very clear—it is not our objective or intention to judge *individuals* for their personal dating preferences: in some cases, individual racism could play little part in why one person marries another of the same racial background. So too might interracial relationships be formed in a context rife with overt racism. Instead, our aim is to call into question the naive views that intimate racial preferences are natural, apolitical, and inconsequential. Indeed, as we show throughout this book, societal forces that insist on a racial hierarchy of desire shape our intimate desires, whether or not we'd like to address that fact.[36]

IS SEXUAL DESIRE A TOPIC FOR PUBLIC SCRUTINY?

People's intimate lives are often eschewed from scrutiny, both because they are hidden and also because the private realm is considered sacred from the purview of the public. However, in the 1980s more and more feminist scholars began to call this claim into question.[37] Kimberlee Crenshaw observed that the "process of recognizing as social and systemic what was formerly perceived as isolated and individual . . . characterized the identity politics of African Americans, other people of color, and gays and lesbians, among others."[38] Indeed, as feminist groups and activists identified how the politics of power and rape, and the intersection between racism and patriarchy, were embedded in the formation of mainstream sexual expression, they argued that sexual desire often goes hand in hand with political power. But this perspective failed to gain mainstream political traction, within both the dominant liberal feminist discourse and nonfeminist discourses of the day.

Today, despite these scholars' efforts, sexual preference is still widely considered to be personal and, therefore, neutral in its relationship to power. If anything, sexual desires and preferences are considered rights that need to be protected from public sanction. As one of our interviewees insisted about racial preference in online dating: "I think it's your choice. It's your body. It's your life!" In this way sexual preference is seen by many as synonymous with sexual freedom.

Yet the reluctance to acknowledge the political implications of sexual desire means that we also frame racial sexual preference as something outside political and social constructs. What happened to "the personal is political"?[39] The concept of sexual racism, first coined in 1976 in Charles Stember's analysis of Black and White heterosexual relations, is gaining new traction today as internet content, ranging from pornography to online dating, makes once-private sexual fantasies and desire abundantly visible.[40] Black feminist and critical race scholars have also long challenged the idea that sexual preference is nothing more than individualized taste. Instead, they point to how the social construction of personal preference masks racism and sexism and how the legacy of slavery and colonialism continues to haunt our erotic lives.[41]

We join this critical inquiry because the rhetoric of personal choice invokes randomness and idiosyncrasy, but our research shows that it maps precisely onto existing racial hierarchies that have been identified and condemned in other spheres. Logics such as whimsical personal preference or natural affinity stem from a false distinction so often drawn between the private and the public spheres—the same rhetoric that drew feminist ire in response to the regulation of women's bodies. If we can acknowledge that race is a social construct, we cannot deny that the categories of desire are *also* socially constructed. In language that presages the Holland quote opening this introduction, Rosemary Hennessy once wrote, "When desire is understood as lust, where lust is equated with a basic human drive, its historical production becomes invisible."[42] We cannot change what we cannot see. Accordingly, we seek to render the very real role of historical production in racialized dating preference *visible*.

INTERRACIAL INTIMACY THREATENS WHITE PRIVILEGE AND POWER

Intimate relations between racial groups have long been viewed as deeply subversive, potentially fueling powerful social change and disruption. In the years following the Civil War and the collapse of Reconstruction, it was the threat of White-Black sexual reproduction that ultimately drove Jim Crow legislation. Racial amalgamation directly threatened the caste system by expanding other groups' access to White privilege and power, not least by making it possible that mixed-race persons might "pass" as White. While the decision in *Loving v. Virginia* in 1967 to ban antimiscegenation laws is sometimes seen as less important than other twentieth-century civil rights cases that ended school segregation and employment discrimination, its impact has been critical in the fight against the legacies of structural racism.

The legal scholar Dorothy Roberts argues that it was, in fact, more foundational than any other case for dismantling White supremacy.[43]

School segregation, for example, was at least partly put in place to mitigate against the kind of White-Black contact that might lead to intimate relations.[44] Later, during the civil rights era, this same fear of interracial sex and procreation still fueled White anxiety. For instance, in a widely distributed pamphlet that also was reprinted in a 1956 an article about school race integration written by a southerner in the *Atlantic Monthly* identified primary school as a site where the South must insist on maintaining racial separation. The author suggested that northern states' support for desegregation revealed their ignorance of the risks of intimate relations, such that

> race preference is not active in the very young. Race preference (which the propagandists miscall race prejudice or hate) is one of those instincts which develop gradually as the mind develops and which, if taken in hand early enough, can be prevented from developing at all. . . . That is the compelling reason, though by no means the only reason, why the South will resist, with all its resources of mind and body, the mixing of the races in its public schools.

The article also states, "Northern support of school integration in the South is due to the failure to realize its inevitable biological effect in regions of large Negro population. If Northerners did realize this, their enthusiasm for mixed schools in the South would evaporate at once."[45] The author's reference to "race preference" is an argument that bubbles up today, sixty-some years later, in conversations about whether sexual preference on online-dating profiles reflects prejudice or natural instinct.

In the United States the state no longer explicitly enforces a racial hierarchy of desire and reproduction. We citizens do that all by ourselves. As we illustrate throughout this book, the media continues to propagate messages and images that exalt men and women who tilt closest to Whiteness, while marginalizing non-White femininities and masculinities. Families and peer networks shape, reproduce, and enforce racialized desire. And individuals internalize the regulatory gaze of antimiscegenation and police themselves in a panopticon-like realm of seemingly limitless mate choices.

The widespread rhetoric in U.S. culture that champions individual choice and consumption in all areas of life obscures the role of history and culture in shaping sexual preferences—despite how strongly people believe those choices to be based on their own autonomous preferences. The extensive data, interviews, and other evidence that we present demonstrates the profound influence of the past in our present-day personal lives through the new manifestation of digital-sexual racism.

In a place like the United States, where subordinate masculinities and femininities have been constructed as antithetical to White hegemonic ideals of beauty and desirability, the choice to match, mate, and love with someone like oneself takes on additional meaning. Indeed, beyond the policing of Black-White boundaries, in the nineteenth century Asian marriage and reproduction were actively suppressed. Asian women were banned from the country, and Asians were constructed, legally and socially, as racially unmarriageable to Whites and unassimilable to the United States. Latinos in the United States have a different history of discrimination—but they too have been targeted in antimiscegenation law.

Interestingly, the long legacy of racial regulation and repression has also prompted minority movements promoting intraracial marriage and courtship. For instance, the curtailment of African American marriage and sexual freedom fed into Black Love and Black Is Beautiful movements that construed same-race marriage as a political obligation aligned with Black pride. When marginalized groups choose to date someone like themselves, we must consider how those decisions are *also* shaped by the power systems that inform the social construction of racial hierarchies, preferences, and modes of resistance.

ORGANIZATION OF THIS BOOK

This book provides an in-depth analysis of dating behavior in the twenty-first century, documenting racial preferences among Asians, Blacks, Latinos, Whites, and multiracial daters across sexual orientations. We have gleaned insights from extensive in-person qualitative research as well as data from one of the largest online-dating websites in the United States.

In chapter 1, "Where Hate Trumps Love: The Birth and Legacy of Antimiscegenation in the United States," we situate current romantic dynamics within the history of U.S. marriages, race relations, antimiscegenation laws (which prohibited cross-racial mixing), and immigration policies (which limited marital choice). We trace how racial preferences were both constructed and legitimated through laws before the civil rights era and how they were recast as benign in the modern rhetoric of individual choice. We illustrate how these legal imperatives aided in the solidification of racial categories, demonstrating the inextricable linkages between the social constructions of race, gender, and personal preference. This manifests itself today in a new online form of digital-sexual racism.

In chapter 2, "From the Back Porch to the Computer Screen: The Rise of Choice in Courtship," we look at the late nineteenth-century transformation of courtship that coincided with the reformation of postemancipation racial identities. As courtship evolved away from family- and community-centered institutions into individualistic behavior, its practices remained nested in nationwide initiatives to reinforce racial distinctions. Thus, the view that Whites and racial minority groups should not mix and marry became self-enforcing as it filtered into individual courtship choices. The advent of online dating represents potential for the highest degree of sexual freedom by lessening dependence on third-party introductions and increasing cross-racial contact, but self-regulation against cross-racial contact has substantially muted this opportunity. The consumption-oriented aspects of online dating allow daters to rationalize this process as akin to a whole constellation of quotidian consumer choices. This dynamic has set the stage for a new form of digital-sexual prejudice that is hidden under the guise of choice.

Chapter 3, "New Rules? Gendered Online Engagement," focuses on several important issues relating to gender construction. Despite the potential for transformation in an online space, traditional gender norms reentrench themselves, with women rarely initiating contact and men driving most interactions. Similarly, straight men are particularly compelled by the physical attributes of potential partners. Straight women, with the notable exception of their fixation on men's height, tend to focus on educational status and personality attributes. Lesbian and gay daters, however, described greater freedom in the online context to experiment and play with gender norms. This raises the question of whether racial hierarchies, like gender norms, play out differently among gay and straight daters. This chapter acts as a gateway into the empirical chapters focusing on major racial groups.

In chapter 4, "A Privilege Endures: Dating While White in the Era of Online Dating," we discuss and dissect the narrative of White masculinity in crisis with relation to intimacy choices. Our analyses show that all groups of women and most gay men respond to White men. In other words, White men continue to be advantaged romantically, even more so than White women. We illustrate the specific operation of anti-Blackness among White men, who tend to accept all but Black women as romantic options when dating online, while White women exclude all non-White men. We consider how racial and ethnic minority groups interpret these trends and explore some Black women's conscious subversion of the White frame.

In chapter 5, "The Unique Disadvantage: Dating While Black," we explore the duality in which digital-sexual racism manifests in themes of simultaneous hypervisibility and invisibility, where Black women and men are simultaneously ignored *and* hyperracialized by non-Black daters. We document gendered patterns of interracial partnership, including how women's intimacy is policed more rigorously than men's in Black communities and how educated Black women prefer same-race, similarly educated partners, while facing significant barriers when they attempt to carry out those preferences. Black women and men's shared disadvantages in the dating market allow us a lens through which to see the ways their romantic experiences are deeply shaped by race *and* gender.

In chapter 6, "The Asian Experience: Resistance and Complicity," we discuss how the transformation of controlling images from "yellow peril" to "model minority" has alienated Asian masculinity while embracing a specific portrait of Asian femininity. Similar to Black men, Asian women are criticized for their relatively high outmarriage rates. They often frame outmarriage as resistance to Asian patriarchy, but such arguments ignore Whites' gender oppression and Asian fetishization. Indeed, many of the Asian women we interviewed exhibited uncertainty about the intentions of non-Asian daters, or what we call "ambiguous fetishization." We find that the prevalence of intermarriage between Asian women and White men is not driven by White men's pursuit patterns, as is often claimed, and that both Asian men and women engage in anti-Blackness in their dating preferences, reflecting their place in the triracial hierarchy.

Chapter 7, "'Hey, You're Latin. Do You Like to Dance?': The Privilege and Disadvantage of Latino/a Daters," turns to the often-contradictory position of Latino/a daters in a racialized and gendered desirability hierarchy. As they have for Asian Americans, controlling images have historically perpetuated stereotypes pertaining to Latino's/Latina's race, gender, and sexuality. These images remain in circulation, at times inciting sexual interest while also limiting a diverse community's power for self-definition. We explore how the intersection of transnational color, family, and gendered hierarchies nest within a traditional racial binary in the United States, such that some Latinos/as see incentives to vie for a better position in the desirability hierarchy of the new digital-sexual racism. Sometimes this leads to anti-Blackness. Often it leads to the internalization of colorism.

In chapter 8, "Postracial Multiracialism: A Challenge to the White Racial Frame?," we explore the experiences and treatment of mixed-race individuals in online dating. We find that multiracial White daters are afforded a relatively privileged status in the desirability hierarchy, apart from both White and other monoracial daters. However, this effect is tinted by gender—minority women generally privilege Whiteness and White multiraciality over minority men, while minority men treat their monoracial minority and multiracial coethnics equally and display a disinterest in Whiteness. The online nature of digital-sexual racism amplifies the sexual objectification of multiracial daters by others who attempt to visually dissect their bodies in ways that reify phenotypes. While holding, in general, a more inclusive view when it comes to dating in *theory*, multiracial daters still reproduce patterns of anti-Blackness *in practice*. Taken together, our findings suggest that the burgeoning U.S. multiracial population will not necessarily undermine the existing racial hierarchy, which remains buttressed by gendered anti-Black bias.

We conclude this book by exploring potential responses to this new racism. We strongly believe that the providers of dating services are responsible for mitigating digital-sexual racism through not only public messaging to their clientele but also a critical examination of the design of their services. They can intentionally frame their platforms to communicate core values of respectful discourse and racially and gender progressive philosophy. The emphasis on search efficiency should not be an excuse to reduce individuals to categories and, in this process, amplify the significance of racial categories. It does not have to be this way.

But more important than what any company can do, we as U.S. Americans must reflect and engage in public conversation about intimacy and race. Individuals bear a social obligation to think deeply about whether and why they have certain racial preferences and seriously consider a commitment to disrupting what may feel like a natural inclination. After all, as we fight racial justice in "public life," we must also remember that every hopeful click and swipe, no matter how trivial it seems, has lasting implications to the racial division in the United States.

A NOTE ON THE DATA AND METHODS USED IN THIS BOOK

Unless otherwise specified, the statistical analyses presented in this book are based on the confidential data we obtained from a major dating website in the United States. We have access to not only the profiles of more than one million users all over the country but also how they interacted with other users of various racial identities. Because these interactions took place privately, they provide a behind-the-scenes portrait of how U.S. Americans make their most personal decisions. Unlike swiping apps like Tinder, in which messages cannot be sent until both daters have indicated mutual interest, this dating platform places no controls on who can send an initial message and who can respond.

As much as these statistical analyses are useful in showing general patterns, they reveal little about the meanings and motivations behind these decisions. To understand how race intertwines with desirability, we thus conducted seventy-seven in-depth interviews with online daters from diverse racial backgrounds and sexual identities. These interviews provide tremendous insight into what we cannot see in the dating-site data: what people *think* and *feel* about race when they decide whom to approach and whom to avoid (at least, what people are willing to admit to researchers that they think and feel). More often than not, we see that daters are aware that race plays an important role in shaping their perceptions of complete strangers. Extensive archival research supplements our quantitative and qualitative analysis by giving us a window into the ways race has always separated people in the United States. We present compelling evidence that gendered racism is still deeply ingrained in our most intimate decisions. More details about our data sources and analytic approaches are discussed in the appendix.

1 Where Hate Trumps Love

THE BIRTH AND LEGACY OF ANTIMISCEGENATION IN THE UNITED STATES

People are trapped in history, and history is trapped
in them.

James Baldwin

Maude Broyles and Jim Torney, two Alabama teenagers, ran away together
in the summer of 1888 with romantic visions of a secret elopement. A
minister's child from Hayneville, sixteen-year-old Jim worked as a laborer
for his fiancée's wealthy father. That hot July afternoon, some 140 miles
northeast of Jim's home town, a group of White men tracked the couple
down on Trout Creek Mountain. They brutally tortured, lynched, and
killed Jim. Maude, also sixteen, "fought her captors with the fury of a
tigress" in a futile effort to save his life.[1] The crime? He was Black and she
was White. From emancipation through the first half of the twentieth century, thousands were killed—often publicly tortured to death by White
mobs—for crossing, or being alleged to have crossed, color lines. Black
men were murdered with impunity for allegedly raping White women, no
matter if there was any evidence they had actually done so.[2]

Long before Europeans engaged in the transatlantic slave trade in the
sixteenth century, the European worldview held particular animus toward
"darkness" and positive associations with all things White.[3] Their long-
standing objection to non-European cultures, especially those with darker
skin tones than their own, was that they were "uncivilized." During the colonial era hostility toward racial intermixing was imported to the Americas by

Euro-Whites. As they colonized the North American continent during the sixteenth and seventeenth centuries—a massive project that hinged on the enslavement of millions of Africans as well as the forced removal and geno-cide of indigenous populations—they established a society that centered around both Whiteness and the capitalist imperative. To maintain their preferred social hierarchy, Euro-Whites introduced antimiscegenation laws to prevent sexual and marital unions that might produce children with the potential to upset the carefully constructed divide between their alleged civilized, virtuous, and deserving people from, well, the *rest*.

One of the first antimiscegenation laws in North America was passed in Maryland in 1664. It prohibited marriages between "'freeborne English women' and 'Negro slaues [sic].'" Fifteen years later a similar law was passed in Louisiana (New France) where the colonial government reasoned that White French men who intermarried with the indigenous population would become less loyal. Of course, there was a clear racial dimension to this law too, expressed by anxieties around "the adulteration that such marriages will cause to the whiteness and purity of the children."[4] Colonial restrictions on marriage both between Whites and enslaved Blacks and among the enslaved themselves would spread through the early republic's states, including non-slave states. Whites often could not marry even free Blacks.[5]

Over the sweep of U.S. history, Black-White intermixing in particular was the subject of White virulent fear and loathing. However, violence of the kind Jim and Maude experienced rose sharply after the abolition of slavery in 1860. Previously, there had been more flexibility in such unions. For example, in the antebellum United States, interracial relationships and even some marriages had not been uncommon among the indentured and working classes of the North and the non–property-owning classes in the South. Among White elites, however, who were more bound by the dictates of social closure, fraternization across racial lines was rare, and marital relations were restricted to alliances within class strata so as to preserve status and social influence across generations.[6] (This is one rea-son why marriage between cousins was common among elites: it tidily consolidated property and power within genealogical lines.)

Because elites used marriage to sustain social status, they sought to control who was allowed to marry whom. Primarily, marital control involved policing the sexuality of White women, a thread that would run through the enforcement of antimiscegenation and antifornication laws forged throughout U.S. history.[7] As historian Peggy Pascoe points out, the very first prohibitions on interracial marriages were gender-specific: White women who married Black men were, along with any children, enslaved by law, while White men who married Black women were perhaps sneered at but not formally punished.[8]

The regulation of women's sexuality was important not just for its practical role in managing bloodlines but also because women's bodies were symbolic repositories seen as demarcating racial identity. This gendered dynamic is reflected in the codification of seventeenth-century status-of-mother clauses, which stipulated that children's status be inherited matrilineally. Intimate relations in the antebellum South among White men and Black women (frequently rape) were tolerated by White society and seldom problematized legally because they did not disrupt racialized norms of chattel slavery, property, and propriety.[9]

In the plantation economy, where additional workers meant additional assets, the sexual exploitation of Black women doubly served the master's interest by creating a new supply for his enslaved labor force. Since they were considered property within the reproductive chattel system, enslaved women were not afforded the protections from sexual abuse granted to White women. They were denied the patriarchal protection of Black fathers and brothers, and the legal system often recast Black women victims as sexual aggressors.[10] This served to further justify their exploitation by White men, while redirecting the anger and disgust of White wives toward Black women.[11] The normalization of sexual violence and blame toward Black men remains a shameful legacy in U.S. society today.

Sexual relations between Black men and White women during the era of slavery was less common—in part, because White society interpreted these relations *only* as rape. As a result, it was much rarer for mixed-race children to be born to a White woman. (Again, we see how a racist mentality of the past still flashes in the contemporary moment: consider, for example, that when Dylan Roof killed nine Black people in a Charleston church in 2015, he claimed it was because "they rape White women").[12] Because of status-of-mother clauses, the mixed-race children of White women were uniquely threatening to the social order that suffused the slavery-based U.S. economy: unlike offspring of Black enslaved women and White slave-owning men, White women's mixed-race children could theoretically be born *free*. To suppress this threat many women who had sexual relations with Black men and did *not* claim rape were punished. In some states such women would be forced into servitude.[13] This disjuncture—where White women's bodies were policed to avoid them giving birth to free mixed-race children, while Black women's mixed-race children were born into slavery—was later utilized by eugenicists in pseudoscientific terms to argue for a historical purity of the White race in the United States (and their racist logics would be adopted, for instance, by the architects of the Third Reich in their attempted extermination of European Jews).[14]

There are two main reasons that intimacy between Black men and White women, while stigmatized by antebellum Whites, was met with ever-more violent retribution by Whites *after* emancipation.[15] The first has to do with the simple fact that during slavery Black men were property whose bodies were economically valuable. The second hinges on threat: unlike freedmen, enslaved Black men were not politically or economically threatening to White men. The institution of slavery superseded all social distinctions. Thus, as Ida B. Wells observes, it was only once Black men gained freedom that the sexualization of race politics began in earnest.[16] Whites had long ascribed sexual licentiousness to Black people, but upon gaining their freedom (at least, from the formal institution of slavery) Black men in particular were recast as rapists and superpredators in need of violent control.

Following emancipation and the collapse of Reconstruction reforms that saw, for instance, the rise of Black elected public officials in the South, the scrutiny of Black men's interactions with White women reached new heights. After about 1877 regional antimiscegenation laws proliferated, and any perceived breach of the social code could—and often did—result in the torture and murder of Black people. The trauma of slavery carried forward: Black women were systematically terrorized through sexual assault. Black men lynching victims were frequently castrated. The sexual specificity of White violence and control in the postbellum United States was innovative in its brutality.[17]

In this context it may seem perplexing that the rate of mixed-race births to Black women increased steadily in the decades following slavery. However, this was not because Black women gained autonomy but because, now that they were no longer legally considered the property of any White man, *all* White men were free to exploit them free of reprisal or rebuke.[18] There was little protection for Black Americans under Jim Crow. Rape and lynching continued as forms of social control such that Black men who retaliated against sexual violence on behalf of family members were summarily hanged. In the classic book *Caste and Class in a Southern Town*, published in 1937, John Dollard describes how White men commonly lost their virginity by having sex with Black women—to whom they saw themselves entitled.[19] Meanwhile, the same White men viewed White women as chaste and virtuous, in need of protection from Black men.

The twin facts of their economic dependence on White employers and the controlling scripts that alleged they were both promiscuous and the rightful prey of White men, have made Black women and girls particularly vulnerable to sexual exploitation throughout much of U.S. history. Considering centuries of institutionalized abuse, it is no surprise that the first lawsuits against sexual harassment were filed in the 1970s by Black women, and it was a Black woman who founded the Me Too movement in 2006.[20] Indeed, whether through enslavement or wage employment, Black women have borne the brunt of men's sexual aggression in the U.S. labor force. Further, the selective impulse of White masculinity, by which only White women are in need of protection—and then only from the sexual predation of non-White men—points less to chivalrous altruism than to a gendered White supremacy that carefully regulates *which* men can dominate *which* women.

The spirit of laws restricting intermarriage that existed in the United States since the seventeenth century was generally termed "amalgamation" until 1864. "Miscegenation" was coined in that year in a presidential election pamphlet at a time in which slave emancipation was the burning issue of the day. The pamphlet, *Miscegenation: the Theory of the Blending of the Races*, was written by two New York politicians who insisted that an independent term was needed to refer to the "mixture of two or more races." *Amalgamation*, the common word for it, also referred to the mixing of metals.[21] And so they combined the Latin word *miscere* (to mix) with *genus* (race) to develop the more scientific-sounding but inherently racialized term *miscegenation*.[22] The term caught on rapidly and appeared as a cautionary cartoon in a New York daily newspaper, which intended to startle and horrify through its depiction of a "miscegenation ball," at which White Republicans waltzed and otherwise intimately interacted with Black women.[23]

Fears of miscegenation were also rooted in questions of identity. At issue during the era of Reconstruction, historians argue, was in fact African American identity itself.[24] Previously, Blackness had been defined as *unfree*. The question of how former slaves and their offspring would enter the national stage as *free* was a pressing concern for a White citizenry whose identity had long been conflated with the idea.

From 1860 to 1920 a patchwork of conflicting standards on racial identity emerged across U.S. states. Among the racial classifications legislators hastily constructed were *mulatto* (the dehumanizing term for individuals of mixed White and Black ancestry that derived from the word for a mule, the offspring of a male donkey and a female horse); *quadroon* (for a person who is one-quarter Black by descent); and *octoroon* (for a person who is one-eighth Black by descent) in others. Each was, by the concept of hypodescent, a way to make clear that a mixed-race person was decidedly non-White and therefore substandard. At the turn of the nineteenth century, the same person could travel to Alabama and be considered a mulatto, but fully "Negro" in neighboring Tennessee.

Such conflicting legal designations reveal a great deal about the construction of race, specifically multiraciality. In their efforts to establish degrees of non-Whiteness and solidify the boundaries around Whiteness, they reified myths about White racial purity and the rightness of White privilege. Before Reconstruction, when White dominance was taken for granted, racial distinctions such as quadroon, mulatto, and octoroon mattered only in those few cities marked by triracial caste systems that more closely resembled Caribbean and Latin American norms. In the absence of slavery, when fears of growing social equality for Blacks intensified among Whites, these designations gained greater importance.

MISCEGENATION LAWS BEYOND BLACK AND WHITE AND THE SPECIFICITY OF ANTI-BLACKNESS

Madison Grant, a prominent conservationist and public thinker of the late nineteenth and early twentieth centuries, publicly lamented that legal shifts since emancipation were allowing Whites to commit what he called "race suicide." He argued that society should fight back by either breeding "from the best" or "eliminat[ing] the worst by segregation or sterilization."[25] Grant was a proponent of scientific racism, which leveraged the language of evolutionary theory, genetic science, and biological determinism to implement a new system of racial disenfranchisement after emancipation. His *The Passing of the Great Race,* published in 1916, greatly influenced U.S. segregationist and eugenicist policies, including the exclusionary immigration acts passed in the 1920s and 1930s, which placed quotas on immigration from countries in Africa, Central America, South America, and Asia, whose populations were not considered a fit with White supremacy and purity in the United States.[26] In addition to advocating for exclusion on the basis of genetic inferiority, Grant explained the already visible persistence of U.S. racial inequality in biological terms, which made racism appear scientific.[27]

Antimiscegenation laws predated eugenics movements in the United States, but eugenic principles were used to broaden antimiscegenation legislation in the early parts of the twentieth century. Influenced by Grant's concerns around race dilution, the notion of hypodescent was key to the rationale for such laws. Commonly referred to as the "one-drop rule," hypodescent was a legal method of categorization that generally defined any person with African American ancestry, and sometimes Native American or Asian ancestry, as "colored" or "negro" and redefined Whiteness to refer only to persons without mixed racial ancestry.[28] Well into the twentieth century, states called on the one-drop rule as they developed antimiscegenation laws. Its legacy remains a powerful influence on the way modern U.S. Americans comprehend race and social status, as well as partner desirability and procreation.

The best-known example of these laws is Virginia's 1924 Act to Preserve Racial Integrity, which expanded the definition of miscegenation such that any marriage between a White person and a person with *any* non-White ancestry was a felony (as opposed to an 1866 law, where people with up to one-quarter non-White ancestry were considered White by the state of Virginia).[29] Now not only a person's racial identity but also their entire genealogical heritage proscribed whom they could or could not marry.[30]

The one-drop rule originates in the property interests of slaveholders, yet it tells us something important about the social construction of race and sexual preference. For one it produced a racial taxonomy upheld by a monolithic notion of Blackness. That is, to be White, it asserts, one cannot also be Black, and to be Black, one cannot also be White. Put differently, Whiteness is legitimate only to the degree that Blackness is negated. Perhaps most telling is the fact that the law stipulated that a White woman could give birth to a Black child, but a Black woman could not give birth to a White child.

Monolithic notions of White versus Black were naturalized through the legal policing of individuals' sexual preferences—behaviors that in today's age are often seen as entirely a matter of personal choice. It took a great deal of effort, both by the state and by individuals, to produce and reinforce boundaries around race and sex. Sexual preference did not have to do with merely whom one desired. Rather, sex and reproduction were avenues by which property, citizenship, and propriety could be expanded to (or withdrawn from) individuals. They allowed White supremacy continued control over the postemancipation expansion of social equality to Blacks.

Although the rule of hypodescent most aggressively targeted Afro-descendants in the United States, other groups—including, by the language employed in the laws of the time, Native Americans, Asian Americans, Malays, Hindus, and Mongolians—were controlled by antimiscegenation laws.[31] Even in these cases a Black-White binary often shaped how the state understood interracial liaisons between Whites and non-Whites.[32] At its core this strain of laws was deployed "to prevent the dilution of the White race." Thus, all immigrants could be "negroized" as the state required, to both reconcile the eradication of slavery and uphold White supremacy.[33] This ever-shifting hierarchy of Whiteness did not deviate on one thing: closer to White was positive, and closer to Blackness was negative. That logic would become a defining feature of U.S. Americans' intimate relations, courtships, and marriages. Indeed, as we will see in later chapters, the same "preference" patterns are still evident in personal racial preferences of daters today.

Asians

People of Asian descent have, throughout U.S. history, been cast as non-White and unassimilable. Chinese immigrants to the United States in the nineteenth century were mostly men, labor migrants who settled on the West Coast and took low-skilled jobs in agriculture, mining, and railroad construction. In 1870 Chinese men outnumbered Chinese women in the United States by fourteen to one.³⁴ The disparity intensified with the California Gold Rush of 1848–55 and the building of the First Transcontinental Railroad (1863–69), both of which increased the Asian population in the West and South. For example, after the Civil War, when free Black labor became more scarce (emancipation, to be sure, did not end the exploitation of Black labor but often displaced it to near-slavery economic arrangements like sharecropping), immigrant men from China, often referred as "Coolies," were recruited and coerced into hard labor.³⁵ In Louisiana Chinese men were imported as cheap and exploitable labor to fill the vacuum of chattel slavery, for instance.

The growing presence of this newly racialized group in the West and South was met with enormous backlash. Many working-class White citizens saw the Chinese, similar to the newly emancipated Blacks, as a threat to their livelihood. Thus, as historian Ronald Takaki describes,

> Racial qualities that had been assigned to Blacks became Chinese characteristics. . . . Heathen, morally inferior, savage, and childlike, the Chinese were also viewed as lustful and sensual. Chinese women were condemned as "a depraved class," and their depravity was associated with their almost African-like physical appearance: they were "fair [of complexion] but [physically] a slight removal from the African race."³⁶

The existing racial paradigm influenced the reception of immigrant newcomers.

Although Asian labor fueled westward expansion after 1850, Asian enclaves springing up in western cities such as San Francisco further aroused fears of an impending "Asian takeover." As eugenicist ideology aided in solidifying notions of monolithic Blackness, eugenicist "yellow peril" discourses constructed Asians as threats to the Western world. Particularly because most such immigrants were men, propaganda depicted Asian men kidnapping and killing White women, often evoking biological threats such as disease or infection.³⁷

Again racialized fears bolstered by racist laws would become taken for granted by many White families, affecting societal notions of desirability over centuries. In response to xenophobic and nativist backlash of Whites, first state and then federal laws were initiated to block the entry of "unassimilable" Asians to the United States. The Page Act of 1875 restricted the immigration of Chinese women, coded as prostitutes and polygamists, while the Chinese Exclusion Act of 1882 broadened bans to all Chinese immigrants.[38] The first was named for its sponsor, Representative Horace D. Page, who stated that the act would "end the danger of cheap Chinese labor and immoral Chinese women."[39] The Japanese would become targets for exclusionary laws almost as quickly as they began to immigrate to the United States. The 1907 Gentlemen's Agreement between the two countries required the Japanese government to stop issuing passports to emigrants if the United States allowed Japanese Americans the right to family reunification.[40] Enforcing prevailing notions of racial and ethnic hierarchies, many states extended or enacted new antimiscegenation prohibitions to include Asians, "Hindus," and Filipinos in the decades after the Civil War.[41] Notably, the explicitly gendered component of the Page Act returns our attention to the gendered racial constructions being leveraged by Whites.

Combined, these acts restricted the reproductive freedom of Asians by ensuring the availability of a neutered Asian male labor force that could fill temporary demands but discouraging permanent settlement and the emergence of Asian American families.[42] White men were prohibited from participating in intimate relations with Asian women by law and by the legally inscribed construction of Asian women as a threat to the White American bloodline.[43]

Nativists during the nineteenth and twentieth centuries warned that miscegenation was inevitable should the United States allow any Asian immigration. Ironically, the situation feared and controlled by the anti-Asian backlash actually resulted *from* U.S. policy, which necessarily resulted in an extreme sex ratio imbalance among Asians in the United States. Offspring of Asian-White unions were often referred to as "Eurasian" and represented by the media as problematic "half-castes" who threatened the nation's development.[44] In 1890 a *Harper's Weekly* article read,

> Around the gutters, playing on terms of equality with other gamins, may be seen a few boys whose features betray their mingled blood. . . . Many of the

Chinese, however, unable to bring their wives from the Flowery Kingdom, have intermarried with the Irish. Whether they prefer Irish, or are unable to win other women, no outsider can say; but it is a fact that all, or nearly all, the women who have married Chinamen here are Hibernians [an Irish Catholic Organization].[45]

Editorials frequently invoked the specter of "half-castes" and "half-breeds." And the 1907 Expatriation Act threatened that White women who married not only Asians but any non-White men with the forfeit of their citizenship.[46] No such laws applied to White men. These racialized ideologies took shape in a context in which race was directly associated with social status and economic well-being. Thus, they would set in motion deep and enduring racialized perceptions of desirability for marriage and procreation in the United States.

The case of Chinese men in the Mississippi Delta is relevant here. The first wave of Chinese came to the Delta after the Civil War, substituting the labor of Blacks who fled the sharecropping economy. Due to the restrictive immigration law curtailing Chinese women's entrance into the country, many of these men married Black women. Antimiscegenation laws had been primarily interested in regulating the boundaries of Whiteness, so these relationships met little state sanction. Chinese were racialized similarly to Blacks in this region, and so Black, Chinese, and mixed-race children were all relegated to the same segregated schools in the Jim Crow South.

Eventually, many Chinese began to engage in what Vilna Bashi Treitler refers to as an "ethnic project"—the attempt to construct a higher place for one's group on the racial hierarchy.[47] To distance themselves from the bottom rung of a social hierarchy, the Chinese began to avoid the grueling work of sharecropping and instead opened shops in Black neighborhoods. They sought alternative schooling arrangements for their children, raising funds to found a Chinese Baptist Mission School in the Delta in 1936, which allowed them to bypass placing their children in segregated schools with Black pupils. Then the Chinese community began to more stringently police Chinese-Black liaisons, though not Chinese relationships with working-class White women, who might help Asians scale the racialized social ladder.[48] The enforcement of anti-Blackness among other non-White groups is a stunning testament to a pernicious White supremacy that has marked U.S. history since its start. And it continues to influence intermarriage and race relations today.

Latinos/as

The same racial structures that celebrated proximity to Whiteness and demonized Blackness and indigeneity have limited Latino/a intermarriage in the Americas. For example, after the War of Independence, the Mexican state hoped to attract foreign investment and permanent settlement, and so it created immigration paths for Whites. Under the law Whites who married Mexican women could receive citizenship and trade opportunities.[49] Perhaps needless to say, the offer did not extend to the indigenous or free Black population.

After a decade of clashes between Mexicans and U.S. settlers in Texas, the republic of Texas achieved self-government. The republic's land policies drew from an extant racial hierarchy by which only "Texas Whites" or "Spanish-Mexican" household heads could purchase land (and even then only if they could prove that they possessed no African or indigenous lineage). The significance of Whiteness was clear to José María de la Garza when he petitioned the republic of Texas court for land. He stated that he was "of Texas parents and is a free White person of Spanish and not of African blood."[50] As the republic of Texas "represented the culmination of Anglo-Saxon beliefs in the racial inferiority of Mexicans as a result of centuries of racial mixing among Spaniards, Africans and Indians," de la Garza, though technically Mexican by birth, had to prove his Whiteness. He did this by making claims regarding the presence of Spanish and the absence of "African blood."[51] Again the negation of Blackness—or at least distance from it—was used to push another group toward the virtuosity (or at least the privileges) of Whiteness.

When the United States emerged victorious from the U.S.-Mexican War of 1848, it forced Mexico to cede one-third of its territory as well as many of the Mexican citizens on that land. It was politically expedient to define Mexican citizens (regardless of skin color) as White, and thus miscegenation laws never came to include Mexicans. Nevertheless, intermarriage between poor Mexican men and White American women was informally policed. White social networks saw Mexicans as "mongrels," presumably due to their mixed-racial ancestry.[52] So while they had been given White status by U.S. law, Mexican ethnoracial identity emerged as a multifaceted identity. In daily life most Mexicans were often identified as non-White, while only Spanish-descendant elites were recognized as Whites.

Upon Texas's statehood in 1848, these hierarchical racial dynamics caused interracial intimate relations to play out in deeply gendered ways. Wealthy Mexican landowners, eager to see their families climb the class and race hierarchy, regularly emphasized their Spanish origins to attract wealthy White men to marry their daughters.[53] Other Mexican men and women, those who did not have resources that interested Whites in this way, were rarely afforded a White racial status in practice. Like Asians exploited to help supplant the lost labor of Blacks, poor Mexicans of indigenous and African descent suffered racialization and labor exploitation. They were frequently recruited to substitute for freedmen's labor on farms owned by wealthy White Anglos and White Mexicans. In the beginning of the twentieth century, industry and agribusiness leaders, eager to maintain a flow of cheap labor, successfully loosened Mexican immigration under the claim that they were "birds of passage"—that is, temporary workers who posed no threat to the racial hierarchy of the United States. For example, in the midst of a nationwide campaign against undocumented immigration, the state sponsored Mexican guest-worker program known as the Bracero Program imported four million Mexican workers to the United States.[54] As such, despite many Whites' concerns, Mexican temporary immigration was protected by the state even as racially motivated restrictions were applied to other immigrants. To many southwestern employers, Mexicans were considered an inferior race, one suited for hard and low-wage labor, yet unsuited for permanent citizenship.[55]

Despite employer interest in maintaining a supply of low-skilled Mexican labor, the name *birds of passage* was soon replaced by uglier terms such as *illegals* and *wetbacks* in public and political speech. Even the popular eugenicist Madison Grant inserted himself into the debate concerning Mexicans, stating in a 1923 letter to the House chair of Immigration that the "case with Mexicans today is exactly the same as it was with the Chinese fifty years ago."[56] Mexican immigrants were increasingly policed and criminalized.[57] Their access to state-sanctioned Whiteness faded as the narrative of illegality increasingly racialized

Mexicans as non-White. For a brief period, from 1930 to 1939, the U.S. Census officially designated Mexicans as a race separate from Whites. This change led to a number of Mexicans being denied U.S. citizenship and placed trade relations between the two countries at risk. Henceforth Mexicans would be formally recognized by the U.S. Census as White, though ethnically as Hispanic.[58]

Europeans

None of the United States' antimiscegenation laws ever applied to any European groups. However, racial hierarchies in the United States have always been in flux, and there have been liminal moments in which the Irish, Italians, and eastern Europeans such as Polish and Russian immigrants were each seen as being of a different race than the nation's English Protestant predecessors.[59]

Though it is sometimes forgotten today, the election of John F. Kennedy in 1960 presents one example. It was a victorious moment for many, in which the Irish (and, for that matter, Catholics) became White; that is, it was the moment that Irish Americans mark as their transition from persecuted outcasts to politically powerful White Americans. Despite the history of anti-Irish antipathy, the U.S. Census has never treated Irish as a racial category. And Irishness is increasingly perceived and treated as an optional ethnicity by Irish Americans, meaning that individuals have some degree of choice in how they identify ethnically.[60] How is it that a group commonly evoked in nativist and racist propaganda not so very long ago is no longer thought of or treated as a non-White group?

The answer, scholars maintain, is multifaceted. First, immigrant newcomers have entered a U.S. racial paradigm anchored by the stigmatization of Blackness and the valuation of Whiteness, as Vilna Bashi Treitler has convincingly argued, meaning that ethnicized identities have been constructed in the context of racialization.[61] In this sense White ethnic groups' shedding of the negative connotations associated with their ethnic identities and entrance into full Whiteness has been, historically, conditioned on their willingness to distance themselves from the bottom of the U.S. racial hierarchy—that is, from Blackness. The vulnerable period of liminal approximation between Black and Irish Americans during the late nineteenth to early twentieth century, for example, may explain why many among the Irish American working classes were so quick to pick up the drumbeat of White supremacy and antiabolitionism.[62] The same can be said about other immigrant groups such as Italians, Jews, and even the Chinese who, in various periods, engaged intimately with African Americans (whether in terms of work or play) but later aggressively promoted their superiority over Blacks as they vied for the privileges associated with Whiteness.

This anti-Blackness can be seen in the way other European groups also shed their "non-White" status. In the early twentieth century, for example, White southerners saw Italians as both similar to African Americans and as a racial middle ground. Mainly from Sicily and southern regions, Italian immigrants faced large-scale antipathy, targeted by ethnic slurs like "wop" and "dago" and sometimes experiencing violence, including, for example, the lynching of eleven Italian men in New Orleans in 1891.[63] Amid denigration from White society, Italian immigrants embraced a "rhetoric of self-righteousness about their own struggles and of blaming African Americans for society's ills," joining Whites to terrorize Black residents in urban spaces. Over time Italian's "waning ethnicity" signaled their racial incorporation into a U.S. racial paradigm anchored by anti-Blackness.[64]

Immigration laws also played a role in constructing these racial hierarchies, instructed by White supremacy and creating the scaffolding through which it would be propped up. They influenced ideas about who one could or should marry as they built racialized preferences and anti-Blackness into the very architecture of the nation. The Immigration Act of 1924 reconstructed a variety of national categories that had previously not been considered discrete or natural units of classification. Before 1924, aside from several racialized exclusion policies (like those targeting Asians), immigration border control was barely a legal concept and policy. For example, immigration was altogether unrecorded by the U.S. Census before 1820, emigration was not recorded until 1907, and politically defined nation-states were not commonly used in formal classification systems. But the Immigration Act of 1924 introduced the social and political concept of "national origins" as well as a quota system stipulating the number of people who could immigrate to the United States during a given year. African descendants residing in the United States by 1890 were not even considered in the calculation, as they were imagined as having no country of origin and thus were not legally considered immigrants.[65]

An extension of the Chinese Exclusion Act, the 1924 Origins Act excluded all immigrants from Asia with the creation of its "Asiatic Barred Zone," which stipulated that Asians were ineligible for citizenship. As a result, racial exclusion and immigration laws, like antimiscegenation laws, would have powerful repercussions for how race, cross-racial intimate relations, and the institutions of marriage would evolve.[66] Indeed, the quota system of 1924 also codified people from all European countries (regardless of quota status, in the case of eastern Europeans) as officially White, including those who had been and often continued to be unofficially racialized as closer to non-White.

WORLD WAR II AND THE WAR BRIDES ACT OF 1945

Although the racial ideas that underpin how intermarriage is understood in the United States can often be tied back to how state and federal governments codified racial subordination, such regulation also occurred beyond this country's borders. One important example is the massive deployment of the U.S. military during World War II, which resulted in large numbers of interracial relationships between U.S. nationals and foreigners. These influenced important shifts in ideas about interracial marriage, particularly as regarded intermarriage with Asian women.

Stateside racial politics affected how military personnel conducted their intimate lives during overseas deployments. For example, military personnel were required to seek permission to marry, and their superiors commonly drew on familiar proscriptions against interracial marriages to inhibit such unions on foreign lands.[67] Those who did marry foreign spouses faced obstacles in bringing their spouses to the United States. However, in a notable shift, Congress enacted the War Brides Act of 1945, which enabled servicemen to marry and naturalize women from countries whose citizens were otherwise prohibited from migrating to the United States.[68] To be sure, the War Brides Act and other related laws directly contrasted with the Page Act and the Expatriation Act.[69] While the latter restricted Asian men's access to Asian wives, the former explicitly expanded White soldiers' access to foreign, often Asian, wives.

Even so the war years brought an intensification of anti-Asian policy, specifically policy aimed at the Japanese. In 1942 President Franklin Roosevelt's Executive Order 9066 initiated the forced removal and incarceration of Japanese and Japanese Americans within the United States into concentration camps. Japan's involvement in the war was the ostensible motivation for the executive order, but the way it was carried out drew on long-standing yellow-peril traditions that postulated that the Japanese (and other East Asians) were dangers to the Western world.[70] Determining the racial status of individuals with Japanese ancestry became a fixation, and hypodescent, or the one-drop rule, was leveraged to carry out this executive order such that any trace of Japanese lineage or "blood" could trigger expulsion. However, the legal definition of Japanese was later redefined under a "Mixed Marriage Policy," then revised again to stipulate that those with 50 percent or less Japanese blood in the family or individual could be exempted from internment. This case illustrates how the implementation of hypodescent in the United States was systematic when it came to Blacks, whereas for groups like the Japanese, it was randomly applied, often in more idiosyncratic local and historical contexts.

The period after World War II would begin a new phase in the history of racialization in the United States, as a number of major social movements would begin to challenge policies that promoted the social hierarchies of hegemonic Whiteness. Ultimately, these social movements would remove the legal restrictions on intimate relations across racial lines. Nevertheless, historical racial hierarchies would remain in place, continuing to influence U.S. Americans' racial preferences for sex and courtship.

BREAKING DOWN CENTURIES-OLD BARRIERS

The question of whether states should or could wield control over marriage and sex has played out in legislation and court cases since the birth of the nation. Antimiscegenation laws, and later immigration laws, were central to such debates. In 1948 the California Supreme Court, in *Perez v. Sharp*, became the first court to invalidate an antimiscegenation law.[71]

But the U.S. Supreme Court was the only governing body that could invalidate antimiscegenation laws *nationwide*.[72] Civil rights activists were well aware that antimiscegenation laws were pivotal to upholding Jim Crow, yet they engaged the issue with more caution than other issues, such as housing, education, voting rights, and employment. The landmark case that ruled school segregation policies unconstitutional, *Brown v. Board of Education,* for example, was decided in 1954. It would be another decade before the U.S. Supreme Court took up antimiscegenation laws. Why did it take so long?

Back in 1944, in the now-classic *An American Dilemma: The Negro Problem and Modern Democracy,* Swedish economist and social commentator Gunnar Myrdal observed a paradox. Whites, he noted, were less resistant to expanding rights to African Americans in the public sphere than they were in presumably private matters: they "put their highest priority on maintaining the bar against intermarriage and sexual intercourse involving White women."[73] Myrdal's observation points to the singular importance of intimate relations—particularly those surrounding Whiteness and Blackness—to U.S. racial policies and racialized social hierarchies. It also points to the reason why, during the twentieth century, activists' political strategy prioritized pursuing cases of racial injustice in areas such as housing and voting rights but avoided pursuing laws against intermarriage.

Once *Brown v. Board of Education* outlawed segregated schools in 1954, it became more likely that antimiscegenation laws could be dismantled. Yet, in the midst of the civil rights movement, Whites were becoming more attached to such laws. Their demise would undermine not only one pillar of Jim Crow segregation but cut to the very core of White supremacy. For civil rights activists it was a matter of strategy to delay court challenges to intermarriage prohibitions. Whites' aversion to interracial intimacy was so ingrained that NAACP litigators and activists believed stirring up this aversion might risk major political efforts, specifically the Voting Rights Act of 1965 and the Civil Rights Act of 1964.[74]

In the meantime nearly a third of states with antimiscegenation laws had repealed them by 1963. The state of Virginia, however, was its own domain. Virginia's Racial Integrity Act of 1924 served as a precedent for institutionalized White supremacy such that it was considered the linchpin of the Jim Crow racial regime; that is, Virginia was a symbolically and politically important state for civil rights activists as well as those invested in the racial status quo.

On June 2, 1958, some four years after *Brown v. Board of Education*, Richard Loving, a White man, and his Black and Native American partner, Mildred Jeter, drove from Virginia to Washington, DC, to marry. Their marriage was used as grounds for their arrest, and the couple was formally banned from the state of Virginia for twenty-five years. In 1964, six years into their exile, the Lovings filed a motion to appeal with the backing of the American Civil Liberties Union (ACLU). The initial appeal was dismissed. In 1965 the Virginia Supreme Court of Appeals also turned it away, upholding the constitutionality of Virginia's 1924 Racial Integrity Act and referring to its 1955 decision in *Naim v. Naim* (which upheld state efforts "'to preserve the racial integrity of its citizens,' and to prevent 'the corruption of blood,' 'a mongrel breed of citizens,' and the 'obliteration of racial pride'").[75] But in 1967—three years after the passage of the Civil Rights Act and two years after the Voting Rights Act—the Lovings appealed to the U.S. Supreme Court with the backing of civil rights activists.

In the end the U.S. Supreme Court decision in *Loving* established a landmark precedent: antimiscegenation statutes were in violation of the Equal Protection Clause of the Fourteenth Amendment and thus wholly unconstitutional. The extension of protection into "private" domestic space radically altered the southern racial regime, which utilized family and personal relationships to promote White supremacy. However, one of the key implications of this decision would be unrealized for some time. As the courts were actively striking down laws that for centuries had allowed racial preferences in the public sphere, the *Loving* ruling asserted not only that racial choice in the private sphere be permitted but that, from a legal perspective, it was conceptually logical that the race of one's most intimate partners was *a matter of personal preference.*

THE LEGACY OF ANTIMISCEGENATION LAWS

Loving v. Virginia, along with the Voting Rights Act of 1965 and the Civil Rights Act of 1964, occurred in the context of the United States' absorption of political colorblindness. Thus, its success seemingly represents a contradiction: the case determined that the state had no role in regulating the private sphere, and its colorblind logic paradoxically made it possible to discount discrimination occurring in the private sphere; that is, if the racial state legally transformed into a colorblind one, personal racial preferences were deemed legitimate—or at least beyond state purview.[76]

For centuries the state had told people which sexual relations were permitted and how to interpret those intimate relations. *Loving v. Virginia* could undo those laws, but it could not undo the social realities and hierarchies that were now associated with interracial intimate relations. In other words, by the time of this legal decision, the work of the court officials, eugenicists, politicians, law enforcement officers, families, and vigilante citizens who together enforced racial separation around sex and marriage had already been done. The social facts of race and racial preference had been solidified and reproduced by individuals through the quotidian politics of everyday life. Within the private sphere, a space now legally marked by the liberal right of "choice," racial preference was anything but a public matter.

Another half century later individual stakeholders—that is, rental agents, home owners, employers, educators, legal clerks—cannot *explicitly* evoke the language of racialized "personal preference" when justifying whether or not someone is a suitable tenant or a job candidate is fit for a position. The ongoing civil rights movement has extended marriage rights to same-sex couples and led to the growth of an interracially married and partnered population.

Yet racial prejudice and violence endure. When Alabama and South Carolina decided to remove their vestigial legal statutes against intermarriage from their books in 1998 and 2000, 41 percent of Alabamians and 38 percent of South Carolinians voted to retain them.[77] The United States has seen the election, and reelection, of its first mixed-race, Black-identified president but also the election of a White president who expresses overt racial prejudice and dismisses the importance of high-profile incidents of racial violence and rallies for White supremacy. The past is not gone, as the disproportionately high murder rate of Black people at the hands of police and stand-your-ground vigilantes illustrate or as the 2017 "Unite the Right" rally of White supremacists makes so horrifyingly clear. By no coincidence the rally took place in Virginia—a state that has played such a key role in the institutionalization of White supremacy in the United States. Hate groups that once occupied prominent social positions in the U.S. South have again found openly expressed support and solidarity, while exposure and backlash on social media points to how technology affects the ways race is viewed and acted on in U.S. society. Indeed, with phones now capturing videos of once-hidden criminal behavior and the use of photos on social media to expose the identities of participants in White supremacy rallies, antiracist activists are exposing the names and faces of those who would spread hate.

In the United States today, the internet is where social issues, including race, are negotiated and renegotiated. In the digital world one can comment, post, and browse topics anonymously with little fear of repercussion. Similarly, online dating allows people to express sexual preferences for Whites or Asians or Blacks without public judgement, leading to a new form of digital-sexual racism. But before we get to the age of internet courtship, we need to look at how pre-internet courtship became inextricably bound to the history of racial politics in the United States.

2 From the Back Porch to the Computer Screen

THE RISE OF CHOICE IN COURTSHIP

The place of all others to court a young lady is in her home.
The only right way for a young lady to receive the addresses
of a young man is with the knowledge and consent of her
mother, and under that mother's own supervision.

George Hudson, 1883

Historically, U.S. courtship followed a chaperoned home-calling model, like the one described in the late nineteenth-century *Marriage Guide for Young Men* excerpt in the epigraph.[1] The evolution of courtship from the colonial era to today is a shift from a formal process involving intense third-party mediation to an informal process that has elevated the role of the individual's interest ahead of family or community demand. It has reflected changes in the U.S. economy, family, and society amid a growing emphasis on individual choice.

Gendered racial oppression has been part and parcel of U.S. courtship all along. As we discussed in chapter 1, it has been central to the state's enforcement of sexual boundaries for at least three centuries. Indeed, the invention of dating in the early twentieth century reduced the roles of the state and family in individuals' marital relations in ways that paralleled the precipitous decline of the agrarian family economy.

At the same time, though not at all coincidentally, postbellum antimiscegenation laws solidified legal definitions of race in the United States. Along with the emergence of consumer culture, codified racial categories created a context in which a prospective partner's race was increasingly framed as one among many dimensions of individual preference. We might call it consumerist discrimination.

In the chapters that follow, we document the way the legacies of U.S. racial and gender hierarchies and notions of personal preference have shaped its citizens' approaches to online dating, resulting in a new form of digital-sexual racism. To help bring these legacies into view, however, we first explore how race and gender came to be bound up in the evolution of dating and courtship in the United States—and how laws and institutions that prohibited sexual intimacy across the color line were, in turn, internalized and actively reasserted through daters' self-regulation.

MARRIAGE AS COLLECTIVE CHOICE

Despite all the sentiments associated with romantic love and fidelity, marriage has always been, at its heart, a contract. This was particularly true in preindustrial, agricultural societies. For White elites, marriages cemented political alliances and consolidated intergenerational transfers of wealth. But even for free families with few assets, marriages established social status and sanctioned a stable production of offspring into a family unit, ensuring mutual subsistence vis-à-vis each family member's labor contribution.

For these reasons courtship during the U.S. colonial through Victorian eras was commonly conceived as a family undertaking. Parents had great incentive to monitor their children's sexuality. They were also in charge of finding the right family with which to form the union, and their decisions were supported by the state and religious institutions. Such marriages were sometimes arranged prior to sexual maturity, particularly among the White upper classes. Where marriages were not arranged early on, parents were actively involved in the courtship process upon their child's sexual debut. This kind of third-party influence—in which the parties of a marriage follow not only their personal preferences but also those of family, community, and religious institutions—dominated marriage decisions among free peoples until the twentieth century.

In contrast, calling courtship among the elite typically took place in the woman's home under the supervision of her parents. In some cases the visits were prearranged through consultation between the parents of both prospective husband and wife—a tradition still evidenced by some contemporary marriage practices such as fathers symbolically "giving away" their daughters in wedding ceremonies and by grooms asking the bride's family for their blessing before engagement. Both the original and the vestigial practices, of course, reflect women's historical role as property to be exchanged between father and husband.

A young person's family's social networks also largely determined who they could court and marry throughout U.S. history. Because the purpose of eighteenth- and nineteenth-century marriages was often to facilitate property inheritance (especially among land-holding, White families); reproduction; and social cohesion, parents desired unions that maintained the family's status. Familial control of courtship in this way also ensured formal racial separation of Whites from both slaves and from the free Black population, leaving little room for even a strong-willed woman to select a mate outside her own race, religion, or class. Endogamy, or marriage limited to same-group members, still generally characterizes the typical U.S. union, as we see in the introductory chapter of this book.

To be sure, the right to marry is enjoyed widely in the United States today, but that is a very recent and not at all settled development. Significant swaths of U.S. Americans have been denied the right to marry, including lesbian and gay Americans. (But for our purposes here, we must delve into the marriage exclusion as it related specifically to enslaved peoples.) Legal recognition of marriages among chattel slaves would jeopardize White families' lines of inheritance (given that the people themselves were treated as heritable property and a form of intergenerational wealth), yet some slave owners encouraged *informal* marriage among the enslaved. Slaves' marriages were seen as bolstering a more stable workforce and reducing attrition via runaways. They also produced children, whose very existence expanded Whites' property portfolios.[3]

Marital unions and courtship rituals under slavery, then, did not function as an economic system to the benefit of slaves as they did for young Whites. Instead, these relations emphasized companionship, emotional support, and mutual protection in ways that interestingly presage contemporary love-marriage narratives.[4] But lack of sociolegal protection plagued slave unions with uncertainty and evanescence, with many unions dissolved at the auction block. Marriages among the enslaved were also decoupled from sexual exclusivity: enslaved women often had no choice in reproductive matters and were frequently forced into sexual relations that would expand their master's "property" (whether the children were fathered by the owner, a woman's common husband, or another enslaved man, all were considered property at birth).[5] Thus the precariousness of slave life led to furtive unions of "unauthorized beginnings and inexact endings"; nevertheless, the historical record indicates that slaves established emotionally fulfilling courtships in a proliferation of forms: within plantations, "abroad" at other plantations, and in mixed-status (free-slave) couples. Some enslaved men and women traded their freedom for the ability to stay in proximity to their husbands or wives, as well as children and other kin.[6] Archival evidence also shows that enslaved parents and their kin were at times actively involved in their children's courtship process. They sometimes exerted influence on their children's choice of courting partner, and, though they were largely without property, many patched together resources to form the couple's new household.[7]

Nineteenth-century immigrants to the United States, free Blacks living outside of slave states, and other poor and working-class U.S. Americans theoretically enjoyed the legal protection of marriage and its benefits.[8] However, they had far less status or property to protect than the elites. That meant fewer reasons to police their offspring's sexuality and secure proper matches. Thus, while marriages still played an important role in economic production and cementing social ties within these communities, working-class youth had more autonomy in their romantic explorations. The church exerted a strong influence on the sexual mores of the poor and elite alike, but this prevalence of consensual unions among the poor and working classes came with a more accepting stance toward premarital pregnancies.[9]

That calling courtship had competition among the working classes does not mean that it was absent. Many of the same calling courtship practices undertaken by White elites were as important to other classes, such that, for example, the chaperones who had become part of the highly ritualized calling culture of the Victorian era commonly enforced gendered social virtues among the working classes, particularly those groups with strong religious ties. Jane Addams, in 1909, noted that those among the "Latin races" of immigrant families in Chicago, for instance, exercised "careful chaperonage over their marriageable daughters."[10] Susan Cahn, documenting what she called the competing moralities of southern Black communities, evidenced similarly how well-to-do Black families restricted the sexual access of their appropriately aged daughters through a supervised calling culture referred to as "keeping company."[11]

Among the Black American community, traditional gendered ideologies also played an influential role in monitoring courtship processes.[12] Given the hardships endured by enslaved families, many Black elites believed that the traditional model of marriage and procreation countered pervasive racist stereotypes about Black femininity and masculinity that so often demonized African American family life. Marriage therefore signaled "proper conduct," understood by elites as necessary for the advancement of the African American community. This imperative also involved the "promise of patriarchal protection" so that Black women could access economic, legal, physical, and sexual protection within matrimony.[13] A politics of respectability ideology, therefore, became the guiding principle of the intellectual and political work of many Black leaders, including W. E. B. Du Bois.[14]

Still, working-class Black adolescents had relatively more sexual freedom than either White or Black elites. As argued by Shirley A. Hill, many Black women insisted on forming families that challenged patriarchal ideals of courtship and marriage as they reclaimed their independence and sexuality.[15] Some Black parents, aside from cautioning against pregnancy and the sexual predations of White men, viewed adolescent sexuality as a natural and expected stage in the process of becoming an adult. Thus, supervision carried less urgency. For example, in a newspaper column published in 1887, Belle Dorce advised on Black teenagers, "Her courtship is free. If the girl has been properly reared by her parents there should be no fear to let her meet her lover alone. When we watch her, we tell her too plainly that we do not trust her."[16] And, as W. E. B. Du Bois observed in *The Philadelphia Negro*, Black families might lack the funds to follow every formal social ritual. Thus, many working-class Black men and women lived together and had children without marrying.[17]

Taken together, pre–twentieth-century U.S. courtship was, with variation, marked by third-party interests and oversight. Whether it was the state via antimiscegenation laws, the church enforcing religious doctrine,

or parents overseeing the sexual morays of their children, personal preference had less claim to primacy over community interest in marriage
compacts.

MATRIMONIAL ADVERTISEMENTS, THE FIRST AMERICAN SINGLES ADS

As the nineteenth century inched toward the twentieth, this third-party
power over marital decisions began to erode. The decline was evident, for
instance, during the large-scale nineteenth-century immigration to the
U.S. West, when individuals left family behind as they moved in search of
work and land. Distance from family, along with economic opportunities
gained by the forced appropriation of indigenous land, freed many White
colonist men from depending on elders for land or financial support. The
westward migration also led to gender imbalances, such that more young
White men than women were in the Great Plains and West Coast.[18]
Starting with the gold rush in the 1840s, this period of movement and
resettlement sparked the very first U.S. singles ads.

While family-centered courtship dominated the more heavily populated
East Coast, advertisement-mediated marriages were more common in the
West. Amid looser community control, a small industry cropped up to
attract women from eastern states and Europe to the male-dominated
frontier country. Soon there were a variety of periodicals and catalogs
devoted entirely to singles ads—by 1900 there were at least twenty in
operation.[19] The highest circulation weekly was *Matrimonial News*, published in Kansas City, Chicago, San Francisco, and England from 1886
through 1901.[20] In forty words or less, nineteenth-century singles detailed
the attributes of their desired mate and their own nuptial bona fides.

The ads were generated largely by men, but women sometimes posted
their own ads. Reflecting the gendered demand and supply of the market
among the western states, women's ads were posted free of charge. By
necessity the ads were short and direct, essentially precursors to the classified newspaper singles ads that emerged in the late twentieth century.
They frequently referenced physical appearance, including age, height,
weight, and sometimes skin tone or ethnicity. For example, one ad pub-

lished January 8, 1887, reads, "A widow of 28, 5 feet 2 inches tall, black eyes and hair, weighing 125 pounds, wishes to make acquaintance of some dark complexioned gentleman of 25 to 45; am a first rate house-keeper."[21] Straightforward, these ads tended to reference the economic, not romantic, aspects of partnership. Most expressed a preference for finding a partner of means or stipulated specific incomes and real estate the seeker would bring to a marriage.

Importantly, the western context meant a lessened parental influence and the general lack of an entrenched slavery system. This meant that cross-race pairings were far more likely in western states than eastern—a legacy that persists today.[22] Indeed, throughout U.S. history new immigrant groups have had higher rates of intermarriage, largely because many of the first immigrants from any country were likely to be men.[23]

In its specificity the catalog-marriage industry also expanded the opportunities for White ethnic minorities to find someone of similar faith or ethnic background. Abraham Calof, a Russian Jewish immigrant living in the desolate prairie of North Dakota, sought a Jewish spouse with an ad placed in an 1893 issue of the *Matrimonial News:* "A wife of good, strong character is what I seek, but it is optional. To be of Jewish faith is mandatory."[24] To Calof religious identity outweighed even integrity in the hierarchy of marital needs. Ultimately, he married an eighteen-year-old Russian immigrant named Rachel, who would chronicle their homesteading life and raising their seven children in a memoir.[25] Today these kinds of targeted advertisements still exist, and ads like Abraham Calof's bring to mind websites like "Jdate," which launched in 1997 and specialized in pairing Jewish singles.

The development of catalog-marriage advertisements was an important harbinger of future courtship in particular ways. It not only indicated a shift away from parental arrangement and other third-party oversight, giving more agency to individual daters, but also impelled daters to consciously articulate what they sought in a partner. In this way these advertisements are one of the earliest nineteenth-century formal expressions of racial or ethnic preferences in the process of searching for intimate partners. Although many records document people's racial or ethnic preferences before this time, these ads marked a moment in which it became common to clearly state such expressions as part of the effort to find inti-

mate partners. Some of these advertisements were outright discriminatory. The negative sentiment against the Irish and southern and eastern
Europeans, for example, was blatant. One May 1873 advertisement published in a San Francisco paper stated,

> I am 33 years of age, and as regards looks can average with most men. I am
> looking for a lady to make for my wife, and I am heartily tired of bachelor
> life. I desire a lady not over 28 or 30 years of age, not ugly, well educated and
> musical. Nationality makes no difference, only I prefer not to have a lady of
> Irish birth. She must have at least $20,000.[26]

The catalog-marriage industry was a notable departure from third-
party oversight, but it operated within the prevailing racial system of late
nineteenth-and early twentieth-century United States. While undesirable
subcategories of Whiteness, such as Irishness, were actively spelled out in
the ads, restrictions against cross-racial pairings went without saying.
Postbellum antimiscegenation laws criminalized and mapped culturally
taboo practices onto a color line, creating a folk wisdom that said racial
separation was normal. Even in the West, where outmarriage was more
common, people still self-regulated in their individual courtship choices.
Race still continued to dictate norms around U.S. courtship.

COURTSHIP IN THE AGE OF CONSUMPTION

Industrialization sparked the twilight of arranged marriage and the slow
but inexorable turn away from full-fledged parental involvement in U.S.
courtship. The Industrial Revolution and the rise of capitalism led to
growing demands for wage work. In turn, people were pulled away from
rural farmland and into urban centers. As these economic changes arrived,
they brought with them new gender and labor dynamics. For example,
late nineteenth-century Victorian ideology promoted the idea that wage
work was only for men, keeping many women out of the paid labor force
for another century. This added new layers to women's reproductive roles,
alleging their natural instincts for caregiving and homemaking over paid
work. Couples had once labored together to care for their children and
produce goods in a family economy, but now the home was starting to be

seen as a "haven in a heartless world," in which men could seek refuge from a ruthless workplace.[27] Put differently, gender roles were reconstructed to cast women as unsuited for wage labor and men as unsuited for raising children and domestic work, though maternal and paternal roles had overlapped for centuries prior.

Meantime, many poor and minority women, whose husbands did not have access to a family wage, had no choice but to participate in wage labor, and they did so at considerably lower wages than men earned. Indeed, the lived reality of racialized minority communities in the United States challenges the emergent separate sphere ideology that emphasized women's alleged appropriateness for caregiving and men's appropriateness for breadwinning. During slavery African American men *and* women shared the status as enslaved laborers. During the postbellum period and into the twentieth century, African American women continued to work—indeed, they were coerced into work through vagrancy laws—and were often relegated to the least desirable and lucrative occupations, including farm labor, jobs on the industrial fringe, and domestic work.[28] Asian, Native American, and Mexican women in western and southwestern states were also restricted to poverty-level jobs for much of the nineteenth and twentieth centuries. As Evelyn Nakano Glenn reminds us, in many instances a racialized division of reproductive labor meant that women of color were disproportionately represented in precarious, low-wage work. These homemakers, cooks, and caregivers often carried out the feminine responsibilities of class-privileged White women before returning home to carry them out in their own homes.[29]

The migration of wage workers from farms to cities and mill towns led to an increasing independence among young adults in their late teens and early twenties. Urbanized lifestyles made smaller families more economically advantageous, while ushering in a variety of other economic, legal, social, and ideological transformations. Greater life expectancy and survival rates during this time meant that married couples were spending longer periods of their lives as companions outside of parenting roles. Parenting practices thus gradually shifted from expectations of filial duty and obedience to a focus on their children's *happiness*.[30]

As industry rose, more women were recruited to wage labor in the twentieth century. This trend further reduced family size and decreased women's economic dependence on husbands and fathers. Such changes shifted the norms and expectations associated with sex and marriage—increasingly, as women and men became more autonomous and economically independent, they began to have sexual relations before marriage. Intimacy and pleasure became more central to their relationships as the first glimmerings of a general shift from male-headed households to dual-headed households were felt.

The midtwentieth century was a transitional period in many ways. One marker was the invention of dating.[31] Rather than supervised, formal calling courtship, dating often involved unchaperoned excursions away from the home and into the world of parks and penny theaters. Poor urban youth, often living in cramped tenements, were central to this change. Calling courtship in the home was difficult for them, and new recreational activities and rising consumption marked urbanized cities.[32] These young people worked in factories and were often expected to contribute to the family economy. But even a small amount of spending money introduced a degree of youthful independence that would have been impossible in an agrarian economy.

National advertising systems promoted leisure, and dating was one such lucrative activity. These campaigns found that products and consumption behaviors sold best when gilded with the promise of romantic love. Thus, one 1907 article noted, "But here is what would happen if courting of the popular sort were to cease tomorrow: Theater, florists, confectioners, jewelers' profits would decrease 33%. Restaurants, haberdashers, night cabs and a score of similar industries would suffer accordingly."[33] Across broad swaths of the U.S. populace, decisions about intimate partners were being based on personal choice and preference rather than family and community choice.

One other implication urbanization had for love and lust in the United States was the emergence of gay life. Those forced to live on the margins of society, without social spaces in which they might form a firm identity based on sexuality, found in cities a sort of critical mass.[34] LGBTQ courtship would remain largely hidden, constrained within small, discreet subcultures until the gay liberation movements in the 1970s. Even then U.S. gays and lesbians would find safety in urban enclaves and specialized spaces, such as gay bars.[35] There would be violent yet legal responses, but nevertheless the transition to an industrial economy was essential to a future proliferation of alternative households. By the end of the twentieth century, a newfound consciousness of sexual identity emerged such that gender preference had become an expected variable in any search for a mate. Earlier, though same-sex desire and practices occurred, it would have been almost unthinkable to wonder whether a young person preferred anything but a different-sex partner.

Dating, today, seems almost wholesome. But it was once scandalous. The term *date* originated in urban slang for scheduling a slot with a sex worker, and women who dated were sometimes scorned as "charity girls," who exchanged in-kind gifts, such as meals and entertainment, for sexual favors.[36] Date venues, from cafes to ice cream parlors and movie theaters, were seen as dangerous "vice resorts."[37] But in the 1930s prostitution, once used by many U.S. men of all social classes, receded as a common practice due to its increased criminalization and the institutionalization of dating as a courtship practice.[38] Almost as soon as dating became accepted, mainstream societal concerns over its similarity to prostitution were soon forgotten.[39]

As Beth Bailey shows in *From Front Porch to Back Seat*, dating had become the normative form of courtship by World War II. Early dating often took place in nickelodeons, which began to populate cityscapes in 1905, and in dance halls by the 1920s. Because people from different racial backgrounds all favored these places, early dating was a source of great anxiety for parents who feared cross-racial dalliances.[40] A 1930 article pointed to the diversity among people at one dance hall in New York: "A languorous and fragile blonde floating gracefully in the arms of a Filipino! A little black haired flapper in the close and questionable embrace of a Chinaman! A Negro orchestra blaring out jazz tunes. All around, Orientals—Filipinos, Chinamen, Japanese dancing with white girls."[41] Alongside White families Black elites voiced reservations about the questionable influence of "lower anti-social cultural groups" mixing with their children. In his 1927 book William Henry Jones, a professor at Howard University, compared dance-hall behavior to "lascivious orgies": "Many of the modern dances are sexual pantomimes. . . . A careful investigation disclosed the fact that the originators of these extreme forms of behavior have clearly in view a sexual end."[42] The anxieties that both Black and White parents felt about the potential for intergroup contact was tied to the possibility of sexual exploration and, indeed, violent retribution, in the absence of chaperoned courting.

Still, with the rise of dating, parental roles in mate selection receded dramatically. The oversight of intimate relations shifted from the woman's family to, in theory, the couple. But, given new gendered economic norms, practice shifted such regulation to men and not women. As Bailey's shrewd book title suggests, power transitioned from the paternalistic front porch to the backseat of the suitor's automobile. Social acceptability norms quickly arose to reinforce this gender divide, dictating that only men could ask women on dates and that only men should pay for dates.[43] Under the calling model, it had been the opposite, with women or their families inviting men to call. Now, as social norms restricted even working women from spending their earnings in the new dating system, sexual favors, or the potential for sexual favors, became women's currency of exchange. Dating flourished even during the Great Depression and became a mainstream activity for most U.S. youth across income levels.[44]

Likewise, the beauty and fashion industries found dating a profitable enterprise. They could sell more products when they played on women's desire to attract men's attention. Cosmetics sales exploded by 1910, in a way that would have been unthinkable when these were but the instruments of stage actors and prostitution's "painted ladies."[45] Similarly, women's fashions turned to the invitation of the male gaze. Clothes exposed more skin. Dancing during the Roaring Twenties revealed ankles and legs and arms, opening a new market for the depilation industry, which profited from portraying women's body hair as shameful and disgusting to potential suitors—which is to say, the advent of dating marks the point when consumer femininity became especially associated with making oneself sexually alluring to men.[46]

Yet, while heteronormativity assumes that men and women are to be intimately involved in courtship and marriage, racial boundaries are anchored by the presumption of cross-gender desire. Early twentieth-century discourse of a hegemonic White femininity assigned greater feminine value and beauty to Whiteness—or closer to Whiteness—and acted as a symbolic "yardstick" for all femininities.[47] This was clearly represented in popular culture, which signaled White women's gender subservience to men yet also emphasized women of color's, particularly Black women's, feminine inadequacies. Pervasive controlling images of the "mammy," for example, constructed Black women as aggressive and hypermasculine and represented light skin, fine features, and wavy or straight hair as part and parcel of hegemonic ideals of feminine beauty.[48] The growing twentieth-century ethnic beauty industry around embodied beauty practices such as hair relaxers and skin lighteners also resulted, in part, from how women of color have had to spend more time, resources, and energy to, as Devon Carbado puts it, "make themselves up women."[49] In this sense hegemonic femininities also create intrahierarchies of beauty among women.[50]

According to courtship researchers, dating itself evolved through two phases. In the 1930s and 1940s, a competitive form of "dating and rating" arose, which emphasized popularity and status as reflected in the number of first dates one could garner.[51] Serial monogamy came to define the post–World War II form of dating, with dating transitioning quickly into the process of "going steady."[52] The shift to universal attendance at high schools across the United States during this period institutionalized the practice with its elevation of peer-based socializing norms over family-based social life. Thus, dating became the norm not just for college students but also for high school students, and third-party mediators shifted from the church and family to peers. In the 1940s couples most frequently met through family connections; in subsequent decades they most frequently met through friends.[53]

Yet the autonomy linked to the rise of dating didn't bridge racial divides or transform the long-standing racial hierarchies in U.S. life. Indeed, dating exploded onto the scene just as antimiscegenation laws and racial segregation took hold. Groups on the cusp of "becoming White," such as Italians and Irish in the early twentieth century, often pressured members against fraternizing with African Americans and other non-White stigmatized groups. Such social control operated through the institution of the family, through socialization and ostracism.[54] Among African Americans the pressure had a different source. The history and ongoing reality of sexual assault against Black women and violence against Black men who consorted with White women led to community scrutiny and ostracism of White-Black pairings. As a result, even as greater interracial fraternization and dating arose, interracial dating and marriage remained stigmatized.

Into the twenty-first century, social pressures conflicted with the rise of personal preference in intimate partner choices. Even as the latter rose, the former remained in force.

The trend toward dating over courtship in the twentieth century reflected other forces chipping away at the homemaker/breadwinner Victorian ideal. The development of personal preference in dating is also tied to increased economic and social opportunities. In the 1950s we saw earlier marriage and high birth rates, but by the 1960s the nuclear family ideal (which, as Stephanie Coontz reminds us, is an untraditional family form) was beginning to show wider cracks.[55] More women entered the labor market, and birth control helped prevent unwanted pregnancy. Economic independence combined with reproductive freedom meant that dating and marriage declined as means of survival—they become ever more optional. Gender roles were in high flux, with women demanding more social, sexual, and economic power both inside and outside of marriage. Two books, *Sex and the Single Girl* and *The Feminine Mystique,* heralded second-wave feminism.[56]

The narrative of a gender revolution most resonated with middle-class White women, who were the ones to primarily benefit from increased opportunities for self-development. Still, women's increased power over economic and sexual lives led to changes in marriage patterns and relationship models too. With most women entering the labor market full-time by the 1970s and 1980s, the age at first marriage rose, as did the prevalence of nonmarital monogamous relationships. By the end of the twentieth century, the couple relationship had become increasingly untethered from the economic exigencies of marriage. Women were theoretically now more able to make autonomous partner choices based on compatibility and personal preferences, just as men (albeit, White men) had been freed to do so a century earlier.

In these advanced stages of capitalism, the monogamous relationship is much more than a context in which to raise and socialize children—first and foremost, it is now a cultural symbol of romance and individual self-fulfillment.[57] Accordingly, the state's oversight of the family receded, as exemplified by the rollback of antimiscegenation laws in 1967, the passage of no-fault divorce laws, and the legalization of contraception and abortion in 1965 and 1973, respectively. This series of changes would also usher in the legalization of gay marriage. All would remain socially contentious and variably legislated. And amid seemingly monumental changes, discriminatory practices would remain largely intact. They were simply repackaged, with racialized preferences for intimate relations now rhetorically rendered *private* and *personal* choices rather than social impositions.

Widespread access to high-quality contraception starting in the 1970s, in tandem with women's lessening economic reliance on marriage, made it more socially acceptable to seek sexual and emotional fulfillment outside of marriage. In this sense, women became culturally conceived as "free" subjects. Yet, like the notion of colorblindness in intimate relations, this appearance of agency was complicated by continued power inequities. Despite social recognition of women's autonomy in their dating and sexual lives, gendered expectations around men's control of the initiation and course of courtship remained firm.[58]

During the 1960s and 1970s, most universities coeducated and dismantled strict single-sex dormitory policies, which relaxed institutional responsibility for the management of students' sex lives. Attending parties and bars became increasingly common alongside dating culture as an alternative means to meet other singles. These developments laid the groundwork for what became a new phase of U.S. courtship beginning in the 1990s: "hookup" culture. Journalists and scholars began to observe and debate the "hookup" as the dominant pattern of sexual and romantic socialization. While dating often relied on friends and family to introduce potential partners to each other, hookups introduced a degree of randomness to the encounter, with initial meetings often occurring at a party or bar, initiated by the individuals and facilitated by alcohol. In this way hookup courtship further centralized the role of the individual in determining mate choice.[59]

And, of course, just as new dating behavior had scandalized onlookers in the early twentieth century, the hookup became the subject of much pearl clutching. Articles and books whose titles gasped in horror at the death of the date abounded: "Campus Romance, Unrequited: Dating Scene Fails Women, Study Says"; "Love on Vacation? Romance Displaced by Flings on Modern College Campus"; "Romance Went the Way of the Dodo"; "Hookups and Sexual Regret among College Women"; and *Unhooked: How Young Women Pursue Sex, Delay Love and Lose at Both.*[60] Hookup culture and its celebration of individual choice are likely to have consequences with respect to race. For instance, studies of predominantly White colleges indicate that minority women and Asian men have fewer

hookup opportunities than White peers.[61] This will have important implications for how these groups experience online-dating culture, which, we
argue, has truly reified the role of individual choice in the racialized sexual
marketplace.

THE LONG ARC FROM COURTSHIP CALLING
TO ONLINE DATING

The transition from calling to dating in the late nineteenth and early
twentieth centuries both reflected and further spurred on changing familial and gender roles in U.S. life. Calling culture didn't disappear, but it
receded as dating and hookup behaviors became more prevalent—new
courtship practices haven't *displaced* but *reordered* their preceding practices. Thus, dating changed the order in which calling took place, with
only serious dating relationships eventually leading to parental exposure
and vetting. Similarly, hooking up hasn't displaced dating but altered the
order in which dates occur, with only some hookup partners pursuing a
possible dating relationship.

The ongoing trajectory of courtship across these three stages reflects
one singular thematic arc—the deconstruction and casualization of how
U.S. relationships begin. Each shift underscores the rising centrality of
individual autonomy and the incremental recession of third-party intervention such that casual sexual relations are normalized and marriage is a
possibility with, rather than a necessity to, socially acceptable sex. Yet all
these changes are still framed by ongoing racialization. Although the state's
oversight receded with the rollback of laws about marriage and reproductive matters in this period, our innermost preferences were imprinted with
the sexual-racial hierarchy, and racial segregation in public and private life
continues to reproduce racialized patterns of interpersonal relations. The
media continues to propagate harmful images and stereotypes of people of
color. Rules once codified by the state are now enforced through the personal preferences explicitly leveraged in online dating.

In some ways online dating is twenty-first-century catalog marriage.
Catalog romance emerged in response to structural changes wrought
by eighteenth-century colonial and frontier migration, which disrupted

traditional ways to meet. Similarly, online dating reflects efforts to expand the pool of potential partners—and, in some circles, resistance to hookup courtship.[62] High school and college are no longer prime venues for meeting marital partners now that individuals delay—or opt out of—marriage. U.S. Americans also began to work longer hours, further reducing their exposure to the dating market.[63] Bars and clubs arose to take the place of educational settings as meeting places. To some extent people also turned to singles ads placed in papers, but "lonely hearts" pages were stigmatized and lacked wide appeal because of the per-word cost and, perhaps most important, their lack of photos. Other kinds of dating services, such as matchmaking agencies and phone and video dating were even more costly.[64] Miss Manners weighed in on the matter in 1998, lamenting the fact that friends and family had become too busy to set up their single friends. She saw dating services as the "embarrassing and unattractive" outsourcing of blind dating.[65]

The internet changed everything.

Online dating, at first reverently referred to as technodating or cyberdating, evolved informally vis-à-vis email communications and chat rooms. It was free and it was private. Unless we count the platforms on which people were communicating, there was no third-party involvement. The now-iconic romantic comedy *You've Got Mail,* in which the protagonists meet in an AOL chat room for people over thirty, hinged on the novelty of such a romance, and a 1994 article about chat-room dating quoted a frequent user—"it's safe, it's cheap, and you don't have to sit in a smoky bar and drink"—before cautioning against "cyber-cads."[66]

In the mid- to late-1990s, internet dating became an explicitly consumer space. In 1995 Match arrived on the scene, followed shortly by one of the first niche dating sites, the aforementioned JDate (specializing in matching Jewish singles). Chat rooms would be remembered as emblematic of 1990s-era innocence almost before the 1990s were out. Unsurprisingly, many online-dating programs began on college campuses, ground zero for the paradigmatic hookup scene. Between 1996 and 2002 college-specific dating programs such as Harvard's Datesite.com, Brown University's HUGS (Helping Undergraduates Socialize), Yale's Yalestation. com, and Wesleyan's WesMatch.com debuted, operating alongside the hookup culture that was settling in as a normalized social activity.

Interviews in college newspapers suggested that these early ventures were, in fact, a response or example of resistance to hookup culture. When asked why he developed HUGS in 1997, Brown undergraduate Rajib Chanda said he saw it as an antidote to the typical practice at Brown in which "you meet, get drunk, hookup and then either avoid eye contact the next day or find yourself in a relationship."[67] Of WesMatch.com, its student founder said in 2004, "We're not just in it for hookups, we're trying to foster real relationships, real compatibility."[68]

Key to the present study, interviews also reveal how such efforts signaled a hope that, in the future, young people might transcend same-race pairings. Chanda, for instance, spoke of how his dating program would allow students to bypass traditional social barriers: "We're very segregated in different groups—by ethnicity, sexual orientation, fraternity, race. You don't meet new people. I always thought that was the biggest problem we have as students." Just a decade and thousands of newly spawned sites later, online dating was the second-highest–grossing paid content in the internet industry.[69]

Online dating further evolved with the advent of apps. Arriving in 1998, Lovegety, a Japanese mechanical device, can be seen as the earliest harbinger of location-based dating applications, but the arrival of the smartphone would see a near-instant flourishing.[70] Grindr debuted in 2009, billed as a hookup app, expanding the pool of potential partners for gay men, and Tinder, catering to straight people, followed in 2012. From there we have seen a profusion: apps for farmers or famous daters, apps geared toward religious or racial and ethnic communities, apps that match users with people they've passed on the street during the course of their days, and apps for specific subgroups among population segments. To heighten the likelihood of good matches, online companies have developed a number of innovations, including personality questionnaires that build on (and iteratively inform) algorithms and cross-platform connectivity with social media accounts (both for identity verification and for further refining the pool of eligible daters).[71]

Some measures suggest that nearly 40 percent of the single U.S. American population has used online dating—which, again, is barely twenty years old.[72] Its growing acceptance is indicated by large numbers of U.S. Americans who see it as normal, especially college graduates, who no longer distinguish between the terms *dating* and *online dating*. A full 58 percent of college graduates have friends who date online, and 46 percent have friends who met their partner or spouse through web services and apps.[73] A majority of Americans (60 percent) believe online dating is a good way to meet people, and 80 percent of online daters think so. In 2001 Ilana Bagell could barely contain her disdain for such practices, asserting in an interview in her college newspaper: *Agreed*

> I think it's totally pathetic that people in college would resort to online dating services. Every day you are surrounded by thousands of students in your age group. If you've reached the point of online dating, not only have you reached a new level of desperation, but you might want to consider developing some social skills.[74]

A decade and a half later, a large survey found that 70 percent of college students—the *last* group most companies assumed would be interested in online dating—are, in fact, seeking out partners online.[75]

The internet is now a central way that heterosexual and same-sex couples enter committed relationships.[76] One-third of current marriages begin online, according to one study, while an industry survey of engaged couples and newlyweds reports that meeting online is now among the most common ways to meet.[77] As an example of how online dating has led to a shift away from third-party intermediaries, the number of couples meeting through friends, family, school, neighborhood, church, and work has taken a major downturn in the twenty-first century.[78] Since 2013 meeting online had surpassed meeting through friends, becoming the number one most common way couples met.[79] Even though hookup courtship often involves strangers and acquaintances, friends are still involved to the extent that they go together to the parties and bars where they find hookup partners. But the turn toward online dating almost entirely removes friends and community ties from the courtship process.

McDating, the Mass Marketization of Love

Detractors argue that online dating commodifies and cheapens love. We argue that it represents one end of a long trajectory of courtship under capitalism, where the individual increasingly operates as an agent of consumption. We established earlier that marriage has always been as much an economic institution as a social one. And, in fact, the emergence of dating culture in the 1900s, which is often looked on by today's standards as wholesome and old-fashioned, was the bellwether of conspicuous consumption.

Today there is ever more slippage between the market and our personal lives. In her book *Cold Intimacies,* Eva Illouz calls this emotional capitalism. She posits that the emotional and economic spheres have converged, with market-like transactions defining our emotional relationships, and interpersonal relationships becoming the "epicenter" of economic relationships.[80] Some of the people we interviewed for this book used transactional and objectifying language to describe online dating. One compared it to looking through a shoe catalog. Another asked, "Are you really just out shopping for your next dog, your next husband, your next life? Is that the kind of transactional interaction you want to have with your soulmate?" This criticism is actually quite similar to early concerns about dating raised by the sociologist Willard Waller, who lamented dating culture's exploitative emphasis on the quantity of first dates and the competitive rating system to which individuals were objectified.[81] New forms of courtship are consistently met with both suspicion and the romanticization of past practices.

The ideology of love easily conceals the transactional underpinnings of courtship and marriage, but these are more clearly revealed by the process of online dating. Metaphors of market transactions like "shopping" for a sexual partner through online dating are widespread. Yet these metaphors have already been in use to describe dating for more than a century: "playing the field," "shopping around," singles "advertisements," and "why buy the cow when you can get the milk for free?" spring to mind. What online dating introduces is a revolutionary transition from scarcity to abundance in the romantic match market.

The investment of time and anxiety people have historically made from seeking mates has been greatly reduced by the arrival of real-time databases. These can keep track, for instance, of people within a designated geographic radius who have declared themselves single and interested in, well, mingling. Individual networks are dwarfed by the pool of possible mates represented by online-dating platforms. For most daters this is a major and obvious improvement, yet there is an understandable sense of loss. One of our interviewees lamented that the fatigue associated with online dating has replaced the "old-fashioned" and presumably wonderful feeling of being swept off his feet—in part, because having learned (or selected) so many of their qualities in advance, he no longer feels the butterflies of nervousness when first meeting someone. Another person described online dating as so "direct and intentional" that it seems discordant with the "romantic notion that we will somehow find true love landing in our lap without effort." It is indeed difficult to maintain an it-was-meant-to-be frame when there are clearly so many suitable candidates waiting to be winnowed down in the spreadsheet.

Because humans have spent so long courting and pairing off under conditions of scarcity, it can be difficult to adapt to the sense that abundance is impersonal. Jordan, a Black twenty-seven-year-old business owner, compared the efficiency to fast food, telling us, "It's like going to McDonald's or going to Wendy's or going to a place where you're trying to get something real quick." Another felt overwhelmed by the choice, warning, "You can't be on it for too long because the facial recognition stops working as well until they start, like, blending together." Many of our interviewees described the process as comparison shopping; a notable simile compared choosing among dating profiles to selecting from the massive menu at the Cheesecake Factory. *everyone knows what is out there*

What was once a personal, limited market is now a public, commercial market. To manage the volume daters are forced to make calculated choices—a process for which a cottage industry of data analytics and app hacks has sprung up, promising to game the system of love in their customers' favor.[82] It makes sense that individuals feel like the spontaneity and serendipity of dating has been routinized and rationalized along the way. As we talked to more and more daters, we noted that every interviewee referenced their preoccupation with crafting profiles designed to set themselves apart from the masses then with searching for strategies to sift through so many choices. These strategies are frequently described as ways to follow personal preferences. However, our data suggests that at least some of these preferences map onto the history of racialized social order.

Is the Expanded Online-Dating Market Increasing
or Decreasing Homophily?

Research on assortative mating consistently shows that individuals tend to pair with others of the same race, education, and religion. In this chapter we have traced how the role of third-party matchmaking has gone from prominence to recession, as mate finding moved from the domain of the state and the family to the domain of friends and peer networks to the self (and the platform). Online dating may expand the landscape of choice, yet the question remains: Will people begin to look outward, searching among all the possibilities now available, or will they become *more* conservative by winnowing an enormous potential pool of partners down using blunt instruments like race?

The reason behind assortative mating remains unclear. Did a selection of "like" mates result simply because predigital daters had fewer opportunities to meet people outside their social groups? Or are people inherently more interested in coupling up with people who share characteristics like race, neighborhood, socioeconomic status, and education? The mass online-dating market provides a litmus test for these questions. Who we know in real life no longer limits who we want to know. Beth, a White dater we interviewed, described how, with online dating, "there isn't a barrier of entry to it, so you can just join and make a profile and you could in theory talk to anyone on there." In this regard, online dating allows people to bypass traditional group boundaries and instead seek out partners based on attributes that may better predict compatibility, such as shared interests and worldviews. And, indeed, early evidence is already suggesting that online dating leads to greater exogamy.

This may come as a surprise to online daters, who turn out to be poor predictors of their own mate preferences. One experiment showed that daters' stated ideal partner preferences, including physical characteristics, did not ultimately correlate to those with whom they most connected in a speed-dating event. In his research, which highlights daters' unexpected outcomes (and outmarriages), Dan Slater quoted a dater named Kelly at length. She appreciated how dating online enabled her to meet people apart from "the mold of who everyone expected her to be with." Similarly, one of our interviewees for this book project, Helena, a Brazilian Jewish

American woman, told us about her Italian American boyfriend, whom she met on a dating app:

> He's from an upper-class suburb. I'm from inside the city. He's really into brand name clothing, and I love thrift stores. I like to read a lot and I try really hard in school, and he doesn't love to read as much and wants to go into his family's restaurant business.

Helena mused that

> it's funny that I ended up with him sort of, because he is not exactly—I always thought I would end up with a nerdy guy who wore glasses and listened to NPR. . . . And he said, "I never thought I'd be dating a Jewish girl. I never thought I would be with someone who is so artsy and weird and proud of it." But he said, "Now that I'm with you, I couldn't imagine anything else."

Despite social class, religious, and ethnicity differences, Helena and her partner came across each other in the boundless space of the internet. They had, by the time we spoke, been together for over two years.

To what extent does online dating enable people to find partners across racial boundaries? Historically, this is one of the most stigmatized forms of exogamy. Christian Rudder, for instance, points out that personalities differ little over racial groups—factors such as religion and political stance matter much more than race for ultimate compatibility. Yet race still dominates among OkCupid dater preferences, suggesting these daters believe they will find better matches in their own racial or ethnic group.[83]

Many dating websites specifically tout their algorithms' ability to perfect matchmaking. For example, eHarmony's dating website describes its "compatibility matching system" and trumpets how it goes deeper than photographs to help users find a quality relationship. OkCupid touts its use of mathematics to match people based on personality traits, and Match sells its unique insight into couple chemistry and shared interests. If these claims are true, users should be shown compatible matches regardless of racial background.[84]

Indeed, based on our interviews, people with specific racial preferences were still exposed to daters of other racial backgrounds. This includes White daters, but also minority daters searching for similar others, especially when they are living in primarily White spaces. In one study of

White daters that allowed users to specify their racial preference, only 41 percent of White men and 27 percent of White women indicated that they were open to dating someone of "any race."[85] The rejection of non-White daters is sobering, to be sure. But the result also indicates that about one-third of Whites now have the opportunity to meet people of other races through online dating, even though they remain quite segregated in their offline lives. The twenty-first century marks a new world, where daters of various racial and ethnic backgrounds—particularly Whites who have long been self-segregating—have the opportunity to opt into interracial interactions in an era where internet dating is the norm. Indeed, from the perspective of racial and ethnic minorities, this also means that they too will confront Whites in cyberspace, for better or for worse.

In the recent history of courtship, we have seen how first parental oversight and then peer oversight receded. Similarly, the state's paternalistic oversight of the family and interracial marriage has also diminished. Thus, the freedom and autonomy of the individual in online dating has, in theory, the potential to increase interracial contact.[86] But this optimism is plausible only if we forget that the idea of individual choice was born in an era of racialized regulation. Even today we find that individuals employ online dating to self-regulate and self-discipline as they are looking for a date, ejecting particular suitors out of the running for fear of parental or social retaliation and taking for granted that certain groups just should not mix. This Foucauldian argument is especially relevant in the absence of coercive, state-led measures.[87] Antimiscegenation laws no longer act as a formal mechanism of social control, yet the power of racial hierarchies operates in our bodies and minds. With the help of the new digital technologies of the twenty-first century, individuals voluntarily monitor themselves to ensure conformity with cultural norms. Through a process of digital-sexual racism, socially constructed racial "folklore" simply allows racial preference to look as though it is solely a matter of personal preference.[88]

As we have seen in this chapter, the history of courtship has also been a history of individuals learning to leverage their own attributes and actively define those they seek in a partner. Given the legacy of the state's intervention in racial matters, it is inevitable that race would become a central attribute of individual identity in the romantic dating marketplace.

3 New Rules?

I found that fascinating too, just thinking of it in terms of
David Attenborough narrating all this stuff, these mating
rituals; it just seemed very like . . . it was like a digital ver-
sion of the male bird of paradise with the feathers who's
doing the dance trying to get a woman's attention.

Andrew, 2019

Antimiscegenation law was, at its heart, a gendered racial project that
sought to keep men of color from marrying and from having sexual relations with White women. It established and enforced strict rules of behavior across racial groups. The history of courtship in the United States—
from the colonial times to online dating in the twenty-first century—has
evolved directly out of that legacy.

Gender, including the social-cultural meanings and ideologies associated with gendered differences, is central to how people engage in intimate relationships, including courtship, marriage, and dating.[1] Although
gender is always present, how gender *operates* varies across racial status.
As a result, any discussion of race must also include a careful consideration of gender construction.

Social norms have changed over time, such that distinct gender norms
and roles are less salient but still important in heterosexual courtship.[2] With
few exceptions studies show that the gender asymmetries in online dating
carry over historical assumptions attached to gender binaries. For example,
women daters prefer partners with higher or equal educational attainment,
whereas men prefer equally or less educated partners; men prefer partners
younger than themselves, whereas women prefer similarly aged or older

men; men are more body- and appearance-oriented in their stated preferences than women are, with the notable exception of height—women
strongly prefer men taller than themselves and men prefer women shorter
than themselves; and women prefer partners who make a higher income,
while men at least profess that they do not feel strongly about their prospective partner's income.[4] These trends, present in dating both on and offline,
point to specific gendered ways that people approach their dating and sexual
lives.

Commonly, U.S. Americans believe that sex ratios on dating websites
and apps grossly advantage women. For example, one Reddit subthread
asks plaintively, "Why Does It Seem Like Every Dating Site Is a Sausage
Fest?"[5] Dating companies that cater to clients looking for sex over relationships *do* tend to be dominated by men, but the average dating website is not
so lopsided. In fact, many niche websites, such as one marketed to bookish
intellectuals and another marketed at singles who prefer country living, as
well as marriage-oriented eHarmony, all report memberships more heavily
weighted toward women. Match and OkCupid, along with other mainstream dating companies, report a more equitable fifty-fifty gender split
(again, gender binaries, in which cisgender womanhood and manhood are
the norm, are persistent, with mainstream acceptance for gender fluidity,
nonbinary gender, and transgender identities remaining out of reach),
while Tinder reports a 45 percent women user base. These numbers can be
taken with a grain of salt: such statistics usually count all profiles, both
active and inactive, real and spam, and they do not tell us anything about
how sex ratios vary by race, age, and location. There may, say, be many
young men on a given site, but very few middle-aged or senior men.

Online-dating companies hold this kind of information close to their
chest since it could have serious implications for business. Since we are
not a business, we can reveal real numbers from the site whose data we
use throughout this book. This site's membership was 43 percent women
and 57 percent men (with the dataset limited to only members who are
active users, unlikely to spam accounts).[7] This gender divide varies only
minorly by ethnicity (see figure 3.1): the ratio of men to women is highest
among Latino/a daters, at 58 percent men and 42 percent women, and
lowest among Asian and Black daters, at about 53 percent men to 46 percent women. White dater sex ratios fall in between, at 56 percent men to

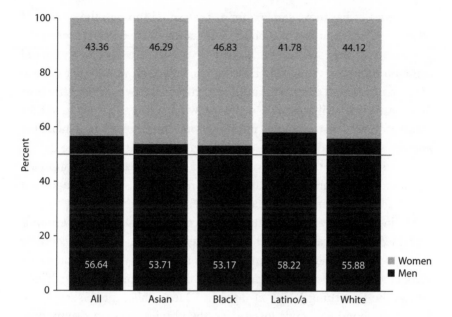

Figure 3.1. Gender Composition by Race of Users on Online-Dating Platform. Sourced directly from our data.

44 percent women. These numbers suggest that the gender imbalance on some dating websites could be greater than the imbalance in famously "lopsided" populations such as China and India.

Besides sex ratio there are several other significant gender differences, all of which relate to the broader empirical analysis that unfolds in the rest of this book. Our emphasis on gender in this chapter is not to say that gender is *more* important than other social statuses, such as race, in online dating. Rather, to understand how racialized hierarchies are continuing to operate in online dating, we need to first outline some of the key ways that intersecting gendered differences are operating there as well.

THE OCCASIONAL IMPORTANCE OF PHYSICAL AND SOCIOECONOMIC FACTORS IN PARTNER SELECTION

One key difference we see in women's and men's approaches to online dating is the importance of physical attraction. When we asked our interviewees what they searched for as they sifted through the profiles of other site users, men and women agreed that they looked for someone with a sense of humor, who they found attractive, and with whom they shared common interests. When we drilled down, however, we saw that hetero-sexual daters found different things "attractive": men who cited attractive-ness meant, primarily, physical attributes, while women specified that they measured men's attractiveness physically but also in terms of personality and economic standing. These breakdowns were reflected in the daters' own profiles: more men than women filled out the income field, support-ing the gendered perception that men's economic status is more important for attracting women than women's would be for attracting men.

During interviews heterosexual women of all educational backgrounds explained that education (which they treated as a proxy for socioeconomic status) was especially important. Janice, a thirty-one-year-old Black law-yer, noted, "My type is educated; preferably an advanced degree. That's always the first thing I look at, literally." Meanwhile, men asked about what they found attractive focused on the physical. Sam, a twenty-one-year-old White undergraduate student, was more general, saying, "I like them not to be fat and just pretty. I'm not really sure how to explain that," while Raymond, a thirty-one-year-old White professor, confessed, "I'm drawn, usually, to thinner women who have longer hair, and usually a pretty light complexion." Both men later indicated that they also value personality, yet, like most of the straight men we interviewed, women's physical attributes got first billing.

Even in the abstract, these gendered differences are not merely benign preferences (as you may have guessed in our discussions of racialized pref-erence in earlier chapters). Instead, they show us how long-standing heteronormative scripts about men's and women's "normative" roles in courtship remain in force, even—or perhaps more so—in the digital age.

Indeed, as we argued in chapter 2, the explosion of dating in the twen-tieth century elevated the concept of embodied femininity—how to look, what to wear—to the degree that women internalized and reenacted scripts related to making themselves sexually alluring to men. A century later such gender norms have changed little. Many women now achieve higher education and greater economic independence, yet, in online dat-ing, their looks remain a high priority among their possible suitors. Taking

this a step further, we suggest that appearance, in itself—usually an indicator only of proximity to or distance from hegemonic norms of White
femininity—is not, and never has been, an objective criterion.

Heterosexual women value appearance, but in a different way. To put
it simply, they measure attractiveness with a ruler. It's all about height.
Women had no qualms telling us that they wanted to date only men taller
than themselves, preferably much taller. The only other preference women
so consistently cited was a universal distaste for men's shirtless profile
photos. Bianca, who is five foot two, told us, "I typically don't go for anybody that is below five seven." I might be moving that up a little bit because
my babies can't be short. That's just not good. It might still happen, but
I want probability to be on my side." Women who used dating platforms that did not include height as an option talked about examining
pictures closely so they could estimate a man's height: "I tend to look for
good pictures to tell for height, because I tend, even though I am five one
and a half on a good day, I tend to go for guys who are much taller. So
group pictures really help me for picking that out." Statistically, taller
women have more difficulty finding matches that fit this standard, given
that the average U.S. man is five feet nine. One woman had lowered her
height requirement: "I was like, 'Gotta be at least six feet in order for me
to, like, be interested in you.' Then I moved it down to like five nine."
Similar to men's preferences for particular body types, women's desire for
taller men fits with common ideas about the ways "desirable" others
should look. Gender norms have been internalized, repackaged instead as
personal preferences.

There are prevailing gender differences that are common across racial
groups, though we also see substantial variation of the kind that was
clearer in the past. While Whites were able to establish families and
extend kinships with marriage, African Americans, and at times Asian
immigrants, were once forbidden by slavery and immigration restrictions.
Upper-class women were able to rely on their partner's income, while
other women (especially immigrant and native-born women of color)
have always been compelled or coerced to labor for wages alongside men.
Some men, particularly racial and ethnic minorities, have historically not
been able to live out the "breadwinning" ideal. These differences suggest
that gender preferences are likely to intersect with racial backgrounds and

socioeconomic status. This gap is even more serious for college-educated Black women, who outnumber Black men with a college degree.

Further, throughout U.S. history the media has propagated stereotypes and images that tie beauty to White European—or *closer* to White—features, hair textures, and body types. Whereas White femininity has been represented in popular culture as beautiful and good, women of color, especially Black women with dark complexions, have been historically represented as less attractive.[8] Hegemonic images have framed White, middle-class masculinity as normative, while subordinating minority men's masculinity as either excessive or insufficient (often in ways that tie Black men to the former and Asian men to the latter).[9] Patricia Hill Collins argues that these images have found particular purchase in the mass media.[10] One major question, then, is whether body type or socioeconomic status—concerns that many of our interview respondents insist are simply matters of "personal preference"—can ever be racially neutral. We already know daters' evaluation of appearance hews to widely held gender norms, but in the next chapter we illustrate that, among White daters, racial preference often *trumps* these norms. This suggests that embodied attractiveness itself is not an objective sorting mechanism but rather a product of both gender *and* racial hierarchies.

SHE RESPONDS, SHE RESPONDS NOT

Dating, as we discussed in chapter 2, took courtship out of the home, shifting advantage from the woman's family to the individual suitor. Courtship had always been shaped by economic interests—inheritance and a concern for within-class matches key among them—but the date made the economics more explicit. Society was at first uneasy with the in-kind transactional expectations between men and women. With barely disguised distaste, the 1930s sociologist Willard Waller wrote about the lack of commitment and meaning he saw in the new morality of the "peculiar relationship known as 'dating.'" Waller observed that the transactional nature of dating had introduced antagonism and suspicion between women and men, with women exploiting men for "presents and expensive amusements" and men seeking "thrills from the body of the woman."

Almost a century and a number of courting technologies later, a similar dynamic has persisted.[11]

One sort of currency in dating apps is messaging, and we see notable gendered differences in message patterns. On most dating websites there is no restriction on who can message first, but in practice straight men are more likely to initiate interactions than women. Counting all the initial messages between heterosexual daters in our dataset, we found that only about 28 percent were sent by women. In the descriptive data (table A1) in this book's appendix, we see that men send more than twice as many messages as women, and the gap is similar across the various ethnic and racial groups presented (see online tables O12A–B at www.ucpress.edu/9780520293458). This suggests that the historical pattern of men pursuing and women waiting to be pursued persists through the performative nature of messaging.

Gendered norms are also made plain when we consider who accrues the most messages: across straight and gay daters, heterosexual women receive the most messages by far. While theoretically, there is no reason women cannot make the first move, the conformity of women to passive dating behavior is surprising in the absence of third-party pressure. Yet the "rules" are entrenched. As Natalie, a White undergraduate student, put it, reflecting a fairly universal sentiment, "Guys message me. I don't message them first. I'm not that interested or eager or thirsty"; that is, Natalie doesn't want to appear too *eager* to gain a man's attention—a negative connotation that evokes social distaste for the "boy-crazy" and even hints at slut shaming. So she waits for men to approach her. It's part of the gender performance she enacts online.

Recently, a few dating apps have intentionally designed their platforms to disrupt gender norms and require that women message first. Yet, even in this scenario, traditional gender scripts often win out. As one man told us, "What I came to find out was that even on apps that make the woman go first, there's still this broad expectation that the man, in a hetero type arrangement, that the guy is supposed to initiate, just carry the conversation, and propel it forward."

Online dating has all sorts of potential to remake courtship, but we find it rarely disrupts gendered and raced power relations. In fact, many of these imbalances have taken on a new form. Many of our interviewee men insisted that this means that they are competing with a formidable deluge of eager men, while women expressed anxiety about whether they were receiving the "right" number of messages.

Besides, online daters are hyperaware of the other's gaze when they have laid out their stats—notes about their physical appearance and career achievement, for example. The depersonalized mass dating market exerts outsized pressure to perform gendered ideals. Straight men certainly noted that they needed to showcase their occupation in their profiles to compete with other men for women's attention, while the importance of physical beauty weighed more heavily on women who more passively wait for men's inquiries.

When these performative acts of gender are carried out, it appears that heterosexual women and men each interpret the same dynamic in opposite ways. For example, Andrew, a forty-five-year-old White-Latino dater, told us that he was struck by the scripted nature of interactions. He had recently entered the online-dating scene after going through a divorce and often compared what he called the "old way of dating" to the new "dating game":

> It seemed to me like the gender expectations were more reinforced than almost any context I had ever seen outside the online-dating situation. It was scripted. It was almost inflexible, the way that things were supposed to go down. If I didn't initiate the conversation, or if I didn't pivot to asking the woman out, nine times out of ten it would never happen. Even in situations where we stopped chatting for a while, then I came back, and I was like, "How have you been?" or whatever. When the topic came up about asking them out, they'd be like, "Oh, I didn't think you were interested, because you never asked me out." Well, you could've done that too, but it's just not even seen as a possibility for a lot of people.

Interestingly, while Andrew read this dynamic as evidence of women's passivity, many women described how letting the man do the messaging gave them more agency in the interaction. One woman we interviewed said, "I think that makes me feel like, I don't know, I don't want to say more powerful, but more in control, I guess." Still, men like Jordan reported, "98 percent of the time, I'm the one that's controlling the conversation. Girls say it on their profiles, 'Message me first. I'm shy.'" Jason also made it clear that he did not like it when women violated this norm: "I know a lot of men are like, 'Oh, well, all the responsibility is always on me to approach,' and it's like, if a girl seriously approached you, you wouldn't know what to do about it. It just feels unnatural and wrong, like she's trying to kill you or something." Elaborating, he explained that such behavior made him nervous that he might wake up after such a date in a "bathtub missing a kidney." Jason may have been joking, but the relatively prosaic behavior of women's initiation, a mere click in the case of online dating, is clearly subject to strong social sanction.

Frustration was a common reaction to the gendered dynamic of communicating on dating sites. "I think that everyone has heard about ghosting," said Connor, a twenty-two-year-old White dater, about the ambiguity of rejection. "People in general in dating are dehumanizing often, like, people don't care, and they treat people . . . as if they were sort of fictional and not real people." Most respondents we interviewed agreed that nonresponse is universally understood to be rejection. As Lisa, an eighteen-year-old Asian American college student, commented, "If I feel like a guy is weird or I'm not into it, I don't feel the need to be like. 'I'm not into it anymore.' I'll just stop responding." Nevertheless, some men insisted that the ambiguity *confused* them. One twenty-four-year-old Asian American online dater named Henry said he could read rejection cues more quickly and better in person, while online,

> the conversation style is different, and if someone is disinterested in the conversation, they can just leave. . . . But, if you're at a bar and the other person doesn't want to keep talking, you can kind of figure that out. I think, you can judge and assess the possibility of this going further, a lot faster.

Many women—for whom the issue of safety loomed larger than for men—noted on the other hand that being able to reject someone from afar rather than risk an angry, in-person confrontation was obviously preferable, provided that nonresponse did not evoke, as it had for some women and gay men in our sample, angry online attacks and cyberstalking.

The gendered sending and receiving patterns among heterosexual daters, coupled with the way the terrain of potential partners looks so enticingly expansive on dating sites, meant that being ignored was frustrating, if not infuriating, for some heterosexual men. But that perception of boundless choice is deceiving. Just because many singles are *visible* does not mean they are *accessible*. Cisgender men we talked to often described the initial illusion of a "feast," which quickly dissipated as they found they received far fewer messages than they sent. Some men we interviewed expressed deep resentment of what they perceived to be women's disproportionate advantage in online dating. Yet, as Eric Klinenberg and Aziz Ansari describe in their book *Modern Romance*, for all the complaints about women's advantages, men still get more attention online than they do in other venues, like bars.[12] Such discontent likely reflects the clash between fantasizing about what appears to be a very large, accessible market of women and receiving a host of nonresponses that feels just as vast.

This feeling is especially amplified for men of color who find their racial status penalized in online dating. For example, Derick, a twenty-eight-year-old heterosexual Black man, explained that had been quite popular with women as a Division 1 athlete in a predominantly White college town. Today, though, he said,

> What I dislike for me personally—I'm a Black man, and it's just. . . . It's awful for me. . . . If I was White . . . I think I would have been very much more successful because I'm seeing my other friends, my other White friends, they literally do not try. It's like it falls in their lap.

Derick's impressions—shared by other men of color—highlight the vastly different understanding of privilege in online dating. They challenge White men's common assertion that women hold all the power by pointing out that White men also have disproportionate sway in the online-dating market. Other men of color pointed to the complexity of the gendered dynamic of contacting others on the dating site. They saw White women and some minority women as feeling scared to respond to their messages, and they speculated that these women may have internalized stereotypes about minority men, such as Black men's alleged criminality and Asian men's alleged effeminacy. Straight Black women had their own complaints about the setup of online dating: far from feeling overwhelmed by an enormous deluge of messages, Black women felt all but invisible. One straight Black woman we interviewed said succinctly that online dating was a "White women's market." While this may also be the case offline, expressed racial preferences and inequities in internet dating are visible in a way they are not offline. Furthermore, some daters expressed anxiety over how online dating had opened up new markets to their same-race counterparts, leading to greater racial competition for their attention.

QUEERING CONTACT, DISRUPTING RACE?

Despite the many qualms we heard about the gender rituals in online dating, many heterosexual men and women have accepted a system in which men felt compelled to lead the courtship. LGBTQ daters, however, played with the norms. Bisexual daters, for example, noted a disconnect between how they interacted with men and women in online dating compared to in person and said they felt empowered to deviate from normative gender expectations. Josie, a bisexual nineteen-year-old White undergraduate student, told us that with men "it's always him texting first," but she likes how she experiences a greater sense of autonomy when interacting with women: "When it is other women, you have that control, too, which is fun. It's good to have that in a way. With girls I'm like, 'Hey.' You know? And then you're starting with your conversation or however you want to take it."

Daters who identified as lesbian or gay constructed their own approaches, reimagining how romantic relationships could begin. Samantha, a twenty-year-old White lesbian college student, noted that the predetermined expectation among heterodaters meant that courtship "goes a lot faster" given men's controls over the direction of the relationship. "Say a guy hits on a girl, and a girl's really into it," she said. "That means that both people are on board automatically. I feel that lesbians will take a little longer to get to know each other because there's not that one dude pushing it forward." While the timeframe of courtship can vary for any couple, she described an appreciation for taking things slow, engaging intimately, and establishing exclusivity with a new partner in an organic way, because neither one nor the other dictated the progression of the relationship. She also resisted the conventional gender frame that is too frequently imposed on queer relationships, a heteronormative frame that implies a power differential:

I feel like the stereotype is that there's one really dude bro in a lesbian couple and one really girly girl. But me and my girlfriend change outfits all the time. We wear the same clothes. No one would even notice. None of us have short, short hair, like shaved off, so it's not like one of us could take that role and be badass about it.

The notion that she and her girlfriend "change outfits" refers not just to gender presentation but also to a power differential assigned to a binary between feminine and masculine, woman and man. She highlights the fluidity of gender roles and suggests that, in her partnership, they also negotiate around gender assignment and courtship, with each partner free to take on different roles.

Queer daters stressed that their decision to express initial interest or wait for others to approach them had less to do with gender norms and more with their state of mind. "It depends," said Cruz, a twenty-nine-year-old Latina who identified as both queer and lesbian. "I'm not one of the people who are like, 'You've got to message me first,'" she continued. "It depends on either whether I matched with them immediately as opposed to getting a notification later and my level of interest. If I'm like, 'Eh, I'm not really sure,' then I may not message ever. If I'm excited, I'll message right then." Respondents like Cruz emphasized how the way they engaged or approached online dating often relied on figuring out what would make them happy as individuals, a reality that they saw as particularly liberating; the ebb and flow of Cruz's willingness to actively engage with others matched the ebb and flow of her emotions.

Ben, a queer, Black, and Asian multiracial dater, told us how his decision to reach out sort of swung on a pendulum. On apps that presented more visual data, like multiple photos of people's faces, he tended to wait for others to contact him because he generally sees himself as a shy person. However, Ben was more likely to initiate on apps that provide less visual data, because the feeling of anonymity made him bolder and less fearful of rejection.

The individualism that some of these daters expressed is a key element of a queer culture in which members draw on a "be true to yourself" philosophy, divorced from many heteronormative norms around courtship.[13] Yet we wondered whether their deliberate challenges of gender norms could also break down racialized hierarchies that have historically been so bound up with dating and courtship? Do queer daters—who are far more likely than heterosexual daters to deviate from a normative courtship script—also subvert racial hierarchies in the same way? Heterosexual online-dating patterns, as we have seen, despite the potential to transform gender norms, instead reform them. What about when it comes to race?

Gender is central to understanding the rules of online engagement, and its manifestation intersects with a variety of status hierarchies. In the area of intimate dating, naturalized hierarchies of gender, race, age, sexuality, and class are interwoven. With this complexity in mind, we begin in the next chapter to explore how, under what contexts, and why Whiteness retains its social privilege in online-dating desirability hierarchies.

4 A Privilege Endures

DATING WHILE WHITE IN THE ERA OF ONLINE DATING

There is something astonishing in this spectacle of so many lucky men restless in the midst of abundance.

Alexis de Tocqueville, 1838

In 2015 two Princeton economists declared a mortality crisis. U.S. American non-Latino White men were experiencing a sudden and unexpected spike in what the researchers called "deaths of despair."[1] For all education and race groups, U.S. mortality had dropped over the course of the previous century, but among White men lacking a college degree, the rate was inching up in the new millennium. Suicide and opioid addiction were almost entirely driving them to early graves. Headlines sounded the alarm: "'Deaths of Despair' Surge among US White Working Class," "Why White Middle Class Americans Are Dying at an Alarming Rate," and "Why the White Middle Class is Dying Faster, Explained in 6 Charts."[2] Even with all this publicity, one important detail was routinely overlooked: U.S. White deaths had increased to *almost but still not quite the same high level* as those of similarly educated Black people. Black men have *always* died at significantly higher rates than White men; in fact, life expectancy at birth in 2016 is four years higher for White than for Black men.[3] Sometimes advantage is taken as a given.

Another rising trend is one of pronounced anxiety around traditional White masculinity.[4] From women's suffrage to emancipation, the closure of the western frontier, large-scale immigration waves, and twentieth-century civil rights legislation, each successive process extending basic human rights to U.S. American groups beyond White men has ratcheted up the sense that White men are under threat. To be sure, White men remain privileged and even benefit from some developments, like the economic and social gains accrued by women and minorities. But as historian Carol Anderson puts it, "If you've always been privileged, equality begins to look like oppression."[5] Entitlement naturalizes advantage so that any diminishment in advantage feels like a deep violation of one's rights. That's how we get the paradox of masculinity's fragility: White men have had so many historical advantages that the perceived diminishments seem to come along more and more frequently. From their privileged vantage point, White men come to see themselves as constant targets, forgetting that they are, nonetheless, looking down on all other groups. In the United States entitlement and advantage have been maintained, in part, through enforcing institutions. Like other social structures, marriage and courtship have privileged White masculinity. Can online dating disrupt its dominance?

WHITENESS AND THE RACIALIZED DATING MARKETPLACE IN THE UNITED STATES

In chapter 3 we look at gender in dating-site messaging patterns. When we focus on how heterosexual men and women interact in this way, we see that they still gravitate toward conventional gender roles.[6] Now it's time to see what the patterns look like when we bring race into the mix. In figure 4.1 we illustrate how open Black, Asian, and Latina women and gay men are to interacting with White men compared to those from their own racial groups. Almost every minority group responds more readily to White men than to men from their own racial group.[7] The pattern is clearest among straight minority women, but less so among minority men, whose smaller sample size makes trends less concrete. Gay Asian and Latino men appear to favor Whites, while Black men, on the other hand, appear to privilege other Black gay men.

White men are even more popular among White daters. Figure 4.2 shows that both White straight women and gay men more often interact

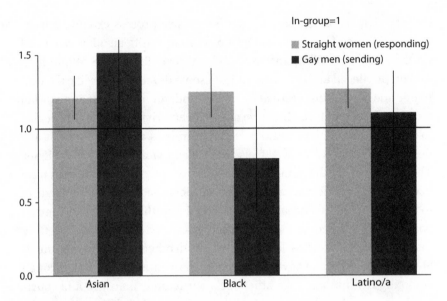

Figure 4.1. *Non-White Daters' Relative Likelihood of Messaging White versus Same-Race Men.* The bars depict the relative likelihood of interacting with White men compared with same-race men among Asian, Black, and Latino/a daters, adjusted for other observed characteristics. The lines depict 95 percent confidence intervals. Interacting with a same-race dater is indicated by an odds of 1.0. Anything above 1.0 shows a greater relative probability of contacting or responding to a White dater than a same-race dater; anything below 1.0 indicates a lesser probability. See online tables O.1 and O.2 (at www.ucpress.edu/9780520293458) for full estimates.

with White men than non-White men do. These differences have taken into account a wide range of factors—including age, education, physical attributes, lifestyles, and personality compatibility—and point to a powerful White male privilege in the online-dating market.[8]

Obviously, the theory of homophily—that like attracts like—is contradicted by White men's overall popularity. Instead of being disregarded by minority daters, we find that Whiteness provides men great advantage in the world of online dating. The pervasiveness of White desire also shows us that racial preference in sexual marketplaces is not merely personal. These "preferences" largely reflect the history of racial oppression and separation outlined in earlier chapters, underscoring how the legacy of state interference in intimacy continues to uphold White dominance. White masculinity

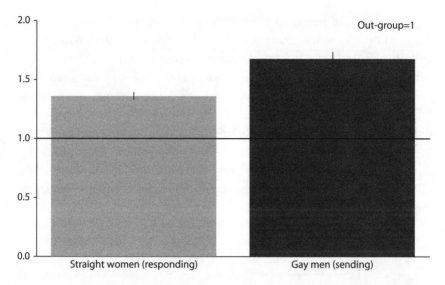

Figure 4.2. White Daters' Relative Likelihood of Messaging White versus Minority Men. The bars depict the relative likelihood of interacting with White men compared with minority men among White daters, adjusted for other observed characteristics. The lines depict 95 percent confidence intervals. Interacting with a minority dater is indicated by an odds of 1.0. Anything above 1.0 shows a greater relative probability of contacting or responding to a White dater than a minority dater; anything below 1.0 indicates a lesser probability. See online tables O.3 and O.4 for full estimates.

and femininity are seen as right, attractive, and good, while non-White, regardless of gender, is constructed as unattractive.[9])

The substantial White advantage is not unique to our data. A study of Yahoo personals showed White women's strong preferences for White men, and one using Match data reported that minority daters were generally willing to date only someone of their own racial group—unless that person was White.[10] In some cases researchers have found that minority daters even exclude same-race daters in favor of White men: one analysis of the LGBTQ profiles on Match found that most Latino and Asian men who excluded their own race from their search filters nonetheless included White men, suggesting that White masculinity may represent an ideal type among certain gay daters.[11] All these studies show that White men are popular beyond racial boundaries.[12]

The concept of hegemonic masculinity is an idealized image of manhood in opposition to femininity and in subordination of non-White masculinities.[13] Indeed, U.S. masculinity is commonly conflated with Whiteness. In one interview Sunan, a twenty-six-year-old Asian man from the Northeast, revealed that he has a deep and lasting sense of not fitting in. Wanly, he listed what he saw as the attributes of the typical man—that did not describe him: "Men should have beards. . . . Men should be White. Men should be hetero. Men should be the moneymaker. Men should be dominant and ask the woman out first and stuff." Other daters were able rattle off lists of the negative stereotypes they saw attached to minority men in dating.

A White-Latino man in his thirties, Roger, told us,

> I would expect that Asian men are viewed as more likely to be stalkerish and creepy. . . . I think there is a general perception of Indian men in particular being very . . . very machista, but in a cruder way than Latin guys . . . more lewd. . . . Black guys, I think, would be usually seen as more likely to send pictures of their junk, that kind of stuff. And probably seen as more likely to be violent on a first date.

What, we asked, were the equivalent stereotypes about White men? Roger was stumped. "And White guys? I think they would probably be seen as . . . Well, I actually can't think of too many stereotypes about White guys." His response was characteristic of the theory of hegemonic Whiteness: as the standard against which other groups are compared and assessed, the hegemonic category has the privilege of going unmarked. There aren't many stereotypes about White men, Roger said, yet the stereotypes he could list about other races were all comparative. *Compared to White masculinity,* stereotypical Black masculinities are inferior because they are *too* physical and threatening. Asian men might have an economic profile that fits the breadwinner ideal, but, compared to White masculinity, the stereotypes charge they are insufficiently dominant and manly.[14] Latinos, despite having been formally defined as White since the 1940 U.S. Census, are subject to stereotypes about machismo, conservativeness, and womanizing and thus are controlled by corresponding emasculating and racialized stereotypes about their height and perceived illegality.[15] As they have been throughout U.S. history, racialized beliefs about racial and ethnic minorities mask racial oppression and justify discrimination. Again daters' racial preferences are anything but personal, ineffable markers of simple sexual attraction.

Many of the minority men we interviewed were painfully aware that they were being penalized by White women using dating websites. Sanjay, a thirty-nine-year-old South Asian American professional from the Northeast, was primarily interested in dating White women, and so he preferred to use double-swipe apps like Tinder rather than sites like OkCupid or Match. It allowed him to bypass the frustration of being unequivocally rejected by White women. He was matter-of-fact when he talked about the experience of online dating as a non-White man:

> The average person probably is in their head like, "I'm not gonna date a brown person." I messaged a dozen people, and no one wrote back. For a person of color, it seems like too much effort for too little return. . . . The double swipe is really good when you feel like you're in a population of people who only certain people might be attracted to or into. It just makes it very easy because there's no guessing or writing a random person, just someone who's already expressed an interest.

Indeed, some White women we interviewed had no qualms about stating their same-race preferences. Those who identified largely as progressive and socially open-minded were more sheepish, sometimes telling us about their process of questioning whether they were being diverse enough in setting their racial preferences. Likewise, a number of minority men expressed suspicions that, if they had White profiles, they would be getting more matches. They drew frequent parallels with their White friends' dating lives. Henry, a twenty-four-year-old Asian man noted incredulously that his White roommate, who he believes is equally as attractive,

> can have a funny face in front of a box of mashed potatoes as his profile picture, and he gets sixty messages a week. I can have [pictures of] our house cat, me playing volleyball and out snowboarding, and all these other things, and I'll get, like, five matches in a month!

The widespread usage of mobile apps has introduced the opportunity for people to conduct mini-experiments to test their hypotheses. The web is full of stories about how a person's experience changed dramatically when they created a false profile or swapped phones with a friend.[16]

Grindr, a popular gay dating app, even created a documentary series in which daters exchanged phones for a day. In one episode a comparably attractive pair was shocked: the Asian dater found getting matches was suddenly effortless now that he had a White profile, while the White man was all but ignored. Furthermore, the White man was surprised at how many of the messages he *did* receive fetishized Asianness and assumed he was a sexual bottom.[17]

FRAMING ONESELF AGAINST WHITENESS

Marginalized racial groups have developed coping strategies with regard to hegemonic Whiteness in the United States. One is what sociologist Joe Feagin calls "resistance counterframing," or adopting a positive, group-affirming mindset that empowers minority groups to resist self-degradation and celebrate their own identities.[18] Another is the internalization of the White frame, a likely explanation for our finding that almost every minority group responds more readily to Whites than same-race men. The White frame explains why, as some scholars have found, Asian immigrants to the United States almost immediately refer to minorities by their race or nationalities, reserving the term "American" for Whites.[19] In this sense, though Latinos/as and Asians may be more socially advantaged than Blacks on some measures, they are also least likely to be seen by *others* as American. One particularly incisive study asked participants to look at photos and rate how "American" the people looked. Whites got the all-American designation, followed by Blacks, then Latinos/as. Asian faces were rated the least American.[20]

Minorities, sensing that they are perceived as "forever foreigners," may adopt a coping strategy that involves enlisting Whiteness—that is, seeking a relationship with a White person as a way to be included in mainstream society or signal belonging.[21] William, a twenty-seven-year-old White graduate student in our study, described how his Asian girlfriend joked that she was a "legend" in her primarily Asian department because she had a White boyfriend. Another interviewee, a college-age Asian American woman, shared that she had exclusively dated Black men until she moved to a White-dominated region:

I would say moving to the Northeast was a huge cultural shocker for me since I've always found White guys super cute, but I grew up in the hood of [a southern city], so I've never ever dated a White guy before, and my type completely changed when I came up here. I was like, "Ooh, maybe I'll date a ginger," because there's so many here, and I've never seen one in real life before. My taste completely kind of did a 360.

Gay men spoke, too, about White men's elevation in the eyes of minority men. Raúl, a twenty-eight-year-old Latino, said,

There are all these Latinos and Asians. . . . They are looking for someone who is White. If they're blue eyed and blond, even better. . . . I talk to a lot of Latinos, and when I try to meet them they are not interested, but I'm pretty sure if I was a White person, they will be responding easily and quickly. . . . I have felt the stereotype like, "Oh wait, you're Latino. You don't have a big dick." You see? Stuff like that. "You don't bottom?" I mean, come on, don't play that.

Latinas brought up family pressure to "date lighter." One referred to the familial imperative *"mejorando la raza"* (improving the race), while another said point-blank that her parents "want Whiter babies" for grandchildren. While the context was more often related to gradations of skin tone within Latino pairings, reflecting residues of colonialism and colorism in many Latin American societies, it also manifested as preferences for non-Latino White men. Tony, a twenty-one-year-old White man told us his Latina girlfriend "jokes about how she likes me because I'm White, but . . . it's more of a joke though, because her parents have mentioned to her that she should try to date White guys, because they're better or whatever."

By now it should be apparent that romantic preference for Whiteness is acutely gendered. For example, some Asian and Latina women associate White men with more gender egalitarian partnerships.[22] This affirmation of White masculinity turns a blind eye to gender inequalities embedded among Whites, with immigrant women often associating White men with the rejection of patriarchy.[23] For some other minority women, White preferences may reflect a desire for acceptance. Intimate unions with White men have historically been an option for some minority women to gain social recognition and economic security.[24] Minority men have historically had fewer options to trade on White women's privilege in this way: White women's partner choices have been more policed and punished than White men's. Minority men's disadvantaged economic status also made them subpar breadwinners. In addition, women's economic and social status has been tied to, and subsumed by, their husband's status. To this extent women's ethnic identities may be experienced as more malleable than minority men's.[25] Antimiscegenation laws more vehemently targeted Black women, disallowing them from marrying Whites but also providing no protection from sexual violence by White men. As we explain in later chapters, gendered and racialized cultural stereotypes of Latina and Asian women typically construct them as desirable and feminine under the White gaze, while Black women are typically represented in the media and popular culture as masculine and less desirable.

Some minority women we interviewed openly discussed a preference for White American *cultural* norms. This kind of preference is often based on racialized stereotypes and finds particular expression in the era of internet dating, when such images are amplified and widely circulated. For example, Mai was a thirty-year-old Asian international graduate student from China who had been living in the midwestern United States for the past decade. She compared how White American men and Asian men acted on dates with her, saying that Asian men "really don't know about the rules about dating, especially the American rules. I summarize it as being very polite in terms of being on time . . . or maybe when you're in a restaurant, you need to pull a chair for a woman sometimes, like chivalry. I think that's the word."

Mai appeared to draw on controlling images of popularly rehashed U.S. expectations of femininity and masculinity to justify her preference for White men. In one anecdote she told us about an Asian man who did not acknowledge her birthday and compared it with the ways romantic relationships looked on TV:

> I feel like in the *Friends* TV series, the guys always do very romantic things for the female characters. I'm like, "If you're watching those things that much, how can you not know and learn from those?" There's a certain bar that you need to hit to please the girls, or at least to show you care for them. I'm really confused. It's not like you have no experience at all.

Some Latinas deployed ethnic stereotypes when they were asked why they did not prefer to date Latinos, at times characterizing White men as more gender progressive than Latino men. On its face this fact contrasts with Mai's desire for White men's chivalry and traditional gender role enactment. But both narratives explicitly compare racialized stereotypes about minority men with Whiteness; though the meanings may be conflicting, those meanings are always superior. As marginalized heterosexual women and gay men collude with and participate in controlling images, they leverage racialized gender stereotypes to justify romantic preferences for Whites over coethnic men.[26]

The deep centrality of Whiteness in U.S. society forces people who are marginalized to constantly navigate their racialized status, online and off. Dating Whites, some minority women revealed, could be challenging, because they have a general lack of awareness around racial oppression and discrimination. Others saw that racial ignorance as a bonus; one Asian woman mused that her Asian friends preferred to date White men because they "felt like they were more accepted, that because their White partners were detached from race as the forefront of their identity, that they were able to kind of talk about their issues without having to push back, having to contest and affirm." Another said, "I've had conversations with people about how dating a White person is sometimes easier because you don't have to have those conversations all the time. You get to take a break."

Navigating one's own social position vis-à-vis a partner's proximity to Whiteness is a complicated issue. Even though many minority women expressed favorable opinions about White men, some women, particularly Black women, pushed back against the notion of a hegemonic White preference. These and others occasionally spoke at length about their preference for same-race partners and general disinterest in White men—more on that in chapter 5.

GAY MEN, WHITENESS, AND THE MYTH OF NEUTRAL PREFERENCE

The gay community has long been known for its progressive thinking and beliefs of inclusivity. As explained by one queer White man we interviewed, people who are looking for same-sex relationships have also been stigmatized themselves for so long, they might actually be more willing to go across races and to reduce those barriers, because they've had to deal with more shit. So they want to be more open-minded because they have had to deal with being in a closed-minded society.

This idea makes intuitive sense. It is certainly possible that transgressing norms in one social dimension may lead gay people to have more socially progressive personal behaviors and empathy toward other types of oppression, such as racialization. However, our findings suggest that dating preferences among gay men, particularly White gay men, deviate little from a White-centered desirability hierarchy. Damian, a Black gay man we interviewed, was annoyed at his sense that other gay men believed, because they were marginalized on the basis of sexuality, that they were incapable of negatively stereotyping others:

> A lot of gay men believe that they can't be racist or sexist. . . . Saying, "I'm gay. I can't be racist" is like, "I'm Black. I can't be sexist. I'm a woman. I can't be homophobic." It doesn't make sense. Because you're a part of a marginalized group, doesn't mean you can't be oppressive to someone else.

The gay community, studies find, does show clear social reproduction of inequalities, and this finds particular purchase within the world of online dating.[27] Offensive racial terms, often in the form of food metaphors, are common on gay dating sites, such as Grindr.[28] "No rice," for example, indicates Asian avoidance, while "Rice Queen" references exclusive interest in Asian men. Latinos are referred to as "spice" and Indian men as "curry." "No Chicken" is taken to mean no Blacks, while "Dinge Queen" indicates Black fetishizing preferences. On both straight and gay dating sites, minorities are disadvantaged, but forthright racialized expressions like these are more common on gay sites. This points to a racialized hookup culture in which queer communities remain centered on Whiteness in expressing objectification and exclusion.

Interestingly, the gay population is also more likely to cohabit and marry across racial lines. If the dating market reveals racial preferences, the fact that the gay dating market is limited results in counterintuitive partnering patterns.[29] Some of the people we interviewed indicated as much. Speaking about the White men he had met online, Trevor, a Black international student, said, "Eventually, you exhaust your White resources, and you're like, 'Okay. I guess I'll hook up with this Black person.' You're bound to have sex with some other different race eventually."

FULL OF SWIPE AND FURY?
THE ANGRY WHITE MALE DATER ARCHETYPE

Classic social-contact theory predicts that cross-racial exposure should lead to positive changes in attitudes and behaviors toward outgroups. In this way online dating, despite being a tool used frequently to hone racial preferences, nevertheless provides the *opportunity* for people to interact across racial lines in ways that could intervene in the historical patterns of hegemonic Whiteness and racialized segregation in the United States. Still, online dating exposes people to a wide range of potential choices, but that greater exposure has a psychic cost, especially for women and racial and ethnic minorities. The online disinhibition effect of anonymized communication over the internet can subject daters to forthright expressions of misogyny and hate—expressions that tend to lay dormant in face-to-face interactions. Reflecting this experience, an emergent online-dating archetype is that of the "angry White male dater." This figure stems both from the perniciousness of White privilege, in the internet and beyond, and from the increase in women's autonomy, such that there is a hint of slippage in White men's entitlement.

The phrase "angry White male dater" specifically refers to men who are enraged by rejection, feeling entitled to the affections of anyone they find attractive. A host of examples are provided by a Tumblr page called "Straight White Boys Texting," which chronicles exchanges within which a self-proclaimed "nice guy" sends a woman what he perceives to be a polite introductory message, then, after a period of nonresponse, lashes out with gendered epithets; "bitch," "slut," and "whore" are part and parcel of such exchanges. The messages vary in the levels of anger and use of offensive language, but some are vehemently racist and sexist:

MAN: lol You're so fucking full of shit just like every other woman on this site. I'm deleting this fucking profile TODAY. I send out tons of messages and never get shit in return. I see girls dating niggers on campus without half as much going for themselves as I do. Fuck this shit. Your probably a fucking nigger lover anyway. Lol. You'll wish you said yes to me in 10 years.[30]

All of the women we interviewed had experienced the "nice guy" treatment. Meanwhile, the White men we interviewed, who all seemed like friendly bona fide "nice guys," expressed frustration with being ignored or ghosted by women they messaged. Roger, the White-Latino man who couldn't think of any stereotypes about White men, spoke about investing time and goodwill in messaging women who looked like perfect matches. He drew a contrast, pointing out that nonresponses spurred him only to change his own profile and the ways he wrote his initial messages, but said, "I do think that a lot of men will end up feeling . . . that these women are Bs or Cs or, you know, those kinds of words, and that leads to them blaming women as opposed to the way they're presenting themselves." Like others, who in our interviews frequently said that men put far less effort into crafting their profiles and selecting photos, Roger claimed that, unlike himself, "a lot of guys don't reflect enough about how their choices might be harming them. They really just want to blame others for their own failings." That Roger saw himself as outside this "angry White male dater" type is interesting in a second way: he felt that there was a clear difference in men's and women's effortful self-presentation and that, by attending to his own, he could gain advantage over other men. Even his take shows how male entitlement intersects with women's growing romantic autonomy and agency.

Another White dater, Tom, twenty-nine, also had a lot to say about women's agency in what he referred to as the "online dating game." Like Roger, Tom felt that he had to compete with other men by constructing a profile that grabs women's attention. He included pictures of himself vacationing to reflect his adventurous side but also included content that highlighted—and indeed exaggerated—his confidence and assertiveness, all qualities that Tom described as encompassing an "attractive masculinity." Tom also admitted that his profile doesn't reflect the real him: "You just kind of get good at building a profile that's not necessarily reflective of yourself and just reflective of what you know the widest kind of archetypal woman would like." While Tom appeared committed to this "online dating game," from which he sought noncommittal sex, he also expressed frustration with women's expectations. In his view his game was one of no-strings-attached conquest, a reality that often clashed with the expectations belonging to the women he met on dating apps:

> You see this in this cultural narrative today, where it's seen as misogynistic, or retrograde, to consider women as trophies or a conquest, you know, but from my perspective that's how they frame the whole dating experience, right? They're just like, "Well, you have to try, and all the responsibility is on you as a man to seduce me and to express confidence and fun and outgoing and take me out and plan out the date and pay for it and do all this stuff," so of course when it works out for me I'm going to have an ego boost and feel like it's a prize to be won, you know? You can't have your cake and eat it too. You can't frame your body as some kind of reward given to a man who is confident, and attractive enough, and then be mad at him for seeing it as a conquest.

Articles and think pieces with titles such as "The Not-So-Nice 'Nice Guys' of Online Dating"; "What Is Nice Guy Syndrome? 5 Signs That a Self-Proclaimed "Nice Guy" Isn't All That Nice"; and "21 Things That Prove Nice Guys Are the Absolute Worst" are countered by the "manosphere."[31] This vast network of online forums and blogs advocates a misogynistic view of women and dating and has played an influential role in the popularity of alt-right outlets such as Breitbart News. The manosphere mobilizes to defend antifeminist men's rights, share pick-up artist techniques for seduction, maintain men's domination in gaming, and share pornography.

Although some see these sites as residual outbursts of a declining patriarchy, the death throes of White male privilege, others argue convincingly that they represent a novel strain of misogyny practiced by young self-labeled geeks and beta males.[32] Online forums, such as 4Chan and various Reddit threads, may have also helped to radicalize such men's sexual frustrations into racial antipathy. It is common in the manosphere to mix misogyny with racial bigotry and resentment, producing a wholesale hostile attitude toward social justice activism. Many men with not unusual sexual anxiety and frustration could be radicalized by such sites into holding misogynistic and racist beliefs.[33]

Lamenting the "rage-inducing sights" of seeing mixed-race couples, Elliot Rodger was a poster child of the manosphere.[34] He was especially active on PUAhate.com, a since-shuttered "incel" website, where men who consider themselves involuntarily celibate (that is, as victims of women who withhold the sexual access to which these men believe they are naturally entitled) gather. Rodger was a biracial White Asian who openly expressed anti-Black racism and cataloged his foundering "life struggle to get a beautiful, white girl." His final manifesto is a disturbing picture of misogyny and anti-Blackness:

> How could an inferior, ugly black boy be able to get a white girl and not me? I am beautiful, and I am half white myself. I am descended from British aristocracy. He is descended from slaves. I deserve it more. . . . If this ugly black filth was able to have sex with a blonde white girl at the age of thirteen while I've had to suffer virginity all my life, then this just proves how ridiculous the female gender is. . . . If women continue to have rights, they will only hinder the advancement of the human race by breeding with degenerate men and creating stupid, degenerate offspring.

Rodger then went on a shooting rampage—a failed attack on a sorority in which he killed three nearby students before dying by suicide. He was an extreme outlier, but it is important to highlight the slippery slope from frustration to violent misogyny and White supremacy. He was neither the first, nor the last, to go on a killing rampage targeting women in the name of the incel entitlement.[35] White men are still advantaged in U.S. society, and many see that privilege as a right they are willing to "defend."

White male entitlement is as evident in the celebration of such violence as much as it is in the deranged acts themselves.[36] The Southern Poverty Law Center (SPLC) has added male supremacy to the racial hate ideologies it tracks. On its website SPLC notes, "In many ways, white supremacy and male supremacy are one and the same," with both groups believing in the decline of Western civilization and placing the blame on women, immigrants, and minority groups. The SPLC website points to the concept of "white shariah" as an example of common ground, the "idea that the submission and rape of white women by white men is the only way to save the white race, since white women tend to leave white men for their non-white counterparts, thus making violence necessary."[37] Just as we have seen in the earlier chapters of this book, male dominance and White supremacy are intimately bound.[38] Thus, while Rodger and others have framed the motives for their attacks in antifem terms, we see even in his manifesto that White supremacy is at least as powerful a motivator. At this point it is almost a cliché that mass shootings are committed by White men who have already tested their capacity for deadly violence by killing women love interests or partners, frequently in response to romantic rejection.[39]

Men murdering women is rare, of course, but complaints about both rejection and women's entitlement are not uncommon among men daters. Their discontent ignores their own biases in pursuing a limited set of women. In fact, whereas only the very youngest women receive the lion's share of attention, men's popularity grows continuously with age.[40] What is more clear than anything else from our data is that non-White men are at much greater disadvantage than White men in their online-dating prospects. This is especially true for Black and Asian men, on whom we focus in later chapters.

WHITE FEMININITY PRIVILEGE?

White women are undeniably privileged in the United States, but they are not so universally desired as White men in dating, according to our data. Instead, both straight men and lesbian daters from minority groups tend to contact women who are from their own racial groups over White women, while White men and White lesbians prefer White women over minorities (see figures 4.3 and 4.4).[41]

What explains the fact that White men receive many more responses from minority women, but White women infrequently receive messages from minority men? One explanation is patriarchy: society still emphasizes men's socioeconomic status and women's physical beauty. Thus, White men continue to hold most of the power and economic resources, while White women access power and economic status predominantly

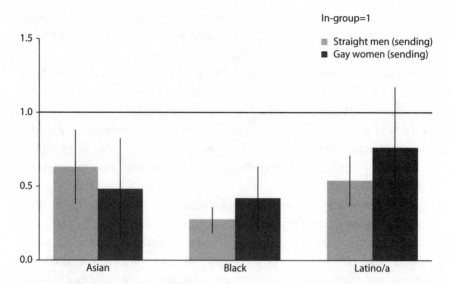

Figure 4.3. Non-White Daters' Relative Likelihood of Messaging White versus Same-Race Women. The bars depict the relative likelihood of sending messages to White women compared with same-race women among Asian, Black, and Latino/a daters, adjusted for other observed characteristics. The lines depict 95 percent confidence intervals. Interacting with a same-race dater is indicated by an odds of 1.0. Anything above 1.0 shows a greater relative probability of contacting or responding to a White dater than a same-race dater; anything below 1.0 indicates a lesser probability. See online table O.1 (at www.ucpress.edu/9780520293458) for full estimates.

through their association with White men. As a symbolic case in point, in our interview with J. T. Tran, who founded an Asian men's date-coaching company, he pointed to gendered aspects of White privilege:

> I get no benefits, like at the societal level, from dating a White woman. I know . . . guys brag. Lots of bragging rights does not give me any sort of institutional hope like privilege. I don't get more money. I don't get more elected. I don't get better access. I don't get any of that privilege. Dating a White woman gives me no White privilege.

In Tran's view his association with White femininity provides no material benefits. Yet his reference to bragging rights does suggest that association with feminine Whiteness does provide some symbolic prestige. Note that, while White men are more advantaged than White women in the

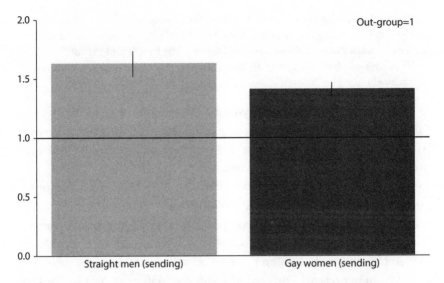

Figure 4.4. White Daters' Relative Likelihood of Messaging White versus Minority Women. The bars depict the relative likelihood of sending messages to White women compared with minority men among White daters, adjusted for other observed characteristics. The lines depict 95 percent confidence intervals. Interacting with a minority dater is indicated by an odds of 1.0. Anything above 1.0 shows a greater relative probability of contacting or responding to a White dater than a minority dater; anything below 1.0 indicates a lesser probability. See online tables O.3 and O.4 for full estimates.

dating market, this in no way suggests that White women are disadvantaged relative to other minority women. Given the power of hegemonic femininity and pervasiveness of beauty discourse that often assigns feminine value to closer-to-Whiteness, minority women navigate a world where they are often implicitly or explicitly told throughout their lives that they are unattractive or less attractive than others.[42] This is especially true for dark-skinned women of color and especially for those Black women who are darker, have broader features, larger bodies, and coarser hair textures.[43] Amid rampant digital misogyny, minority women must also contend with being fetishized on the basis of their racial identities. As such, White women are objectified "only" for their gender identity, while minority women are doubly objectified for both their gender and their race. Mary, a college-aged White woman, alluded to this:

Definitely I feel like I never had to worry about being a fetish or worry about someone not liking me because of my race. I feel like even if someone said, "I don't want to date a White girl" . . . I think I'd be like, "I understand, I hate White people too. It's gonna be okay." I don't know. I never had to even worry about that.

By contrast, Bianca, a twenty-nine-year-old Latina, told us that she thinks White men have differing standards when it comes to whom they will take to bed versus take home to their parents. She said, "I think they prefer White and Asian for marriage. And I think Black and Hispanic mix to date or just fuck." This fits well with social theory around majority-group views of Asians as "honorary Whites" and "model minorities," while reinforcing hypersexualized stereotypes around Black and Latina women.

Some minority or immigrant women actively reframe and resist dominant White culture to reclaim power in a system that devalues them. For example, in her research on second-generation Filipinas, Yen Le Espiritu highlights the gendered discourse of moral superiority that immigrant families use to place Filipino womanhood above White feminism and individualism.[44] In a study of Black women's storytelling around interracial relationships, Amy Wilkins describes these narratives as cultural vehicles used to construct collective meaning that reposition some Black men as preferring White women because they are sexually easy and too meek to say no.[45]

Black women in our interviews often recounted incidents in which White and minority men drew on such racialized and sexualized stereotypes about them. In the fact of this devaluation, Black women often perform identity work to create solidarity and dignity. They may resist racist narratives by flipping controlling stereotypes, for example, painting White women as more sexually promiscuous than Black women. Robert seemed to have absorbed this notion, telling us that White women were more sexually available than Black women, who he said were "more reserved about having sex." Alicia said Black men sometimes pressured Black women like her to be less "stuck up" and more like other women. She mimicked what she described as a stereotypical White woman saying, "I'm okay with having a one-night hookup. It's no big deal to me. I could give you a blowjob. It's no big deal to me, you know." Then, taking on the role of Black men, she said, "They tell me [being sexually reserved is] just being stuck up.

You know, wanting me to loosen up. 'You're just too hard. You're making things difficult.'" While resisting controlling images of the hypersexualized "Black Jezebel" stereotype, such beliefs ultimately pit Black women against White women in a way that has been found in a great deal of scholarly work.[46] Intersectional gender and race politics are such that both men and women may work to undermine racist stereotypes without fully upending the race-gender order.

STAYING CLOSE TO WHITENESS

Among all the racial preferences we find in online dating, none is stronger than Whites' preferences for Whites. Both White men and White women actively seek each other out, reproducing intimate segregation through their exclusivity. The online-dating website we draw data from asks users to answer an array of personal questions to help develop a compatibility score for any prospective match. Figure 4.5 shows the proportions of daters who indicate a strong preference for their same race when asked, "Would you strongly prefer to date someone of your own skin color/racial background?" Overall, White daters are more likely than non-Whites to have such a preference, with variation by gender and sexuality such that racial gaps are largest among women and gay men (16 percent more White straight women and 19 percent more gay men feel strongly about the racial background of the men they date than their minority counterparts).[47]

These are not just beliefs but scripts for action and inaction. Figure 4.6 indicates that White women respond to messages from White men nearly twice as often as they do to messages from Black and Asian men. They respond to Latinos slightly more often than Black and Asian matches but not nearly as frequently as they respond to White men.[48]

As we noted from the start, U.S. Whites have always been more likely than minorities to disapprove of interracial intermarriage, and the difference continues today. Unsurprisingly, these racial norms are still enforced through family influence. Some minority men we spoke to expressed frustration with what they perceive to be paternalistic control over White women's dating. For example, Kevon, a thirty-year-old Indo-Caribbean

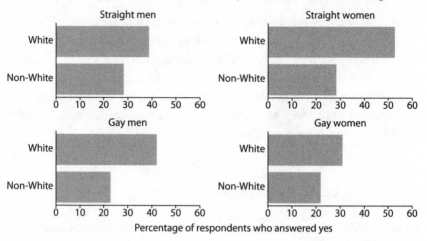

Would you strongly prefer to date someone of your own skin color/racial background?

Figure 4.5. *Proportion Strongly Preferring Someone of Their Own Racial Background.* The bars depict the proportion of daters answering yes to the question: "Would you strongly prefer to date someone of your own skin color/racial background?" Non-White daters include Asian, Black, and Latino/a daters but not those of other racial backgrounds.

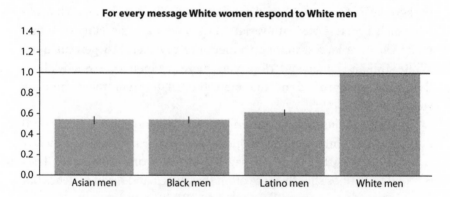

Figure 4.6. *White Women's Relative Likelihood of Responding to Minority versus White Men.* The bars depict the relative likelihood of responding to a message from minority men compared with White men among White women, adjusted for other observed characteristics. The lines depict 95 percent confidence intervals. Responding to White men is indicated by an odds of 1.0. Anything above 1.0 shows a greater relative probability of responding to a minority dater than a White dater; anything below 1.0 indicates a lesser probability. See online table O.2 for full estimates.

American, relayed three instances in which White women told him they could not date him because their parents would be uncomfortable. He vented in the following exchange:

> Women are less open than men because they have to have their daddy approve every fucking thing, and it's the truth. Women who are saying that they're liberal-minded, they're open-minded. . . . Let me make an example here. . . . A friend of mine who I met online, she's so open-minded, blah, blah, blah, and all this. But I told her flat out, "You know, you say all that shit, but I bet you a hundred bucks you would never let me take you out for a cup of coffee." She shut up right away. She was like, "No, I guess not." I'm like, "Why not?" She's like, "Kevon, if you had parents like me, you would understand." She said her family would never accept me. She said that how her family, especially her father, would not accept me. I said, "Why not?" She said because her dad's very conservative, religious, and he feels that she and her sister should not be dating anyone who's nonwhite.

Thinking back on other examples, Kevon added,

> I once talked to another girl I met about dating, if she would like to some-time see each other again so we could go out and have some fun and get to know each other more. She said, "No I don't have any interest in doing that." I said, "Why not?" She said how if I was to date her and she was to bring me home, her father would shoot me on sight.

In addition to his clear articulation of racial violence and of racial prefer-ences as being a form of sexual racism, Kevon's frustrations over paternal control connected to a broader issue: compared to men, women's sexual and personal relationships are and have long been rigorously scrutinized. After four centuries of legal, social, and cultural sanctions aimed at segregating their intimate lives, it is not surprising that even White women who claim a progressive political identity still see dating White men as "natural."

Whiteness scholars have expanded Adrienne Rich's theory of compul-sory heterosexuality imposed on women to specify compulsory *White* heterosexuality to capture the disproportionate application of antimisce-genation laws to White women.[49] As the domestic and reproductive rep-resentatives of the family, women are expected to be cultural bearers of dominant ideologies of sexuality, nation, gender, and race. As such, "the patriarchal production of 'good girls' within the family is inextricably linked to the racist production of 'good (white) girls,'" who are expected to uphold racial solidarity.[50] It makes sense, then, that White women we interviewed often mentioned that dating White men prevented conflict with family members. White men who brought up a reluctance to bring home women of color indicated that it had more to do with a worry that their family's prejudice might offend a non-White girlfriend than it did with any family requirement that they date White women. One White man described his complete mortification at his father's racial insensitivity. When meeting his girlfriend, the father made a number of racialized references, such as remarking that a flooded field they drove past looked like a rice paddy and commenting that, if his girlfriend were in Japan, she could be a geisha. "At that point," the man told us, "I got mad. . . . And I said, 'Dad, you're calling her a prostitute.'" Based on this experience, he concluded, "I would never introduce another girlfriend who wasn't White to him."

More White women than men professed racially aware and progressive views in our sample. However, it did not mean they were willing to enter cross-racial relationships. This may be attributable to patriarchal and gendered family norms, or it might be a convenient excuse to avoid admitting to sexual racism. For example, Clara, a White twenty-one-year-old bisexual dater who dated mainly men, felt guilt over her preferences for White men and described how she intentionally tried to disrupt her predisposition. When we asked if she had ever been in an interracial relationship, she answered,

> No. I've hooked up with people, but not had a relationship. . . . I kind of realized this year that I really hadn't hooked up with anyone who wasn't White. I was like, is there a reason for that? I think mainly it's that there aren't as many people who aren't White. Then, I don't know, I was like I should try to diversify. . . . Yeah. I feel like that sounds kind of weird, so I did hook up with a few Black guys and I liked it, and I would date a Black guy.

If contemporary racial preference trends didn't map so closely onto deeply entrenched social-domination strategies and historical laws and stereotypes, such perspectives *could* be seen as random. But these preferences patterns have been shaped by centuries of social norms and aggressive, state-sanctioned racial prejudice and violence.

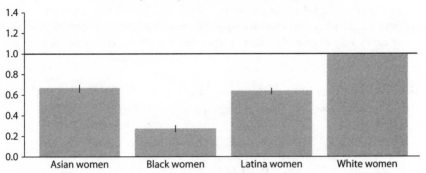

For every message White men send to White women

Figure 4.7. White Men's Relative Likelihood of Sending to Minority versus White Women. The bars depict the relative likelihood of sending a message to minority women compared with White women among White men, adjusted for other observed characteristics. The lines depict 95 percent confidence intervals. Sending to White women is indicated by an odds of 1.0. Anything above 1.0 shows a greater relative probability of sending to a minority dater than a White dater; anything below 1.0 indicates a lesser probability. See online table O.1 for full estimates.

In contrast to White women, White men are less hesitant to cross racial boundaries. As figure 4.7 shows, White men's treatment of non-White daters is very different from White women's. White women reject all non-White men, while White men display a clear preference among non-White groups, contacting Asians and Latinas second and Black daters last.[51]

This mirrors national intermarriage trends. Our data shows that White men's preference falls in line with what triracial hierarchy theories predict, while White women's hew to a White/non-White dividing line—that is to say, in the everyday realm of online dating, which has the *potential* to desegregate racial exposure, White men continue to practice anti-Blackness and White women practice Whites-only filtering.[52]

Few White men specifically brought up Black women in our interviews. Among the exceptions, one respondent, age forty-four, volunteered, "I don't have a type." Then he elaborated, "But I am more attracted to White women than Black women, so I sort by that." He then added, "But I do find attractive Black women." Another interviewee, Sanjay, however, spoke to his White friends' broad lack of interest in Black women:

We were talking once about if he were to date a Black woman. He's like, "No, I would though. I think Beyonce's hot." And I'm like, "Wow, you would date Beyonce. That's really generous of you." It's like, "Yeah, I would date Beyonce or Kerry Washington." But that's not the level of attractiveness you're looking for if it was a blond chick.

Black women, for their part, were acutely aware of the Black-avoidance dynamic operating in online dating—more on that in chapter 5.

GENDERED AND RACED DIFFERENCES
IN DESIRED CHARACTERISTICS

Body weight was another big topic among daters—enough so that we wondered whether body type preferences were significant enough to eclipse racial boundaries. For example, would a White man prefer a non-White but slim woman to a White, fuller-figured woman? How do constructions of beauty influence the racialization of dating preferences?[53]

Figure 4.8 shows that body weight is a significant deal breaker for White men. Looking at the left panel (not overweight men), we see that they prefer women who are not overweight across every racial group of women. But anti-Blackness far, well, outweighs this preference. White men are more likely to send messages to overweight White, Asian, and Latina women than they are to Black woman who are of average size (taking into account all other characteristics). Thus, anti-Blackness operates *in conjunction* with other sorting mechanisms in a way that results in Black daters experiencing *compounded racialized disadvantage*. A similar dynamic also exists among overweight White men (shown in the right panel of figure 4.8), who show a slight preference for overweight women but still rarely contact Black women, regardless of their body types.

Weight was the only factor we found that transcended racialized boundaries—that made some White men reach out to some non-Black minority women. For instance, we noted in chapter 3 the studies showing that men prefer women who are shorter than they are; however, their distaste for taller women is not enough to disrupt the racial hierarchy (see figure 4.9). No matter the height, a White man will contact a White woman over all other races, and he will contact an Asian or Latina woman,

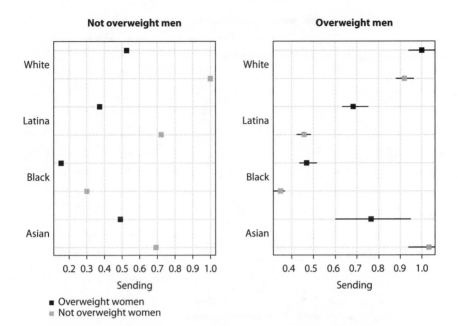

Figure 4.8. White Men's Relative Likelihood of Sending to Women by Race and Body Type. The estimates depict the relative likelihood of sending a message to women of different racial identity and body type compared with White women who share the same body type, adjusted for other observed characteristics. The lines depict 95 percent confidence intervals. The left-hand graph represents the behavior of men who are not overweight, while the right-hand graph represents the behavior of men who are overweight. Sending to White women of the same body type is indicated by an odds of 1.0. Anything above 1.0 shows a greater relative probability of sending; anything below 1.0 indicates a lesser probability. See online table O.5A for full estimates.

even if she is taller than him, over a Black woman of any height. In other words, in terms of compatibility, White men find race to be much more important than height but possibly less important than weight.

Unlike straight White men, straight White women's messaging behavior in online dating demonstrates that their racial preferences are stronger than other physical concerns. And although studies indicate that women have less appearance-oriented partner preferences than men, appearance was rather important in our data. As figure 4.10 indicates, White women, even those who are overweight, care about weight. Still, in all cases White women will respond to overweight White men over slimmer minority men.

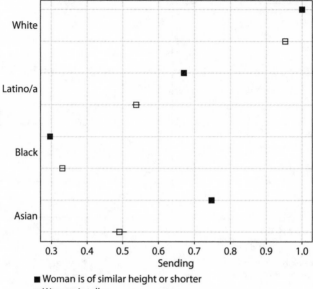

When woman is about the same height or shorter

Figure 4.9. White Men's Relative Likelihood of Sending to Women by Race and Height. The estimates depict the relative likelihood of sending a message to women of different racial identity and height compared with White women of similar height or shorter, adjusted for other observed characteristics. The lines depict 95 percent confidence intervals. Sending to White women of similar height or shorter is indicated by an odds of 1.0. Anything above 1.0 shows a greater relative probability of sending; anything below 1.0 indicates a lesser probability. See online table O.6A for full estimates.

Height also takes the backseat to race when it comes to White women's preferences. Recall that, in chapter 3, many women were insistent that they heavily preferred men taller than themselves. Yet figure 4.11 shows that White women are more willing to date shorter White men than taller minority men.

Throughout our interviews daters were firm about the idea that attraction and personal racial preferences are no different than an aversion or preference for certain types of food or music. Our findings, however, sug-

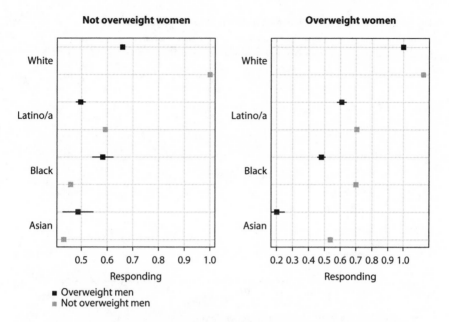

Figure 4.10. White Women's Relative Likelihood of Responding to Men by Race and Body Type. The estimates depict the relative likelihood of responding to men of different racial identity and body type compared with White men who share the same body type, adjusted for other observed characteristics. The left-hand graph represents the behavior of women who are not overweight, while the right-hand graph represents the behavior of women who are overweight. Responding to White men of the same body type is indicated by an odds of 1.0. Anything above 1.0 shows a greater relative probability of responding; anything below 1.0 indicates a lesser probability. See online table O.5B for full estimates.

gest that race and desirability hierarchies are inextricably bound even in the era of supposedly egalitarian online dating. It is not that particular bodies or heights are attractive objectively, but rather embodied attractiveness is often a *product* of racial hierarchy.

WHITE WOMEN AND EDUCATIONAL PREFERENCE: WHERE WHITENESS REIGNS

Further cementing the evidence for the centrality of race for U.S. daters and U.S. society more generally, White women in the United States do not

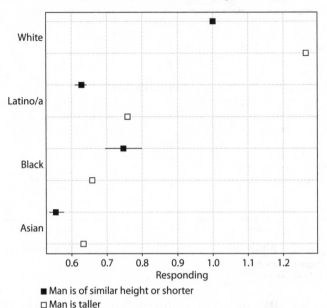

When man is about the same height or shorter

■ Man is of similar height or shorter
□ Man is taller

Figure 4.11. White Women's Relative Likelihood of Responding to Men by Race and Height. The estimates depict the relative likelihood of responding to a message from men of different racial identity and height compared with White men of similar height or shorter, adjusted for other observed characteristics. The lines depict 95 percent confidence intervals. Responding to White men of similar height or shorter is indicated by an odds of 1.0. Anything above 1.0 shows a greater relative probability of responding; anything below 1.0 indicates a lesser probability. See online table O.6B for full estimates.

appear at all swayed by another otherwise significant factor—education level. In general, education levels are a good indicator of socioeconomic status, which is, as we noted in chapter 3, important for many women as they consider potential partners. Education is an achieved status rather than an ascribed status like race, and some have argued that it may be becoming equally or more important than racial identity in the mate-selection process.[54] For example, a study of a European online-dating site concluded that educational homophily was more important than any

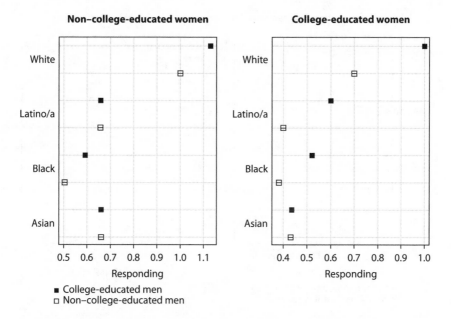

Figure 4.12. White Women's Relative Likelihood of Responding to Men by Race and Education. The estimates depict the relative likelihood of responding to a message from men of different racial identity and education compared with White men who share the same education, adjusted for other observed characteristics. The lines depict 95 percent confidence intervals. Responding to White men of the same education is indicated by an odds of 1.0. Anything above 1.0 shows a greater relative probability of responding; anything below 1.0 indicates a lesser probability. See online table O.8B for full estimates.

other characteristics in mate choice.[55] This is not the case in the United States, where racial divides are wide and deep.

We show in figure 4.12 that, while White women clearly prefer men with a college degree over non–college educated men, they are still more likely to respond to White men of any education level than any other group. The prioritization of race over education is evident among non–college educated, as well as college-educated, women—both are more willing to respond to less educated White men than to non-White college-educated men who contact them.

The internet promises a more connected world, but Whites continue to self-segregate. Just like White women, White men—who, in general, are

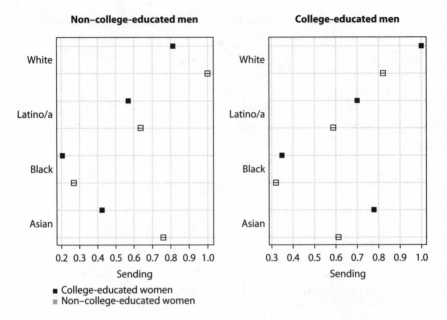

Figure 4.13. White Men's Relative Likelihood of Sending to Women by Race and Education. The estimates depict the relative likelihood of sending a message to women of different racial identity and education compared with White women who share the same education, adjusted for other observed characteristics. The lines depict 95 percent confidence intervals. Sending to White women of the same education is indicated by an odds of 1.0. Anything above 1.0 shows a greater relative probability of sending; anything below 1.0 indicates a lesser probability. See online table O.8A for full estimates.

more open to minority daters—exhibit strong patterns of racialized preferences in education (figure 4.13). In keeping with traditional gender role theory, White men should prefer women with equal or less education, yet the data show that White men ultimately prefer White women of *all* educational levels to all Latinas and Asians, who fall in the middle. Regardless of education level, they are most likely to avoid Black women.

On a dating website, where people believe they act on whim, White women and men move in harmony when it comes to racial preferences. They both see dating another White person as more important than just about anything else. The remarkable findings in this chapter point to the long-standing and devastating racial divide in U.S. intimate life. They map onto the ways that centuries of antimiscegenation and damaging popular images regulated and disciplined who could see and be seen as desirable. White women, historically more subject to antimiscegenatory oversight, still avoid all men except Whites. White men show slightly more openness to minority women, which may reflect their greater historical freedom to cross color lines. Yet they consistently avoid Black women. Surely, pervasive images depicting Black women as undesirable and unfeminine figure into this aversion. State-sanctioned racial separation and imagery regulating sex, dating, and marriage date back to the colonial era. They have been continuously revised, reiterated, and reinforced ever since. Their influence has only intensified in the online era of mass communication, leading to today's neoliberal language of romantic racial preference. This repackaging of antimiscegenation into individual choice is the cornerstone of the new digital-sexual racism.

5 The Unique Disadvantage

DATING WHILE BLACK

"I was trying to figure out how I was going to put myself out there," said Monica, a thirty-three-year-old lawyer. Her initial foray into online dating began when she was a master's student at a large public university.

> I was just interested in figuring out how to meet new people. I wasn't at the bar at five. I lived on campus; I worked on campus. I went to school on campus, and I was going to school with a bunch of college-aged kids. I mean, obviously, there were people in my master's program, but nobody was of interest.

A self-proclaimed introvert, Monica may have initially resorted to using online dating to expand her dating circle, but her intentions were always precise: "My motivations for online dating have always been to find a meaningful relationship that leads to marriage. That was always my expectation."

Monica has spent a great deal of time refining both her profile and her filters on popular dating apps. She is as careful about her search parameters as her photos. Having grown up in a Catholic, Haitian American household in a suburb located in the Northeast, Monica has always wanted to find a man who was similar to her in three key ways: education, religion, and race. Calling herself a lifelong learner, she wants a partner who can "be on her same level," and it's equally important that he's a Black man of faith who will enthusiastically raise their future children in a Christian and culturally affirming household. "I lay it out there 100 percent," she said with a chuckle. "I mention that I'm an attorney, that you can't be an atheist at all, nor agnostic."

Monica had "perfect" matches with a large number of men across the sites, yet the reaction to her carefully constructed profile was underwhelming. Like so many others, she believed in online dating's promise of an enhanced and ever-expansive dating pool, only to be disappointed by who was and wasn't interested in her. Few men shared her desire for long-term commitment, and few similarly educated Black men reached out. She had more recently tried connecting with White men, but hadn't had much luck in that department either: "I don't try to discriminate, but when it comes to White guys I expect more," she said nonchalantly. "The White guys who reach out to me are like welders, contractors. I am highly intellectual. I chose to go to law school for a reason. I just don't think my world and their world would make sense together."

As a proudly "full-bodied, dark-skinned Black woman," Monica had a sense that she simply did not conform to the idealized standard of beauty U.S. society assigns to women who tilt closer to Whiteness, and Monica's tone became tense as she recounted some of the most memorable interactions with White men online. With the click of a button, they could easily send her messages containing a slew of racial and gendered connotations. "I feel like a lot of that is status-based. White men will reach out just like, 'I never dated a Black girl before.'" She added, "Nobody fucking asked you!"

Throughout our interviews Black daters frequently brought up feeling rejected or stereotyped in online dating, such as Lucas, a twenty-six-year-old African American, who just relocated to a small, predominantly White college town in the Northeast. When we talked, he was only a few months out of a messy breakup with Samantha, his long-term Italian American girlfriend. So he turned to online dating: "It's more of a confidence booster for me," he said. "I was having a hard time, so with online dating you're self-validating yourself with just a couple of pictures." Nonetheless, he was getting the idea that his Blackness made him undesirable to non-Black women. That was a major issue, given that the Black women he connected with on the platforms were located many miles away. "My bio is on fleek; I am not going to lie," he said with a smile. Lucas's profile had a straight-forward bio and an array of artfully selected photos. "My bio is pretty upfront, but to the point. . . . It's enough information to show who I am. . . . I felt like I have a really good profile, but still undervalued, unless it's Black women." Because he knew his race could project ideas out of his control, Lucas explained, he limited how long he would communicate with non-Black women on the site. He now preferred to set up a face-to-face meeting sooner rather than later, so that he could "prove" he was more than a racist stereotype.

In our research for this book, we interviewed a diverse set of Black women and men, ranging from a board-game enthusiast who enjoys spending weekends with just a few friends to a social butterfly who can be found at the center of the dance floor of crowded clubs. Their stories of online dating were, however, anything but diverse. Time and again we heard how hard it was dating while Black, even in the internet age.

Many studies have shown a uniquely separate Black experience in online dating, whereby non-Black men and women are least responsive to the messages sent by Black women and Black men.[1] In figure 5.1 we present the distribution of attractiveness ratings by sexual orientation, gender, and race on the one-to-five scale offered by the website whose data we use throughout this book.

While we cannot distinguish the race of the rater in this data, our attractiveness rating is naturally weighted more heavily by the preferences of Whites, because the majority of users on this site are White. There is a clear devaluation of Black attractiveness.[2] Both Black women and Black men are underrated relative to Whites, both falling at a below-average "two" on the five-point scale.

Monica's and Lucas's frustrations with "dating while Black" are common and frequently expressed in online communities such as Reddit, Twitter, and Buzzfeed. Social media threads boast titles such as "Online Dating Is Horrible If You Are a Young and Black Woman," "Online Dating While Black, It Sucks," and "If You Are Black, Don't Bother Using Tinder."[3] The digital expansion of the dating market, along with the normalization of digital-sexual racism, operates in ways that consistently result in the gendered and racialized exclusion of Black daters.

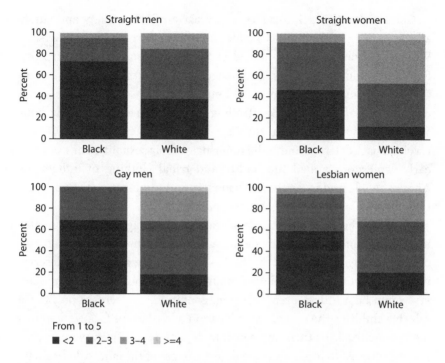

Figure 5.1. Black and White Daters' Website-Based Attractiveness by Sexual Orientation, Gender, and Race. The bars depict the distribution of attractiveness by sexual orientation, gender, and race. Individual users are rated by other users on the website on a scale from one (least attractive) to five (most attractive). Since the ratings are not random, and the vast majority of the users are Whites, the distribution is likely skewed due to racial bias.

GENDERED ANTI-BLACKNESS IN CYBERSPACE

Status-exchange theory posits that people should be able to leverage their socioeconomic status or youth to compensate for other marginalized statuses, but this doesn't appear to be the case for Black daters.[4] In chapter 4 we illustrate that White women and men are less willing to interact with minority daters, even those with more education or "normative" body types, though White men are relatively more willing to include Asians and Latinas in their dating filters. Even that scant openness stops short, though, when it comes to Black women.

Gendered anti-Black imagery is pervasive in U.S. society and surely affects notions of desirability inside the internet's romantic markets. In Western culture Whiteness is held as the highest standard of attractive femininity and masculinity, feminist critical race scholar Patricia Hill Collins reminds us, and racialized heterosexism has suffused the social construction of anti-Black "controlling images" aimed at calcifying non-White subordination.[5] From the start European images of Black people revolved particularly around the othering of their sexuality. For example, early explorers claimed the nudity and tribal clothing of indigenous African people evidenced their debauchery and lewdness, such that it justified their colonization and sexual exploitation.[6]

Later, in the transatlantic slave trade, such images took on greater meaning. White slave owners dehumanized Black men and women, not only by buying and selling their bodies but by using animalistic descriptions to depict them as docile and submissive workhorses for whom slavery would be a fitting, even civilizing, condition. To increase profits via saleable children, the sexual objectification of enslaved Black women was institutionalized. In turn, indefensible depictions of Black women provided a contrast to hegemonic ideals and images of the cult of domesticity and "true" White womanhood in ways that would affect Black women through to the present day.[7]

Black men's sexuality, in the meantime, was guarded. Their potential for sexual reproduction with White women represented a serious threat to the system of slavery, and so any intimate contact between Black men and White women was forbidden. In this world Black men were depicted as hypersexual animalistic aggressors to be feared and controlled; White women were seen as possessing "piety, purity, submissiveness, and domesticity"; and White men painted as stable and desirable breadwinners. The intentional devaluation of nonetheless extremely valuable Black bodies carried over through Reconstruction and the Jim Crow era, continuing to legitimate inequality and make oppression appear natural.[8]

As we have considered in earlier chapters, in the nineteenth and much of the twentieth centuries, intimacy between Black men and White women in the United States was considered rape, while intimacy between Black women and White men could *never* be rape. White male entitlement to Black women's bodies was upheld through the "unrapeability" of Black women. For instance, in 1914 the South Carolina legislature pardoned a man convicted of the assault and attempted rape of a Black girl, arguing that there was "serious doubt as to whether the crime of rape can be committed upon a negro."[9]

The mammy figure, born out of slavery, is one prominent controlling image levied against Black women. As opposed to many schemes in which Black women, like Black men, were positioned as hypersexualized, the mammy figure portrayed Black women as ignorant, exclusively middle-aged or old, obese, and maternal yet also desexualized. She had exaggerated masculine qualities, such as large hands and a raised brow ridge, and she "belonged" to White plantation families. Her loyal servitude and hearty laughter portrayed her contentment with slavery. After emancipation, the mammy image was again leveraged to reassure the superiority of White hegemonic femininity, with the underlying assumption that no White man would choose an obese, elderly Black woman over a refined, youthful White woman.[10]

Stereotypes of Black masculinity also uphold hegemonic White masculinity after emancipation. Powerful images of the Black man as a rapist posing imminent danger to White women were popularized well into the Jim Crow period.[11] Nowhere was this concept evoked more viscerally than in White rationalizations for lynching. The racist brute caricature rendered Black men predators even as Black women were represented as available to satiate White men's sexual appetites. These brute figures were commonly evoked in antimiscegenation propaganda, which saw virtually all forms of sexual relations between Black men and White women as rape. The controlling image of the Black brute also occluded awareness of the widespread sexual abuse and rape of enslaved Black boys and men.[12]

In the post–civil rights era of new racism, as Collins calls it, more modern controlling images can appear to contradict one another, but, rather than underscore their absurdity, the juxtaposition allows for more control.[13] If depicting Black women as "bitches" or single mothers who are hypersexual but undesirable for legitimate relationships is not useful in a given situation, White stereotypes can present them as being too "uppity," masculine, and aggressive.[14] In recent years, for example, we can point to a literal caricature: an editorial illustration by *Herald Sun* cartoonist Mark

Knight, lampooning a contentious moment at the U.S. Open women's final. In the incident world-famous tennis player Serena Williams squared off with an umpire over what she saw as an unfair call against her. In the cartoon she's not an elite athlete contesting a call but an exaggeratedly large, masculine, apelike woman who, having tossed aside a pacifier, is now throwing a tantrum and stomping on her racket. In the background the umpire, Carlos Ramos, is depicted asking Williams's Haitian Japanese opponent, Naomi Osaka, misportrayed as a White blond woman, "Can you just let her win?" Like so many other racialized images of Black femininity, this cartoon—consciously or unconsciously—used a clichéd White feminine foil to maximize the racialized and gendered depiction of Williams and her unseemly athletic passion.

Hypersexualized and violent notions of Blackness are made apparent in the differential criminalization and punishment of Black men.[15] They begin a life of being suspects as early as boyhood vis-à-vis the educational system and play overtly hypermasculine and often criminalized roles in movie theaters and on TV.[16] The racialization continues in the shadows of mainstream culture, such as pornography, a venue that functions as a "festival of social infractions."[17] There Black men are usually found in heterosexual interracial pornography, taking on "gangster" roles of dominance over White women and enacting scripts that reveal a fetishization of the Black male phallus.[18] Black women in pornography also face discrimination due to controlling images and stereotypes about their hyperaccessibility.[19] And while history shows how the propagation of anti-Black controlled images was most enthusiastically taken up by White elites throughout U.S. cultural spheres, these images interplay with digital-sexual racism to shape a broad swath of interactions in online dating today.

HYPERVISIBLE AND INVISIBLE

The operation of digital-sexual racism in online dating renders Black daters as simultaneously hypervisible and invisible. This plays out across online dating and represents some of the key ways that anti-Blackness and hegemonic Whiteness operate in dating life today. For example, both Black men and Black women daters feel that they are contacted on dating

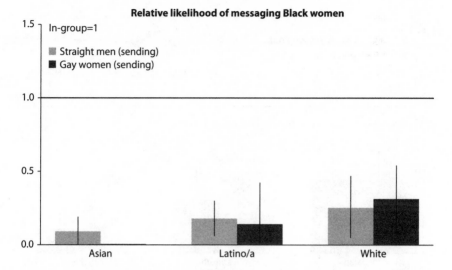

Figure 5.2. Non-Black Daters' Relative Likelihood of Messaging Black versus Same-Race Women. The bars depict the relative likelihood of sending messages to Black women compared with same-race women among Asian, Latino/a, and White daters, adjusted for other observed characteristics. The lines depict 95 percent confidence intervals. Interacting with a same-race dater is indicated by an odds of 1.0. Anything above 1.0 shows a greater relative probability of messaging a Black dater than a same-race dater; anything below 1.0 indicates a lesser probability. *Note:* In separate models that examine response patterns of men to the small pool of Black women who initiate first contact, the results do not attain statistically significant differences. See online table O.1 (at www.ucpress.edu/9780520293458) for full estimates.

sites specifically because they are Black but also ignored by other site users entirely because they are Black.

Indeed, our data show in figure 5.2 that Asian, Latino/a, and White straight men and gay women are all unwilling to send messages to Black women.[20] And, as figure 5.3 shows, Asian, Latina, and White straight women refuse overtures made by Black men.[21] Asian, Latino, and White gay men are also unlikely to send messages to Black men. Though both are deeply disadvantaged in this marketplace, Black women appear to face greater exclusion than Black men.[22]

Our interviews also illustrate that Black daters' experiences are distinct from those of other minorities. Sandra, for example, was a twenty-six-

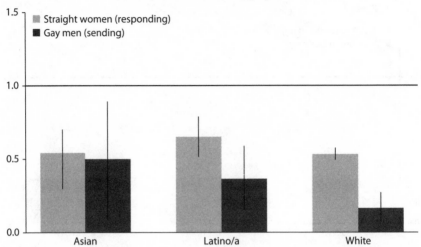

Relative likelihood of messaging Black men

Figure 5.3. Non-Black Daters' Relative Likelihood of Messaging Black versus Same-Race Men. The bars depict the relative likelihood of interacting with Black men compared with same-race men among Asian, Latino/a, and White daters, adjusted for other observed characteristics. The lines depict 95 percent confidence intervals. Interacting with a same-race dater is indicated by an odds of 1.0. Anything above 1.0 shows a greater relative probability of contacting or responding to a Black dater than a same-race dater; anything below 1.0 indicates a lesser probability. *Note:* In separate models that examine response patterns of men to the small pool of Black women who initiate first contact, the results do not attain statistically significant differences. See online tables O.1 and O.2 (at www.ucpress.edu/9780520293458) for full estimates.

year-old bisexual Black woman who described herself as an aficionado of "all things nerdy." Living in a predominantly White town in the mid-Atlantic states, Sandra told us she was constantly aware of her racial minority status. When it came to using online-dating applications, Sandra noted,

> Even when there would be folks that I matched with and clearly they must have liked me, but even when I'm matched with others I still wouldn't get a response. I'm a dark-skinned Black woman. Is that it? I have natural hair and have had natural hair for long before the natural hair movement. Could that be it? At the time I wore glasses. So it's like here, you have this dark-skinned Black woman, natural hair, super geeky looking.

Like many others, Sandra couldn't tell if her experience was shaped by race. But she also couldn't help wondering. In a powerful reminder of how emotions are attuned to the intersectional inequalities enforced in quotidian scenarios, it felt like *something* was not quite right. Sandra had joined the apps to find others who shared her interests in sports, social justice issues, and music. But her interactions seldom went beyond friendly text conversations. Eventually, Sandra started a serious relationship with a woman of color she met online, yet she had few fond memories of the process up to that point. Online dating had been harmful to her confidence: she entered what seemed like a new, big dating world for her but found that her Blackness meant exclusion even there.

Black queer and straight men we interviewed reported similar experiences. Though they could not "prove" racial discrimination, they too said they had a "gut feeling." Like Sandra, other Black online daters spend every day being exposed to both covert and overt forms of racism. This compilation of data renders them sensitive to subtle, quotidian discrimination others might fail to see.[23] One Black queer interviewee contrasted her experiences using online dating to two friends, a White colleague and a racially ambiguous friend. Her White colleague, she said, often "talked about how he would Netflix and chill with a different girl every weekend," while the racially ambiguous friend "dated people that she met on Tinder and from day one got a lot of matches and messages." A Black straight man who lived in a White college town told us he had given up on messaging non-Black women all together. He would wait to use dating platforms until he was visiting his hometown, a larger metropolis where more women of color were using the apps.

Black daters have a "double consciousness" that allows them to understand how daters from other racial groups view them.[24] As they explain, they often feel invisible—a particularly poignant feeling for straight Black women, who are "supposed" to wait for men's contact. Black men and women feel walled off by the demonized and hypersexualized images absorbed by non-Black daters. Yet their invisibility coexists with a hypervisibility. The categorical thinking and filtering of dating apps makes their gendered racial identities seen over all other qualities—as if the hypervisibility triggers *invisibility*. Monica spoke of how users'

snap judgements amplify bias, such that she feels simultaneously objectified and ignored:

> Online dating makes me feel like kind of the way that I feel in school, that
> I'm invisible and hypervisible. And I think it really is very much a White
> women's market, so I feel like all the biases that people have outside in the
> real world, it just comes into effect or comes into play when you're online
> dating. Like, you're extra sexual and promiscuous. There's so many different
> stereotypes about Black women that I feel like come to play in how people
> approach me and I guess other Black women on these platforms. And it
> kind of sucked, especially when you knew all these women, specifically
> White women, talking about, "I have so many messages, and I just can't do
> all this." And I'm like, "I got two messages today and one of them asked me
> . . . if I like White chocolate."

The straight women we interviewed who were *not* Black would frequently joke or complain about "message overwhelm," but that wasn't a
problem for the Black women in our sample, straight or queer. Black
women described feeling "ignored" by most daters and "underwhelmed"
by those inquiries they actually did receive. Amber, who was engaged to a
White man she met on a dating site, told us that the vicissitudes of online
dating had affected her self-esteem:

> I think a lot of people just overlooked me, like period. I've never gotten bom-
> barded. Like ever. So, yeah. Yeah, I hear a lot of, like, people have complaints
> about online dating and I'm just like, I've never had that, like, happen to
> me. . . . I also hear a lot of White women complain and I just think they get
> more attention more than us, so . . . like okay. . . . That's not my reality at all.
> And, like, men are always like, "Oh, well, you guys have men eating out of
> the palm of your hands." I'm like, "Nah man, I'm a Black woman on a dating
> app. That's not what happens."

During our conversation Amber jokingly suggested that she was the
exception that proved the rule: a Black woman who ended up with a White
man; that is, her frustration stemmed from the process of online dating,
not her personal happy ending. Janice, a thirty-one-year-old who had
used dating sites for most of her adult life, related daters' disinterest in
her to the gendered anti-Blackness that saturates societal notions of
desirability:

Oh, I'm 100 percent positive that online experiences for White women differ from Black women. I don't know that I can definitely say in a tangible way how. . . . Through anecdotal information I could say I think that White people, or White women I should say, are generally contacted by more of a diverse group of individuals than Black women. Not to say that I haven't been contacted by them as individuals, but I think that societally speaking, the White beauty is "beauty" whether or not I'm perceived as approachable or beautiful enough. I feel like that is slanted towards societal standards.

On the flip side Black men were used to reaching out to daters of other races but being ignored. If they did strike up a conversation, they were regularly "ghosted." For them it was true that the internet could connect otherwise total strangers, but it could also allow Whites to interact with Black people out of curiosity rather than genuine interest. Jordan, a twenty-seven-year-old Black man of Liberian descent, provided an example by way of explaining the fact that he primarily sought out other Black daters:

> [Online dating] is super segregated. You know what's funny—when I moved to DC and was using the app, I could match with a White girl, and we would talk and she'd just disappear. It was always consistent like that. Are they just doing it for curiosity? "I just want to talk with a Black guy to see what he's like."

Black men such as Jordan saw "curiosity" coming from the hyperracialized and sexualized images of Black men. It represented a desire for a well-storied spectacle, but at a distance. This is significant: some believe that Black men are advantaged in dating, because of stereotypes of hypermasculinity; however, our qualitative data suggests such notions may reinforce the mutual objectification and demonization of Black manhood. Damian, a twenty-four-year-old gay Black undergraduate, told us that he avoided White men because he did not want to be objectified as seemed so common in gay porn. Describing his sexual interactions with White men while online dating, he said,

> Race is always brought into it. Whenever they say they want to flirt you, they always mention, for example . . . "I want your Black penis" or something like that. They always put Black before anything. Black hands, Black muscles, things like that. Black bodies. They always do that. I'm sure within White races, when you get in bed with your partner, you don't say "I want your White . . . "

"Put[ting] Black before anything," in Damian's words, was how hypervisibility turned into invisibility.

Michael, thirty-four, met his Latina wife through online dating. He described how White women were hyperaware of his Black biracial status, often openly espousing stereotypes:

> Yeah. There's always this expectation of our prowess in bed. So, there's that expectation of like, he's kind of thug. I'm like, "I'm kind of a nerd." Some of these expectations, they're wrong to have. It's not like any of us see a White woman, and we're like, "Yo, she could do my taxes."

Black women also find themselves on the receiving end of assumptions about oversexualization. Deborah, twenty-six, noted that the messages she got from White men almost always foregrounded race:

> Like, "Oh, do you like White guys?" Or like people calling me by, like, a food name, so chocolate, caramel, all this other stuff. It's just like, "I'm actually a human. I'm not food." But they always feel like they have to come, they have to approach Black women in that way. . . . They don't treat you like a woman; they treat you like a Black woman. And I love being a Black woman, but don't treat me like I'm some alien version of what you're used to.

Deborah felt less like a woman than a *Black* woman—something different or alien to these men. Given that Black women get very little interest from White men, experiences like Deborah's suggest that even that paltry interest may be driven by prurient interests. White men we interviewed confirmed the notion that Black women were both highly sexual and unsuitable for lasting relationships. One said he had "certainly heard the stereotype that Black women are really promiscuous, and they want a lot of sex." Keisha, twenty-nine, described a White man saying as much to her directly:

> I remember this time with one guy—he was a White guy—he literally said, "Oh yeah no, I don't want to date you for a long time. I just want to have a sex goddess. I'm really into White girls," because he wanted to have sex; that's it. He just kept it simple and rough.

These interactions hearken back to the "Jezebel," or the controlling image of the sexually aggressive Black woman that served as a powerful rationale for the exclusion of Black women from the bounds of "respectable femininity" during slavery and Jim Crow and, shamefully, into the present.[25]

Black women subject to this treatment moderate their online-dating behaviors. For example, Alicia, a thirty-year-old Jamaican American, said she had always been open to dating White men but tended to avoid them on dating sites:

> ALICIA: Certain White guys I talk to online, they're like, "I never had sex with a Black girl. Imagine having sex with you." I said to them, "Is that all you want?" They respond, "I don't know, maybe." I'm just like, okay, this is uncomfortable. One guy said, "I don't think we'll date, but I just wanna have sex with you 'cause I never had sex with a Black woman." I felt so uncomfortable, and I was just so annoyed. It made me very upset. I was just, like, what the heck? That's why I don't date a lot of them online, because I get a lot of that too.
>
> INTERVIEWER: How did it make you feel when he said that?
>
> ALICIA: I just feel like, okay, that's all you see me as. Just someone to have sex with. You don't see anything else? For you to say, "Oh no, I can't. . . . I *won't* [emphasis hers] date a Black woman, but I just wanna have sex." I just felt like I was just gonna be used and that's it. It just made me feel degraded and less than. I just didn't like it. And I think that's the main reason why I don't talk to a lot of them online too, even though I do like White guys.

The more things change, the more they stay the same. The abolition of slavery, the end of Jim Crow, the triumph of Loving over Virginia, the great promise of the internet—centuries later, to some White men, Black women are treated not as potential partners but as sex objects by daters who use online-dating applications where digital-sexual racism pervades.

NON-WHITE ANTI-BLACKNESS

White supremacy is a global phenomenon, and the reach of anti-Black racism expands beyond the United States. Many minority groups exhibit anti-Black racism in their dating choices: their "personal preferences" map eerily well onto the racial hierarchy of the United States.[26] Indeed, the global stigmatization of Blackness is reflected in how Asians and Latinos see distancing themselves from "Blackness" as a way to protect themselves in an oppressive racial system. Within the United States it has been common for new immigrants, such as the Chinese, Mexicans, and the Irish, to work, live, and love alongside African Americans, then limit those associations as they pursued assimilation into the U.S. mainstream (see chapter 1). Today many Latino/a and Asian daters who experience racial discrimination and objectification by White daters nonetheless overlook Black online daters.

Some blame the colorism in their immigrant families. Take, for example, Carlos, a twenty-eight-year-old gay Latino, whose family, he thought, was unlikely to accept him dating a Black man:

> I think if I bring someone [home] who is Black, there would be worry . . . because my family comes from the country I came from. Just as me, they grew up watching the light-skin guy is the good guy, the educated guy, and the Black skin [guys] are the ones that they are thieves, the ones that are not as good as other races, I guess.

As we saw in chapter 4, White women invoke familial explanations when they are avoiding facing their own personal biases. It appears that other non-Black daters use the same reasoning when they explain their anti-Black preferences. A Chinese international graduate student we interviewed, Mai, said first that she "filtered out all the African Americans," and "as long as I have the education box checked it's very hard to bump into them." And when we asked her whether her family's expectations ever influenced these choices, she affirmed,

> I always try to tell them it's about racism; there's really nothing bad about being Black, and then in one hypothetical scenario I asked them, "So if I'm dating Barack Obama, who's like super-successful and is super-cute, what will you say?" Then my dad hesitated for like five seconds, and he said no. I said, "Really? That's Barack Obama. What are you thinking?"

Similar to Carlos's parents, Mai's parents adhered to anti-Blackness in their attempts to control their daughter's dating decisions. Her father could not even agree that the epitome of U.S. success, a wealthy Harvard law graduate and two-term president of the United States, could be both

Black and a good match for Mai. So it went among the Asian, White, and Latino/a daters we interviewed. Many parents, they told us, had expressed disapproval of dating Blacks even if they were otherwise ideal partners. That anti-Blackness is taken up by other minority groups serves to further isolate Blacks in the dating market.[27]

Parental disapproval also helps to illustrate how "personal preferences" are learned. Jazmín, a second-generation Honduran American, told us about her mother's response to her previous boyfriend, a Black biracial man:

> She was very upset, she was like, "You have nothing in common with this person culturally." She just wasn't about it. For me, that was weird. I was like, "Well, Mom, but he kind of was born and grew up in New York City in the proximity. We're American—what do you mean that we have nothing in common culturally? I think we do." But she was just hell-bent that it wasn't going to work out. She cried! She even said, "I just can't stand the thought of a Black man touching my daughter."

The trope of the Black brute, it would appear, is evergreen. To these parents seeing their child dating a Black person represented downward mobility and a failure of a racialized American dream. As shunning Blackness and privileging Whiteness (see chapter 4) appear to coalesce at the polar ends of the U.S. dating hierarchy, romantic gatekeeping becomes one way that immigrants and other non-Black communities of color distinguish themselves from the bottom of the U.S. racial hierarchy.

BLACK DATERS' AGENCY AND RACIAL VETTING

Certainly, Black daters are not merely victims of the racial hierarchies of desire. They too pick and choose. Similar to what sociologist Shantel Buggs found in a study on multiracial women's online-dating experiences, our interviewees described sophisticated vetting strategies to determine who might be an appropriate match. They paid attention to who supported the Black Lives Matter movement and who wore a "Make American Great Again" hat in their profile photos.[28] Black daters told us they took a closer look at the profiles that included Afrocentric symbols, such as natural hairstyles and African or West Indian flag icons, as well as references to "Black love." Describing the symbolism on his profile, Jordan, a Black man who hopes to match primarily with Black women he meets on apps, said,

> I got the Black man dreads going on, you know? I got the Liberian flag. It shows I am in tune with my culture. I would say that girls like to see that. And I would say my smile. I always got compliments when girls would message me and say, "You have a great smile." Also, the fact that I travel, so I always had pictures of me in different countries. So you're like, "Oh this is an interesting person, a world travel person." People always say like, "Oh, you lived in Brazil; you did this and that." Yeah. I would say those three things: my hair, my smile, and my experience traveling.

For many daters like Jordan, dating Black was a way of expressing cultural commitment, a shared commonality and history, and pride in one's history and familial background. Unlike non-Black daters, our Black interviewees were well aware that swiping left or right was more than a personal preference. To them the choice was both personal *and* political—a response to widespread gendered anti-Black racism and devaluation, a desire for a mate who could share an understanding of racial discrimination, and an expression of pride in the heterogeneity of Blackness all at once.

Indeed, straight Black men respondents indicated that they were most likely to search and message Black women. One explained that his first choice was always a Black woman and that he "just swipes or sends messages 'cause how they look. Black and attractive." The data that we have collected suggest that this approach is very common. In general, heterosexual Black men are most likely to reach out to Black women and least likely to reach out to White women (figure 5.4).[29] Black women, on the other hand, are most likely to respond to overtures sent by White men. Yet, unlike other women of color, Black women do not exclude Black men and are open to other men of color as well (figure 5.5). Black straight men and Black gay women, on the other hand, generally send messages to Blacks. Although Black gay men are most likely to send messages to Black men, they are relatively more open to sending to non-Blacks than are straight Black men and gay Black women (figure 5.6).

The vetting strategies employed by Black daters also go beyond filtering through profile content. White daters had to be held up to a particularly

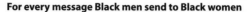

For every message Black men send to Black women

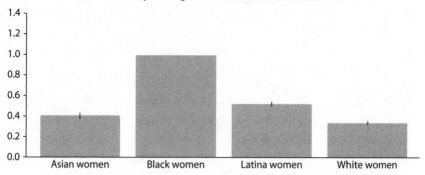

Asian women   Black women   Latina women   White women

Figure 5.4. Black Men's Relative Likelihood of Sending to Non-Black versus Black Women. The bars depict the relative likelihood of sending a message to non-Black women compared with Black women among Black men, adjusted for other observed characteristics. The lines depict 95 percent confidence intervals. Sending to Black women is indicated by an odds of 1.0. Anything above 1.0 shows a greater relative probability of sending to a non-Black dater than a Black dater; anything below 1.0 indicates a lesser probability. See online table O.1 for full estimates.

For every message Black women respond to Black men

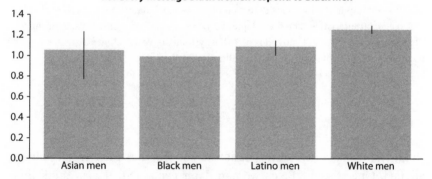

Asian men   Black men   Latino men   White men

Figure 5.5. Black Women's Relative Likelihood of Responding to Non-Black versus Black Men. The bars depict the relative likelihood of responding to a message from non-Black men compared with Black men among Black women, adjusted for other observed characteristics. The lines depict 95 percent confidence intervals. Responding to Black men is indicated by an odds of 1.0. Anything above 1.0 shows a greater relative probability of responding to a non-Black dater than a Black dater; anything below 1.0 indicates a lesser probability. See online table O.2 for full estimates.

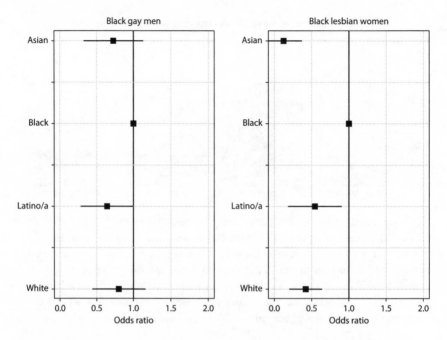

Figure 5.6. Gay Black Daters' Relative Likelihood of Messaging Non-Black versus Black Daters. The estimates depict the relative likelihood of sending a message to non-Black compared with Black daters among Gay Black daters, adjusted for other observed characteristics. The lines depict 95 percent confidence intervals. Sending to Black daters is indicated by an odds of 1.0. Anything above 1.0 shows a greater relative probability of sending to a non-Black dater than a Black dater; anything below 1.0 indicates a lesser probability. See online table O.1 for full estimates.

"high standard," a sort of inspection to see whether their racial politics aligned. One straight Black woman dater explained, "I also think that Whites probably won't respect me in the way I want to be respected. So I used very race specific criteria. I judge White dudes differently than I judge Black dudes." And a queer Black dater remarked, "The type I have for White folk is different from what I have for Black folk. It's different from what I have for Asian folk, et cetera, et cetera." Encounters with Whites were scrutinized to get a sense of their cultural competency and racial politics. Because our interviews took place in the Trump era, many daters of color underscored that White daters' support for—even indifference toward Trump*ism*—was a red flag. Nena, a thirty-two-year-old Black Floridian, made a typical comment:

> A couple of months ago I liked this White guy on Bumble. We exchanged numbers. We were talking about politics and the government and all that stuff. With the president, we were talking about Trump, and he was just like, "I think Trump is the best fit." He just said some stuff to me that was just like, I don't know if that's the person I want. If they believe in certain stuff that Trump believes in, I don't think that's something I want. . . . He tells me, "I love Black women." I could tell he's the type that dates Black women, but the stuff that he was agreeing with Trump. He was like, "I don't like when Black people say 'Black Lives Matter'; all lives matter." We had a discussion about it, and I didn't like it. Then after that I was just like, yeah, that don't make any sense to me. Then I just stepped back.

As Nena found, White daters' *openness* to interracial dating does not necessarily translate to the progressive racial beliefs many Black daters hoped to find in a partner.

Thus, many Black women interviewees explained that they hope to share a racial consciousness with people they meet on dating apps, and they are aware that a Black partnership will be culturally affirming and reduce conflict around family values, especially when raising children in a racialized world. That was a key concern among many of our Black interviewees, who feared that mixed-race children would have to contend with judgmental and racially insensitive relatives. Black women respondents voiced the importance of maintaining a Black identity for passing both racial and cultural heritage to future generations, a sentiment we also found among our Latina respondents (chapter 7).

For example, Alicia said she was theoretically open to all races but reluctant to actually date non-Black men. Her reluctance, she explained, came from the societal lack of understanding of what it means to be Black and a Black parent. Describing her conversation with a White man she met online, she said,

> Well, I had a conversation with him and was just like, but I'm a Black woman. If you date me, there's certain stuff you're gonna have to know. He was like, "I don't care. I'm gonna be there for you, blah, blah, blah." I just wasn't convinced. You know? I just feel like when you see a red flag. . . . I

said, "What if we had kids together? We'll have mixed kids, you know. Do you realize because you're White, that doesn't mean your kids are not gonna face what I go through? You know racism does exist. No matter if you have mixed kids or not, they may have to endure things I endured that you don't have to endure because of their skin color."

To Alicia a shared understanding of racial struggle was one way to protect any future children, who she'd be bringing up in a country with a long legacy of White supremacy.

Besides vigilance many Black daters said they had to learn to cope with having the odds stacked against them in dating sites. Straight Black men were particularly frustrated with the nonresponses they got, because they understood the heteronormative expectation to initiate contact yet were so frequently unable to get a message back. Jordan, for example, returned to the theme of White women either ignoring his interest or going silent in the middle of a conversation: "I would talk to a White girl and nothing would come about it, so I stopped. So then I retaliated in that way: 'Okay, then good-bye.'"

Having been repeatedly "ghosted" by White women, Jordan wanted to take control by rejecting White women altogether. Another Black man, Robert, had grown up in a predominantly White suburb in the South, where he learned, as a teenager, to look to "other races" for dates: "White women weren't really attracted to [him]." Robert understood that his treatment of others was often anticipatory: he generally ignored Whites because he didn't "really expect them to swipe [him] back." For many of the Black respondents in our study, it seemed that the accessibility of dating apps did not mean a world of unlimited romantic possibility but an early—or reinforced—awareness of their racialized undesirability.

Black women also expressed their expectation of rejection; they anticipated that other daters would have little interest in them and were occasionally surprised when they did receive messages from non-Black men, particularly Whites. Black women's beliefs that other groups won't want to date them has been documented in other research. For example, legal scholar Ralph Richard Banks finds that Black women may simply ignore advances by White men, or decide not to show interest in them, due to a

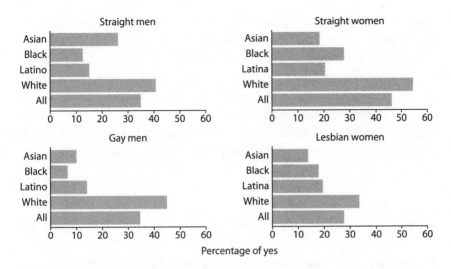

Figure 5.7. Proportion Strongly Preferring Someone of Their Own Racial Background. The bars depict the proportion of daters answering yes to the question of "Would you strongly prefer to date someone of your own skin color/racial background."

prevailing assumption that only Black men like Black women. White men may also assume that Black women have no interest in them. According to Banks, this assumption of no interest on both sides translates to "pluralistic ignorance": relationships never form because of the underestimation of the others' interest.[30] Janice explained that she was in disbelief when she started using OkCupid because "surprisingly a lot of Indian men" contacted her, later adding that "people can assess who they think will be attracted to them too. . . . I feel like the Indian men was surprising. The couple of Asian guys was also surprising too."

While "pluralistic ignorance" may lead to moments of surprise, straight Black women we interviewed stressed that their openness to dating others relied heavily on who sent them messages. This fit neatly with the shared understanding of the gendered dynamics of online interactions among straight daters. Indeed, our data suggest that Black women are quite willing to date White men, under the condition that those White men express their interest first (see figure 5.5). Like Asian and Latina women, they respond to White men's messages more frequently than they do to Black men's messages, suggesting that many Black women may also buy into the White male cultural ideal.[31] Unlike other women of color, however, their openness to other men of color follows closely behind. Yet, when it comes to women daters, the data clearly shows that White women are the most discriminatory (see chapter 4). For example, in response to a survey question about whether they prefer someone of their same skin color or racial background (figure 5.7), only 27 percent of Black straight women said yes, against more than 50 percent of White straight women.

BLACK WOMEN AND BLACK MEN'S RELATIONSHIPS IN THE TWENTY-FIRST CENTURY

As racist and sexist controlled images pertaining to Black femininity and masculinity fuel anti-Blackness and abound in online dating via the operation of digital-sexual racism, the relatively few contacts Blacks, particularly women, have with non-Black daters often take on a racialized and sexualized tone. Inevitably, the gendered expressions of anti-Blackness also affect the online relationships that are forged—or not forged— between Black people.

While there has been an increase in intermarriage in the past two decades, most marriages take place within racial boundaries. And while it's true that Black people have lower marriage rates than the national average and Black men are about twice as likely than Black women to marry Whites, interracial marriages remain relatively rare among Blacks and Whites overall. According to the Pew Research Center, Asian and Latino/a newlyweds are much more likely to intermarry, with nearly 30 percent of Asian newlyweds and 27 percent of Latino/a newlyweds married to someone of a different race.[32] Blacks and Whites, in comparison, outmarry at lower rates: just 18 percent of Black newlyweds and 11 percent of White newlyweds married someone of another race. When Black people do outmarry, it is most often to Whites.

Still, given the intense polarization of Blackness and Whiteness in U.S. society, there has been a constant fascination of anything that involves Black and White interracial mixture, especially when it draws the media's

White gaze.[33] Considering the historical taboo of the union between a Black man and a White woman (chapter 1), some see the growing number of such marriages as representing Black masculine success and power. Others may see it as a betrayal of shared struggle.

Today high-profile Black actors, singers, and athletes who date or marry White women are considered notable—think LaVar Ball, Shannon Sharpe, Kanye West, Hank Baskett, Travis Scott, or Taye Diggs. Black mainstream music videos frequently privilege lightness by showcasing mostly light-skinned women of color (women in videos are generally sexually objectified, but the colorism catches our eye here).[34] And though the vast majority of heterosexual Black men today are married to or dating Black women, the fact that more Black men outmarry is nevertheless a sore spot in the Black community, particularly given its otherwise low marriage rates.[35]

Black women are frequently depicted as having a particularly negative response to Black men dating interracially—these depictions span popular culture, academic scholarship, and everyday social commentary.[36] Some simplistic portraits leverage the statistics to suggest that Black women are embittered or insinuate that they are less desirable to Black men than White women.[37] Rarely do these sensational reports go deeper to unpack the complexity of this issue. Monica, for example, saw many structural factors at play in outmarriage:

> I think it's more a byproduct of mass incarceration in that there just aren't as many Black men out there for us. When you see a Black man with somebody outside their race you feel some type of way. It's not just that Black men don't deserve love. You just wish they would love somebody within their race. I think that's just a race survivalist kind of a sentiment. Like how are we going to outlive this? As far as making sure that Black people have equal opportunities and here we are, we're diluting the race. . . . I definitely know I feel that way just because I do love Black love, and I do appreciate Black power couples and what that means to the Black community.

Monica referred to race dilution, echoing antimiscegenation political rhetoric that has historically utilized the myth of racial purity to enforce racial separation. Yet, as a member of a marginalized group, her internalization of that ideology may reflect more general constraints Black women face in finding a mate. Indeed, Monica contextualized her sentiments within the structural context, pointing to the ways mass incarceration have emptied many communities of young Black men. This situation has led to solidarity among some Black women. For example, sociologist Erica Chito Childs finds that Black women aren't truly angry with individual Black men and White women who engage in Black-White relationships but at what these relationships *represent* for Black women like themselves.[38] Our respondents and Childs's linked their opposition to interracial pairing to their political struggles against systemic constraints on Black women's marriage and dating prospects. These include, but are not limited to, gendered and racialized stereotypes assigned to Black femininity, as well as discriminatory educational, legal, and labor-market institutions that limit Black men's and women's opportunities for social mobility and constrain their dating prospects.[39]

Skin color also matters. In the Deep South, skin color has particular historical resonance. But colorism is rampant throughout U.S. life. Since women are more often judged by their skin color, it is also linked to their self-worth, as evidenced by a Latina in our study who was partnered with a dark-skinned Black woman.[40] "There's a large internalized oppression part," Cruz told us. "My partner and I talk about it, all the time. My partner is darker than me. She talks about how even in the queer community it's really hard to find other members of the community who are Black who will also want a darker-skinned person." And Keisha, a Black woman who described herself as "dark brown," remarked, "I just feel like people feel that lighter-skinned Black women are more attractive." The significance of skin color appears to be amplified in online dating, where all physical characteristics take center stage, and it is well documented that lighter-skinned African American women have clear advantages in both heterosexual dating and marriage markets.[41]

Black men were more likely than Black women to pinpoint their own Blackness as a determining factor in how others perceived them. Black women believed that race *and* skin color were equally salient. As argued by sociologists Maxine Thompson and Verna Keith, the difference we observe may be due to a gendered construction of skin color, whereby skin tone is related to the feeling of self-efficacy for Black men but predicts self-esteem for Black women. This, of course, traces back to traditional gender norms that expect men to be productive, successful, and independent and women to garner adoration and validation from others.[42]

GENDERED BOUNDARIES, GENDERED WOES

Black women are also frustrated that they see all men as having internalized gendered anti-Black racism that frames Black women as undesirable. Alicia scoffed at some Black men's online-dating profiles and the way they suggested they were interested in anyone but Black women:

> I had no preference because I just didn't think any of the Black dudes that I read into on the site was checking for me in any way. And sometimes they kind of explicitly said it, like in their preferences, only like White. But then sometimes they implicitly stated it because they have pictures of like blond White girls. And it's just like, first of all, you shouldn't have pictures of other girls if you're on a dating site. And, second of all, they're all White, so I guess I kind of see what your taste is.

Some participants also took issue with how Black men adhered to gendered anti-Black controlling images that devalue Black women by depicting them as "angry" or resentful. Alicia reflected,

> Black men, they say, "Okay, I don't date Black women because they're bitter" and all this stuff. It hurts me as a woman because I'm like, "Are you just saying because someone is White or because they're Spanish, they're not like that?" For instance, when my ex, when we broke up, he dated a White girl. He was like, "You know, they don't argue. They're more chill. They don't talk back. You know, they don't get upset easily." He would say things like that, and I'm just like, what does that mean? I get upset because if you do something that hurts me, I'm gonna speak up. He was like, "Well, people just brush stuff off versus arguing and fussing." To me it's not arguing, it's you just saying, "Well, this hurt my feelings."

Black people, Alicia demonstrated, are not immune to perpetuating racialized and gendered desirability hierarchies that devalue Black womanhood. Yet there is another dynamic at play here. During interviews our Black women respondents pointed to the gendered policing of intimacy, a form of control they believed applied more stringently to women than to men.

Indeed, for many African Americans, dating and marrying other African Americans remains an important political and cultural choice against a backdrop of racist and sexist devaluation of Black manhood and womanhood. Black feminist scholars have argued, however, that concerns for "protecting" Black women coalesce around this political imperative to sustain Black love, which they connect to Black men's powerlessness to protect Black women from sexual and physical abuse under slavery.[43] Moreover, while some Black women may want to be protected, "a slippery slope emerges between protecting them and controlling them." A double standard within Black communities chastises women far more than men when they cross the color line.[44] Take, for example, the pushback Serena Williams received on social media after her engagement to the cofounder of Reddit, Alexis Ohanian. One online commentator pointed out that the announcement was met with "the shattering sound of angry keystrokes of Black men" as they accused Williams of disloyalty.[45] Amber, a Black woman engaged to a White man she met online, told us about this double standard:

> There are some Black women who they see Black men dating outside of their race with no repercussions, and so it's kind of like, it hurts. . . . If a Black woman dates outside of her race, they call her a bed wench; they call her a traitor. But these dudes they're with White women and it's okay, and they're friends even like dab and all this other stuff. But if you see a Black woman with a White man, it's just like, like you're ruining our race. Where are the next generation of Black children going to come from? Or you're the White man's whatever, add any pejorative term in there.

The pejorative term *bed wench*, for instance, calls on the memory of enslaved Black women forced into sexual submission to their White masters. Again we see the gender dynamics starkly operating within racial boundaries.

None of these nuances are tangential. As we have shown, our data indicate that the operation of digital-sexual racism redeploys historical and contemporary racialized hierarchies in the world of online dating. The internet doesn't remove anyone from social context. It is not a neutral space stripped of history, politics, gender, or race. During interviews both Black women and men often referred to "real world" issues that made it difficult to differentiate the inequality they face online and off.

EDUCATIONAL AND GENDERED RACIAL BOUNDARY WORK

Race clearly matters when searching for a mate, yet some scholars argue that gendered norms make socioeconomic characteristics more important for men. Historically, men have had more opportunities to achieve higher education, obtain professional jobs, and earn high salaries. Women have needed to access status via marriage, and so the decision of whom to date and marry has been far more economically consequential for women than men.[46] These processes have been distinct for Black women and men, given how the pervasiveness of institutional racism in U.S. society results in circumscribed opportunity structures for Black people more generally. Still, the gender gap in educational attainment has narrowed and, by some measures, increasingly favors women. This is particularly pronounced among Black women, who outnumber Black men completing college degrees.[47] And while White women with a college degree are more likely to marry than those without, marriage rates have been declining for Black women across educational brackets since the 1960s.

Indeed, some educated Black women in our study said that they were quick to ignore inquiries from Black men who did not have college degrees or were pursuing risky careers, such as musicians and small business owners. These women wanted racial and educational homogamy, but it seemed out of reach. Looking around their offices and other professional spaces, they could see plainly that most of their colleagues were White. That alone was enough to drive them to online dating. Janice, who hoped to date a Black man, put it this way:

> I do a full assessment of the profile. I would, say, not answer you if you don't have a college degree. For me that's a big deal: if you're in your last semester and you indicate that "Oh, I'm graduating in May." All right, you're fixing to get your degree. Whatever. That to me is a deal breaker. That's weird and I know people are like, "You're so judgmental." I'm like, "No, really it's just a standard."

Janice, a lawyer, had no intentions of altering her standards. And she is not alone. Among the many studies that affirm Janice's desires, sociologist Rocio Garcia's demonstrates that many educated Black women prefer same-race, similarly educated partners and face significant barriers when they attempt to carry out those preferences.[48]

In the same way that Black women prefer same-race partners because of shared experiences, the preference for college-educated Black men among educated Black women creates a feeling of overwhelm on both sides. Some Black men reported that they felt unable to measure up to educated Black women's standards. College-educated Black women in our sample, meanwhile, felt dismayed to find so few Black men in the same educational bracket and that those they could find were likely to outmarry or date non-Black women. Research confirms this frustration: for Black men the likelihood of marrying out increases alongside education, but this trend is less pronounced for Black women.[49]

The inclusivity we see among Black women—their relatively high openness to dating men across races—may reflect the fact that they do not have the power to be "choosy" when so few daters appear to favor them (see figures 5.1 and 5.2). Still, they may face backlash from Black men when they attempt to cross the intimate color line. In our interviews we heard Black men chastising Black women for claiming to be "tired" of the "games" but attributing such behavior to all Black men. Just as some Black women saw Black men marrying White women as a rejection of themselves, some Black men interpreted Black women's choice to date non-Black men as a wholesale rejection of Blackness.

Other Black men respondents claimed that Black women's relationship standards were too high. They thought Black women were searching for an unattainable "African King" or "Prince Jamal," as one dater put it, not a regular guy. One recently laid-off Black man, for example, described how a Black woman he met online rejected his advances after he disclosed his employment status. He argued that women claimed to want honesty, but "if you're totally honest about your situation, and if your situation is bad, it won't work out." Other straight Black men we interviewed called the Black women who rejected them "uppity," drawing unironically on stereotypical notions of Black femininity. Such concerns were particularly voiced by Black men who were unemployed or underemployed. They alluded to how hegemonic ideals of family (i.e., male breadwinners) created significant strains for minority men lagging behind those ideals.

Structural constraints frustrated the intentions of many Black daters in our study. These grievances were at times compounded by Black men's misogyny toward Black women, resulting in stereotypical and narrow views of Black womanhood. What was generally absent from men's qualms was a consideration of how Black women may be particularly disadvantaged and how Black women endure more scrutiny when they do cross the intimate color line. Our goal here is not to chastise Black men and women for expressing frustrations about each other but to highlight the pervasiveness of gendered anti-Blackness and the controlling images that animate it. Indeed, this "gender dilemma," as Shirley A. Hill calls it, exposes the racist, patriarchal, and economic underpinnings of outmoded ideals of courtship.[50]

As we discussed in this chapter, devaluation of Blackness is often accompanied by the privileging of Whiteness in the context of online dating, where people can effectively apartheidize their dating prospects by filtering, rejecting, or ignoring entire groups. However, if anti-Blackness is one anchor of desirability hierarchies, and the privileging of Whiteness the other, what can be said about daters who self-identify as neither Black nor White? It's time to consider the dating patterns of Asians and Latinos/as, groups commonly theorized by scholars as occupying a "racial middle ground" in U.S. society.[51]

6 The Asian Experience

RESISTANCE AND COMPLICITY

Maxine Hong Kingston's *China Men* opens with a mythical retelling of an epic Chinese tale, following warrior Tang Ao as he wanders into a North American Land of Women. He is captured and conditioned to accept humiliating servitude. His captors threaten to sew his lips together. His feet are painfully broken and bound, his ear lobes punctured, and his face plucked and painted. It is a double metaphor, in which Kingston explores both Chinese patriarchal traditions and the oppression that early Asian immigrants experienced when economic, immigration, and antimiscegenation policies pushed them into low-paid, often feminine-coded jobs and denied them the right to form a family.

Kingston's work was part of a major surge in new Asian American feminist work. When it was published, it drew ire from some fellow Asian American writers. Critics saw her critique of misogynistic cultural practices as an act of betrayal to the emergent revisionist movement, which was seeking to reclaim Asian masculinity from dominant White cultural narratives. A number of artists, most notably, playwright and author Frank Chin, sharply rebuked Kingston and other Asian American feminists for cultural inauthenticity and promulgation of a "white racist stereotype."[1] Yet this rebuke had itself reified sexist notions of masculinity, which demeaned Asian women to assert an Asian-specific masculinity.[2] Such debates are common in social movements, as racial and ethnic minority groups in the United States know well the contours of double consciousness. The burden of group representation often invokes conflict and anxiety among minorities over how they are seen among themselves and how they wish to be perceived by the White establishment.

These debates are particularly contentious in the Asian and Asian American community because Asian women are much more likely to out-marry than Asian men are. Filipino American artist Joshua Luna created a controversial image, titled *Reconciliasian,* to call attention to the differ-ing racial pressures that Asian men and women face, often leading to gen-der strife instead of alliance and resistance.[3] His work depicts Asian women as participating in White supremacy against Asian men under the guise of feminism and Asian men participating in misogyny under the guise of racial justice.

Some suggest that Asian Americans have failed to develop an overarch-ing group identity able to resist racial oppression. Partially, this is due to the lack of a shared history—Asian Americans, as a group, include a mul-titude of different ethnicities and nationalities who migrated to the United States during many different periods. The failure to cohere may also stem from the fact that Asian Americans, by virtue of their socially bestowed proximity to Whiteness, have more to lose in challenging existing power structures and underscoring their racial difference. Activists Frank Chin and Jeffery Paul Chan, pioneers in the early Asian American civil rights movement, have described U.S. racial stereotypes as falling into two mod-els under White supremacy: under the *unacceptable* category fell Black Americans, Mexican Americans, and Native Americans, while Asian Americans fell into the *acceptable* category. "The unacceptable model is unacceptable because he cannot be controlled by whites. The acceptable model is acceptable because he is tractable," they wrote, such that the unacceptable races were met with "racist hate" while Asian Americans were uniquely met with "racist love."[4]

What does "racist love" under the White gaze mean for Asian Americans in dating? While it suggests the assignation of a higher minority status over other minorities, the model-minority image manifests very differ-ently, in romantic terms, for Asian men than for Asian women. For men their relative socioeconomic successes come with an exchange—the erasure of traditional manhood. But for women racist love has meant the *magnification* of traditional femininity.[5] The prescribed endgame for both Asian men and women is equally coercive—model minorities, no matter how close to Whiteness in a U.S. racial status hierarchy, should not threaten the existing social and sexual status quo of White supremacy.

FROM YELLOW PERIL TO MODEL MINORITY TO DESIRED AND EXOTIC

Asian men have not always been branded model minorities in the United States. For instance, like Black men, Chinese men were routinely depicted as predatory threats to White women. Yet they were racialized under different historical contexts: the framing of Black men as sexual threats emerged most forcefully upon emancipation, but for Chinese men it was most vehement with their mass labor immigration in the nineteenth century. These men, recruited by U.S. businesses to expand the railroad and mining industries, were shocked to be received as invaders taking jobs from Whites. The path to Asian demasculinization began with economics but soon circumscribed their political and even their sexual freedom. State by state Asian men were pushed into low-paid "women's work," such as cooking, cleaning, and laundry—jobs that White men avoided.[6] They were systematically denied citizenship and, with it, the right to vote and own property—both basic tenets of U.S. manhood at that time.

Asian sexual and reproductive rights were also suppressed through legislation in the nineteenth and early twentieth centuries. A patchwork of antimiscegenation laws emerged to target, in turn, Chinese, Japanese, Korean, "Mongolian," "Malays," "Hindus," Asiatic Indian, and Filipinos. Such laws served a double function, both codifying immigrants into distinct racial groups and reinforcing their "otherness." The Page Act of 1875, which banned the migration of Chinese women to the United States, along with the 1882 Chinese Exclusion Act and the federal legal designation of all Asian as "aliens ineligible for citizenship" in the Johnson-Reed Act of 1924, functioned as a tripartite policy stripping Asians of their economic, political, and sexual rights.[7] David Eng calls this a form of racial castration, by which men once viewed as overtly virile and threatening were subjugated and emasculated as a matter of policy.[8] Yet the Page Act also targeted and racialized Asian women. Far from later twentieth century stereotypes that would have them as passive as "lotus flowers," Asian women were also viewed as threats in this period, often depicted as treacherous and unassimilable prostitutes undermining both public health and, symbolically, U.S. morality.

The emasculation of the East as weak and feminine was pushed along by the twentieth-century U.S. military occupations in Asia.[9] As explained earlier in chapter 1, this cultural imagination materialized in the relations between U.S. soldiers and Asian women during wartime, as the former came to see the latter as needing rescue and protection. Rather than unassimilable, Asian women were repainted as alluringly exotic and, importantly, sexually accessible. These controlling images of Asian women were shaped, in part, by U.S. military occupation after 1945 that encouraged soldiers to frequent Asian sex workers and to intermarry with local women.[10] The resulting association between Asian women and sex work manifested in popular stateside characters like Suzie Wong and Miss Saigon.[11] Because Asian women were seen to serve the needs of White American men, the cultural image of Asian sexuality was transformed in this period from threatening to possessable. Postwar policies permitting the migration and citizenship of servicemen's Asian wives created an exception to the "yellow-peril" exclusion laws of earlier periods.

Indeed, the "Orient" has a longer history as a site of Western male power fantasy. The relationship between Asian countries and the United States cannot be separated from racialization, colonialism, and U.S. militarization. In this context popular U.S. representations of Asian women have vacillated between that of the dragon lady prostitute and that of the chaste, submissive victim in need of redemption by White saviors. Which stereotype depended on whether the Asian country in question had been militarily subdued or not. "Japanese War Bride" films that depicted White military men returning home with Japanese wives both reflected the growing numbers of interracial couples during World War II and gendered constructions of "pacified" Asian women as subservient to their White American husbands. Other such controlling images of servile Asian women are the popular twentieth-century fixtures of "lotus flowers," "geisha girls," and "china dolls."[12]

As Asian migration reopened in the mid-1960s, these images were still fresh and provided a backdrop for the rise of the model-minority stereotype. Lisa Lowe summarizes this process: "The material legacy of the repressed history of U.S. imperialism in Asia" was "borne out in the 'return' of Asian immigrants to the imperial center."[13] With the Hart Cellar Immigration Act of 1965, hyperselective requirements were imposed on Asian immigrants, and these would remarkably alter the demographic composition of this community.[14] Whereas past Chinese migration flows consisted of working-class men concentrated in ethnic enclaves, these shifts brought Asian immigrants who were more educated than the average U.S. citizen, bringing them into closer proximity to Whites both geographically and socioeconomically.[15] Today Asian Americans experience less segregation than Latinos and African Americans and are far more likely to come into contact with Whites than other minority groups. While 90 percent of Whites and just over 40 percent of Black and Latino/a Americans live in neighborhoods where their own ethnic group is the majority, only 11 percent of Asians do.[16]

Some critique the Asian model-minority stereotype for its patronizing definition of a group that, through hard work, stoicism, and perseverance, has risen above other groups to attain socioeconomic success and a "better life." Indeed, the stereotype is a gross generalization of a heterogeneous population, and the term itself exists in opposition to what are presumably *nonmodel* minorities. Implied in the term *model* is good behavior, such as political and social compliance to the White status quo in contrast to other minority groups. Yet the accompanying term *minority* suggests a permanent distinction from White.[17] Thus, the yellow-peril narrative may be dormant, but it is never absent.[18] Asian Americans form an alleged racial bourgeoisie between Whites and other minorities—a buffer zone of people who are not quite White but not entirely minorities in the pejorative sense.

Asian educational achievement is accompanied by racial tensions too. Recently, scholars have found many White families moving to particular school districts to avoid placing their children in "competition" with Asian students in certain California districts.[19] Others note that elite colleges set implicit quotas for Asians by reserving admissions spots for White legacy students. These developments indicate that admiration quickly tips to threat when the model minority shows signs of becoming a model majority in *any* domain.[20] Such instances underline the reality that Asian Americans are not seen by many as fully American but rather as "forever foreigners."[21] And, as the United States becomes increasingly dependent on China for imported goods and to hold its debt, threat narratives disguised as patriotism have again become common.[22]

When Vincent Chin was beaten to death by White Detroit autoworkers in 1982, the racial precariousness experienced by so many Asian Americans was brought to the fore. Chin, a Chinese American celebrating his bachelor party, was misidentified as Japanese and made to pay the price for the success of the Japanese auto industry. Despite similar incidents, the average U.S. American views Asian Americans as the least discriminated-against group, at about the same level as Jewish Americans.[23] Indeed, there are a number of similarities between these groups. Both have been vilified *and* praised for their economic and scholarly successes. In the first half of the twentieth century, in fact, the Ivy Leagues' legacy policies were created to ensure that White Protestant students would continue to have seats as they competed for incoming class slots against highly qualified Jewish applicants.[24] And, like Asian Americans, Jewish Americans are experiencing an enormous rise in hate crime victimization in the contemporary United States and elsewhere around the world.

Indeed, yellow-peril discourse continued to rear its ugly head alongside the emergence of the global COVID-19 pandemic. Despite the World Health Organization's guidelines that reject new infectious diseases from being labeled based on geographic location, President Trump's relentless references to the "Chinese virus" intersected with long-standing, pernicious stereotypes about Asian people, ushering in detrimental consequences.[25] In the United States and abroad, the pandemic unveiled the stark reality that "yellow peril" is not a matter of the past, with Asian and Asian Americans facing frequent coronavirus-related acts of racial violence and harassment.[26]

ASIAN MASCULINITY ECLIPSED

It is perhaps because Asian Americans are so often depicted as successful that many people we interviewed seemed comfortable reciting negative

Asian stereotypes, particularly about Asian men. Typical stereotypes that we heard White women, and some women of color, use about Asian men were "quiet," "nerdy," and "smart." A twenty-one-year-old straight White-Latina woman from California, went into more detail, describing the stereotype of Asian men as "high-achieving" but dorky. In her words, he "wears glasses, [has] kind of patchy facial hair, overweight. Maybe more of first-generation, who has an accent when speaking English."

As we see here, the model-minority stereotype can easily be flipped such that a reputation for scholarly achievement, for instance, undermines any possibility of social desirability. John, a thirty-year-old South Asian engineer, was well aware of such stereotypes and felt ambivalent about his online-dating prospects. He remarked, "When do you have the hots for someone who is Asian or someone who's Indian? You don't hear that often. You just hear of them being tech geeks or doctors." Ironically, doctors and other high-status professionals are traditionally considered desirable spouses, but John associates such occupations with his own ethnic group and thus identifies them as undesirable. Still, at least one woman we interviewed embraced the relationship appeal of certain aspects of the model-minority stereotype. Beth, White and twenty-seven, told us she was specifically attracted to Asian men:

> Asian guys tend to be very smart and well educated, and have really good jobs. A lot of them are doctors, engineers. I look for guys who are ambitious ... and they also tend to be more interesting and have more hobbies and things going on in their lives or at least they're like more open about talking about it, whereas some of the White guys, that I see on these apps, are just like, I don't know. They just seem like typical party bros.

The most pervasive of the stereotypes we heard from White women about Asian men was that they had heard (though not experienced) that Asian men had small genitals. Despite the fact that there is no statistical correlation between penis size and race *or* height, it is a widely repeated trope.[27] In one convenience sample, almost 70 percent of Asian Americans reported being aware of the stereotype that Asian men have small penises, and 46 percent had heard someone else say that they wouldn't date Asian men.[28] Even star athlete Jeremy Lin has been targeted with this stereotype, in a particularly infamous tweet penned by a competitor.[29] The ubiquity of this belief, even when it is repeated in jest, is nothing more than evidence of racial ideology at work.

J. T. Tran, who runs a dating-advice service marketed toward Asian men, told us that he believed, based on his own dating experiences and those of the men he consults, that many such stereotypes about Asian men are driven by other men. In turn, Asian American men internalize these messages, becoming less confident about approaching women. During our interview J. T. commented,

> Almost 90 percent of the time that comes from White men in my experience. It's always White men that bring up my penis to me, right? . . . So there is that shame and then you throw in the additional sort of face-saving, shame-based culture of East Asian culture, and so it's definitely amplified. There is a deep, deep shame when it comes to . . . relationships and sex.

This is not limited to heterosexual dating. Sky, a twenty-four-year-old White dater, said they had dated men of different races and believed that Asian men were unfairly desexualized and undervalued in queer online apps and websites. Sky said,

> I mean there's a larger discourse of "no fats, no femmes, no Asians." That's, like, first of all, the fact that you would even be able to call it up as a slogan means it's prevalent enough that it was turned into a slogan. I would say that of queer sex icons very, very, very, very, very, very, very, very, very few of them are Asian.

Trevor, a similarly sympathetic Black gay dater remarked, "[Asian men are] either expected to be submissive, or they're actually completely invisible. [Other races] don't notice Asians; they don't look for Asians." Levi, a White bisexual dater, also commented on the invisibility of Asian men on gay dating sites:

> They are just seen as not desirable at all and totally erased. Even within their own community, Asian men are seen as asexual or not desirable, or just totally demasculinized. I've heard from so many people like, "oh I will never date an Asian man." It's like, why? You can't say that an entire group of people is not desirable to you.[30]

Mathew, a queer twenty-eight-year-old Chinese-White multiracial American who grew up in a conservative, mostly White city in the

Midwest, was on the other end of this invisibility. Even when daters interacted with him on the dating sites, he got messages like "I thought I'd give
you a shot, but I'm just not attracted to Asian guys." Mathew said,

> I found that very hurtful, because it's just something about myself that I'm
> definitely never going to change. It's not like if they told me I was too fat,
> then I might lose weight. So it kind of made me feel hopeless, like, yeah,
> that's definitely what most people want, and they're just too nice to say it.

These are examples of sexual racism that, in digital form, manifests itself
so directly as to be undeniable.

At the same time, online dating has provided greater opportunities for
gender-transgressive behaviors. Queer daters often described to us how
the internet helped them explore their sexual desires and many identified
online dating as a catalyst for how they came to terms with their own queer
identity as young adults. Yet dating online can also be a regressive experience for Asian daters. Some got unexpected inquiries, like the straight
Asian man surprised to get interest from gay women on dating apps or the
gay Asian man who went out on a date with an "extremely masculine,"
straight White man who was "interested in Asian men, because he thought
we seemed feminine." Not a single non-Asian man in our sample related a
similar experience, highlighting the ways that a specifically gendered
racialization conflated Asian men's race with femininity.

In online dating an internal pecking order becomes visible among
Asian daters. Some Asians we interviewed discussed how colorism and
nationalism were a constant presence. For example, a Southeast Asian
man whose siblings had lighter skin than his own, would sometimes hear
from his aunties and uncles: "Oh, you're so dark! You're never gonna get
married like that." At one point his aunt recommended a skin-whitening
soap. He asked us, rhetorically, "That really ruined my self-esteem, didn't
it? At a certain point, I definitely wanted to be a lighter-skinned Asian
guy." This worsened upon his foray into online dating. He noticed that his
lighter-skin East Asian friends seemed to have better experiences when
using dating apps:

> I've talked with my friend who's Korean about this before. He's like, "Yeah.
> I'll be real with you, dude. . . . Let's be real. I'm a light-skinned Korean guy.

I'm more of the standard Asian person, and if a person is going to date out-side their race or ethnicity, they may feel more comfortable going for what they know."

Notably, the friend's comment revealed the tendency to mistake Asians as necessarily *East* Asian and to reinforce White cultural beauty standards by privileging lighter-skin tones, even within Asian (and other non-White) communities.[31] To this man the apps reified anew Asian skin-tone strati-fication via colorism.

Linh, a queer Chinese and Vietnamese American, had empathy for her brother and cousins trying to date:

> It's just really difficult, because they're already trying to figure out their identity in terms of Western masculinity, but that is a typical standard that a lot of women use. How do you negotiate that if you are a really skinny Asian man who likes computer science? It doesn't really matter how much money you make if no one sees that you're a person who is capable of being in a relationship romantically and sexually.

At the same time, she saw how the quantification aspect of online dating elicited digital racisms of their own. Recalling how her cousin told her he wasn't attracted to South Asian women and sees them as non-Asian, she said with a smirk, "It's also, like, Asian men need to critique that in them-selves. Double-edged sword, racism is hard."

This pecking order, in which some Asians routinely express preference for others based on how closely they appear to standards of Whiteness, is frequently expressed by Asian Americans. For example, Sanjay discussed the feeling that East Asians, in particular, were not interested in Indian American men like him. He saw it over and over as he navigated dating apps:

> I have felt very much that Asian women are not interested in South Asian men. . . . I'm pretty open to dating an East Asian woman, and I don't know. . . . I've been on 1 date I think in four years with an East Asian woman out of, like, 150 dates I've been on.

Sanjay's suspicion was shared. Some East Asian men also believed that East Asian women avoid them in favor of White men. In popular culture this phenomenon is salient enough to have a shorthand—WMAF, referring to "White male–Asian female" pairings. Meanwhile, on Reddit, embittered discussions among charged Asian men are met by Asian feminist condemnations of what they see as unfair judgement and misogyny.[32]

Just as it seems more socially acceptable for people to voice negative sentiment about Asians because of their model-minority status, Asians often bring up stereotypes about themselves. Esther Ku, a comedian, is one exemplar, frequently disparaging Asian men in ways that are often echoed by other Asian women.[33] The movie *Crazy Rich Asians,* publicly lauded for its careful avoidance of Asian male caricatures, was famously altered from the best-selling book, in which the main character declared she did not date Asian men.[34] J.T., the dating service owner we mentioned earlier, described this as a near universal experience and that Asian women were often "telling me she and her girlfriends never talk to Asian guys. They don't want to ever date Asian guys, right? And there have been times when Asian women were trying to warn off their White girlfriends from me because I was Asian."

Tim, an adventurous and athletic DC-area twenty-three-year-old second-generation Taiwanese American, was outgoing—the kind of guy who likes to dance and enjoys chatting up Uber drivers. Online dating, he told us, had made him "quite familiar with the totem pole," explaining, "where White males and Asian females are at the top and Asian males and Black women are at the bottom." Tim, who is heterosexual, described receiving only a couple of matches a week. By contrast, Asian women in our sample described receiving lots of messages. But how does this play out in statistics? Is there a totem pole like the one Tim alleges? It turns out Tim is about half right.

Figure 6.1 indicates that, in fact, a number of non-Asian women are quite responsive to Asian men. Black and Latina women are just as likely to respond to Asian men as to the same-race men who contact them. White women and gay men, as well as gay Latinos, however, prefer their own groups to Asians.[35] The idea that Asian men are the most penalized group of all men on the dating market is widely cited, yet it is not supported by our data.[36] Unlike Black men, who are ignored by all groups except Black daters, Asian men are primarily ignored by White women and gay men. And, as we see in chapter 4, White women do not specifically avoid Asian men any more than they avoid Black or Latino men. In the end, not being

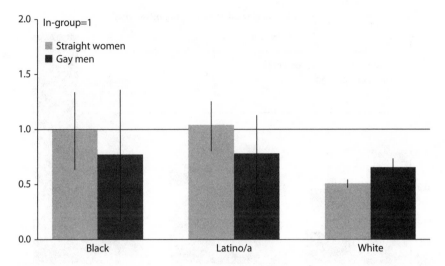

Figure 6.1. Non-Asian Daters' Relative Likelihood of Messaging Asian versus Same-Race Men. The bars depict the relative likelihood of interacting with Asian men compared with same-race men among Black, Latino/a, and White daters, adjusted for other observed characteristics. The lines depict 95 percent confidence intervals. Interacting with a same-race dater is indicated by an odds of 1.0. Anything above 1.0 shows a greater relative probability of contacting or responding to an Asian dater than a same-race dater; anything below 1.0 indicates a lesser probability. See online tables O.1 and O.2 (at www.ucpress.edu/9780520293458) for full estimates.

in last place is hardly reason to celebrate, but it is a point that is often missed among Asian men looking for romance online. These results suggest that it's an exaggeration to say Asian men are at the bottom, though they do support J. T.'s frustration about Asian women passing over Asian men for White men. Our data, in Figure 6.2, also show that Asian women and gay men are most responsive to White men, with Asian men as their second choice. They are more likely to interact with Asian men over Latinos and Blacks, but they are most interested in White men.[37]

Some argue, provocatively, that such a preference for White men by Asian straight women and Asian gay men represents a form of internalized racism. Studies of people's dating profiles indicate that Asian women are more likely than other women to exclude their own race in the list of preferred racial backgrounds.[38] In a similar study gay Asian men express

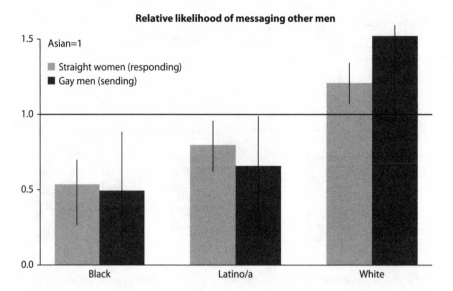

Figure 6.2. *Asian Daters' Relative Likelihood of Messaging Non-Asian versus Asian Men.* The bars depict the relative likelihood of interacting with non-Asian men compared with Asian men among Asian daters, adjusted for other observed characteristics. The lines depict 95 percent confidence intervals. Interacting with an Asian dater is indicated by an odds of 1.0. Anything above 1.0 shows a greater relative probability of contacting or responding to a non-Asian dater than an Asian dater; anything below 1.0 indicates a lesser probability. See online tables O.1 and O.2 (at www.ucpress.edu/9780520293458) for full estimates.

the highest disinterest in Asian men—being more likely than White gay men to prefer dating *only* White partners.[39]

It is difficult to separate such preferences from White masculine hegemony and racial hierarchies.[40] We see similar internalization among other minorities, but Asian Americans appear more complicit in subscribing to the value of Whiteness in online dating.[41] This may be due to a relative lack of race consciousness around marriage and dating. Unlike members of Black communities that emphasize the revolutionary act of "Black Love," Asian Americans have a less unified history through which they can construct a collective identity. Indeed, the fact is Asian American women outmarry more than any other group in the United States, despite the fact that Asian men most often have the socioeconomic characteristics associated with gendered courtship ideals.[42]

Why would racial identity eclipse a man's high socioeconomic positioning? This dynamic is likely a manifestation of the way that race is constructed through gender in the United States. While Black Americans must contend with the overmasculinization of Black men and women, Asian Americans contend with just the opposite. In a heterosexual marketplace that still falls under the White gaze and traditional gender norms, Asian women are at a greater advantage than Asian men to pair with Whites.

An alternative explanation of the WMAF phenomenon is that Asian women seek White men as way to resist Asian patriarchy.[43] Such a notion was brusquely expressed by comedian Esther Ku, who tweeted, "White men shouldn't have to be made to feel bad about their attraction to AF's [Asian females]. They make nicer partners than wife beating Asian men."[44] Kumiko Nemoto calls this romanticization of White men by some Asian women "egalitarian knighthood."[45] Some scholars see such resistance as flawed, not just because White men are complicit in gender oppression but because women's critique of Asian men often reproduces Westernized anti-Asian racism. While Asian men should not be absolved of cultural misogyny, neither should the specific racial marginalization of Asian men in these critiques go unaddressed. For instance, Asian men may deploy patriarchy as a way to compensate for emasculated masculinity in the United States. Pierrette Hondagneu-Sotelo notes in her work on machismo that masculinity performances of racially subordinated men should not be confused with those of men acting from structurally constituted sites of power.[46] Wesley Yang elegantly captures this contradiction in The Souls of Yellow Folk, in his discussion of the liminal space occupied by Asian men in discussions of gender and race. As an "honorary white" man, the Asian man's claim to being a person of color is "taken seriously by no one," while at the same time he benefits in no meaningful way from the advantages of White masculinity. He writes,

> In an age characterized by the politics of resentment, the Asian man knows something of the resentment of the embattled white man, besieged on all sides by grievances and demands for reparation, and something of the resentments of the rising social justice warrior, who feels with every fiber of their being that all that stands in the way of the attainment of their thwarted ambitions is nothing so much as a white man. Tasting of the frustrations of both, he is denied the entitlements of either.[47]

The argument against dating Asian men because of Asian patriarchy also obscures the plurality of Asian cultural traditions and generational change. Indeed, White women's exclusion of Asian men reproduces racialization by assuming homogeneity. In our interviews Asian American men discussed how their marginalization, which they have found amplified online, had made them more aware of and empathetic to Asian women's specific oppressions. Both men and women also mentioned that the global ascendance of Asian economies and the globalization of the musical genre K-pop is a cultural phenomenon that diversifies the way U.S. Americans view Asian masculinity. Another study of White, Asian American, and Asian immigrant college students split Asian men into two gender typologies: those with more flexible views who tended to view masculinity and femininity as less rigid categories than did White counterparts, and those with more rigid gender views than White men.[48] Of all men, these scholars reported, Asian Americans were most willing to say they would take on domestic household roles.

J. T. shared that Asian men were more polite and respectful toward women and less inclined to "play the field" than other men, making them "safer" in terms of the threat of sexual assault and rape. "I've actually argued that it's more dangerous for Asian women to be in White space if you look at the sexual assault crime rates."[49] Yet, he lamented, these characteristics are more often a penalty than a prize. Women, he believed, saw Asian men's "politeness" and "niceness" as evidence that they were less masculine. Nevertheless, it contrasts notably with the stereotype that Asian men are abusive misogynists.

RACIALIZED AND GENDERED ASIAN FEMININITY ONLINE

The gendered racialization of Asian women operates in reverse, such that they are fetishized.[50] Many of our interviewees discussed how normalized they had found this dynamic to have become in the massive dating market of the internet. People frequently cited hearsay as they identified specific types of White men as most likely to fetishize. Asian women daters derided the men online who fetishized them as "creepy" "geeky White guys who are into anime" and gender-conservative older men. Linh said she could spot them from a mile away:

Their profile will always be like, "I'm into anime; I'm into manga; I'm into Japanese culture." Yeah, I'm rolling my eyes, too, in the back of my head. . . . There was this one White man who had a picture of him and the Great Wall . . . in like a bamboo hat.

In some ways the WMAF cultural trope was reproduced by our respondents in forms that echo other interracial tropes, like the stereotype that Black men prefer to partner with overweight, unattractive White women.

Of course, the Asian woman and "nerdy" White man trope may also reproduce stereotypes about Asian women's sexuality. Yet Asian women's criticism of this trope also represents their resistance to the fetishization of Asian femininity and to the framing of White masculinity as necessarily attractive. Indeed, each Asian woman we interviewed spoke about dating experiences in which they had felt sexually degraded because of their racial identity. Rae shared, "I think one of the times that I felt the most disgusted on the app was . . . [when] one of the guys started a conversation with me and literally just said, 'I've never fucked an Asian before.' And I was like . . . What!?" Others attested to feeling "pornified" and upset by expectations that they be "docile, submissive, good in the bedroom." It wasn't only White men who held such views, however; one woman worried that non-White men she met online were also looking only to "fulfill this fucked-up fantasy of having a submissive Asian woman." She shared a powerful anecdote about an Afro-Latino man whose keen interest in her Asianness made her uncomfortable. She decided to stop seeing him after one sexual encounter:

> He was a really big dude, six three. His bicep was the size of my head. He was trying to make me submit. He was trying to do like a dom-sub type of relationship, and I didn't give him any consent to that. He would keep talking about how small my vagina was . . . too often.

It is clear that racial imagery, once constructed, is not constrained by group boundaries. Many people, including marginalized minorities, perpetuate societal narratives of racialized desire. These narratives are sometimes so animated in the online context that many daters saw it as the dominant interaction.

Feeling regularly stereotyped, most Asian women we interviewed described a gnawing feeling of uncertainty. Repeatedly, they told us they were not sure whether the men they met online were interested because of who they were or simply that they were Asian. Rae said, "It always feels like it's just like a sexual 'I want to experience an Asian woman,' rather than you're a person who is also Asian. . . . It's like, is that the only reason why you swiped on me?" Another mentioned a White dater who was disappointed when they met in person because she lacked an Asian accent. Asians already face accent discrimination socially and professionally, and now her date expected her to fit an exotic image of Asian womanhood in which a foreign accent and broken English were desired.[51]

To cope with fetishization, many Asian women develop a sophisticated vetting strategy. Wen, for instance, called her "in real life" meetings with White men underwhelming, a feeling she attributes to their lack of interest in her cultural background. In reference to a recent date, she stated, "I don't think he had any particular curiosity in probing more about something that he doesn't know. He's happy to jump in to comment on something that both of us are interested in, but whenever I mentioned something about Chinese, he didn't want to probe more."

Asian women also looked for negative indicators—specific images, words, and props that could signal White conservatism, which they tied to racial intolerance. Like many other daters of color we interviewed, Asian daters told us that symbols such as posing with dead animals and guns were deal breakers after Trump. Fairly or not, they saw it as representing that the person was okay with overt racism and sexism. Stacy, a queer multiracial Asian dater put it this way:

> Well, at this point, I'm much more politically picky than I would have been before. Like, I mean, before the whole Trump era, I was more open to, you know, some people believe this, some people believe that. But now I would never date someone who, you know, considers themselves a Republican, under the current climate. . . . Well, I just think they have to be a very irrational person or a very bigoted person to justify voting for Republicans at this point.

And Ana told us about a *Get Out* moment, when she discovered that her White ex-boyfriend, whom she had met online, might have a particular interest in Asian women:

> I would just say it really does worry me because I can't tell if someone is contacting me just because they have this weird Asian fetish. . . . And I

didn't really realize it until we were [together], because I asked him the question . . . and I said, "Oh, you have dated a lot of Asian women then?" And he's like, "Oh, no, not that many. Probably only 40 percent." Which is kind of a lot! And so I was looking at all of his photos of his past exes, and every single one had the same exact body type as me. Very, very similar to me. . . . We were all Asian. . . . So, it really pissed me off because I felt like, no, he doesn't like me because he thinks I'm so great. He likes me because I fit his Asian smart mold.

In the article "Why Yellow Fever Isn't Flattering," scholar Robin Zheng documents similar anxieties among Asian women respondents.[52] Racial fetishization, she concludes, sexually objectifies and depersonalizes, placing a negative psychological burden on Asian women who must navigate doubt and uncertainty. But, as Ana alludes to in her story, some men's interest in Asian women extends beyond the sexual to model-minority stereotypes. For example, Paul, a thirty-year-old White-Latino from the Northeast, who told us he had "never been particularly attracted to Asian women based on physical appearance," nonetheless indicated that many of his White friends see Asian women as a "really safe choice." He explained,

> "Safe," as in they are less likely to cheat on you. They are going to be someone you can bring home to the parents, and the parents will be satisfied. They are safe in that . . . likely to be well educated or responsible, those kinds of things. And I think that's, at least within my friend group, the stereotypes, and those are stereotypes that I would hold myself, if I'm being perfectly honest.

Scholars have theorized that the cultural fetishization of Asian women may lead to a "mutual attraction," which drives the disproportionate number of White man–Asian woman intermarriages.[53] Some White men's exoticization of Asian women then is of a piece with some Asian women's cultural valorization of hegemonic White masculinity. This, of course, fits with the scholarly view that Asian women leverage cultural stereotypes to gain closer proximity to Whiteness. But Nemoto emphasizes that "what has led these women to engage in feminine subjugation is not their subservient nature in a stereotypical sense, but rather the culturally embedded imaginary discourses that promise their upward mobility and realization of self."[54]

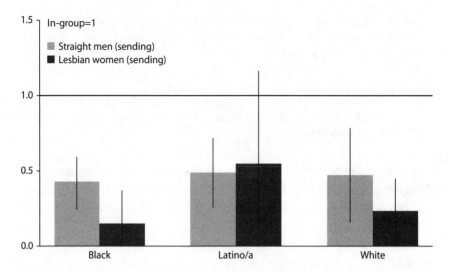

Figure 6.3. Non-Asian Daters' Relative Likelihood of Messaging Asian versus Same-Race Women. The bars depict the relative likelihood of sending messages to Asian women compared with same-race women among Black, Latino/a, and White daters, adjusted for other observed characteristics. The lines depict 95 percent confidence intervals. Interacting with a same-race dater is indicated by an odds of 1.0. Anything above 1.0 shows a greater relative probability of contacting or responding to an Asian dater than a same-race dater; anything below 1.0 indicates a lesser probability. See online table O.1 (at www.ucpress.edu/9780520293458) for full estimates.

Upward mobility and a sense of belonging are powerful motivators, and in a White supremacist society, a desire for proximity to Whiteness could very well be a driver for WMAF couples. Asian women *are* more likely to respond to White men than to Asian men (see figure 6.2). Yet when we run similar models predicting men's behavior, White men do not appear to be more interested in Asian than White women.

In figure 6.3 we compare the messaging patterns of heterosexual non-Asian men and lesbians to Asian women. It shows that White, Black, and Latino men are all less likely to send messages to Asian women than to women of their own racial group. Lesbians are even *less* likely to send messages to Asians.[55] So the data does not support cultural narratives around an active seeking out of Asian women by non-Asians. More prevalent is Asian women's interest in White men—an interest shared by Black

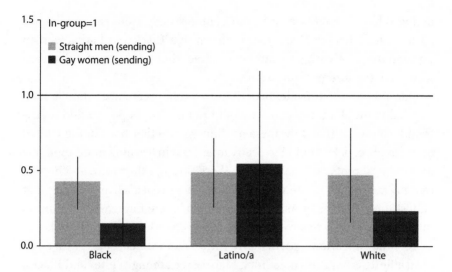

Figure 6.4. Asian Daters' Relative Likelihood of Messaging Non-Asian versus Asian Women. The bars depict the relative likelihood of sending messages to non-Asian women compared with Asian women among Asian daters, adjusted for other observed characteristics. The lines depict 95 percent confidence intervals. Interacting with an Asian dater is indicated by an odds of 1.0. Anything above 1.0 shows a greater relative probability of contacting a non-Asian dater than an Asian dater; anything below 1.0 indicates a lesser probability. See online tables O.1 and O.2 for full estimates.

and Latina women. Together these results reflect the power of hegemonic White masculinity and that Asian women are not necessarily passive in WMAF pairings.

Commenting on Asian women's White preference, Jeremy Lin, the famous basketball player, flipped the term *yellow fever* when he was asked about dating in a press conference: "You don't see a lot of non-Asian girls going for Asian guys.... Like when they say 'yellow fever' growing up, it wasn't like all these White girls are going for Asian guys. It was the Asian girls going for White guys."[56] Indeed, one analysis of dating profiles reports that 11 percent of Asian women exclude White men from their dating searches, while 53 percent of White men exclude Asian women (55 percent of Latino men and 71 percent of Black men exclude Asian women too).[57]

Despite the apparent interest among Asian women in White men, our data suggest that Asian men and Asian lesbians are far less interested in dating White women (see figure 6.4). Interestingly, from earlier (chapter 5) and later (chapter 7) analyses we learn that Black and Latina women respond frequently when Asian men contact them. Still, most Asian men focus first and foremost on Asian women.

Our interviews provide insight into such preferences. Some men stressed cultural affinity and national origins. Tim hoped to find a girl-friend who was either Taiwanese or Chinese, whether born in the United States or abroad. He said, "I'm pretty interested in learning more about my own cultural roots and maintaining those through the future and hoping that my kids in the future will also retain those roots." Given the fact that almost three-fourths of Asian American adults are foreign-born, cultural influences are likely to strongly shape peer networks and dating pools.

Yet other interviews, particularly with Asian women, suggest that cultural affinity is not the whole story. Like we see among Whites and Blacks, politics and patriarchy also influence dating priorities. As we mentioned earlier, proximity to White masculinity may symbolically "buy" power. Patriarchy binds women's identity in ways that may help explain some Asian women's greater orientation toward White men. Still, the power of hegemonic masculinity is that it legitimates intramale hierarchies.[58]

Indeed, it was interesting how often White men indirectly figured into Asian men's discussions around their partner preferences. For example, Arthur, twenty-seven, had grown up in the Northeast, where men in his Cambodian community invoked fears around racial competition over women: "A lot of the guys would be like, 'We need to make sure that these White men don't take our women!' or 'We need to make sure that we pre-serve our values as Asian men.'" When Arthur's brother brought home a White girl, he faced social stigma: "My brother dated a White woman in high school, and he would get shitted on in different ways. They're like, 'You can't hang out with us cause you're not dating an Asian woman' . . . and he'd have to deal with that stuff." While the literature often discusses how immi-grant women may be forbidden by their families to outmarry, Arthur's nar-rative adds a twist: within ethnic enclaves there can be a sense that com-munities are imperiled by all outmarriage and that cultural vitality requires both men and women to seek intimate association within their racial group.

Another way White men play into heterosexual Asian men's prefer-ences came up in our interview with J. T. In addition to preserving cultural roots, J. T. felt that many Asian men avoided dating non-Asian women because they don't want to invite male aggression. Racism was an ever-present hazard, he said,

> but the problem with [walking down the street with] a White woman is that it's like every single block . . . when it comes to the White men at a bar, club, people are—drunk; they get activated. They get triggered. And I've been physically accosted. I do this every weekend, so I know how to deal with this, but it does cause physical risk. . . . One of the biggest fears as Asian men—I have a lot of students that are literally . . . yeah, they won't tell you, right? Because admitting that kind of fear makes them 'less manly'—but there is a very large fear of White men and Black men beating them up and just that physical violence.

The belief that being with a White woman would call unwanted attention or even violence may appear staggering, but it was a common fear shared by early Asian immigrants who lived under White supremacy and restrictions over their sexual freedom. It also reflects how White women are still often painted as victims of men of color—including Asian men.

Another commonality we found between Asian men's and women's dating preferences was their disinterest in Black daters. In fact, compared to how they treat all other groups, Asians interact with Blacks least (figures 6.2 and 6.4). Wei, an international graduate student from Taiwan, described how when he first moved to the U.S. Southwest, he was primarily interested in White men, which he attributed to U.S. popular media and culture. But after some time he said he began to appreciate "the beauty of different races." Even so, he admitted that online dating had helped him develop a racial dating hierarchy with Asians at the top, followed by Whites and then Latinos. When we asked about Black daters, he said,

> I rarely have this conversation with other people, but . . . I'm talking right now. Just when I'm thinking about this, sometimes I think that doesn't make me racist, but just because I'm just less into Black people when it comes to intimacy, relationships. The way I justify it is my best friend here is Black, so I don't think I'm racist. I don't know. That's how I see it.

Ironically, Wei's closest friend was Black, but he was unable to achieve intimacy in romantic relationships with Black people. In this sense, Wei draws from a familiar frame of color-blind racism by tokenizing a Black person as he justifies the anti-Blackness of his intimate life.[59]

These experiences were also supported in our interviews with Black daters. For example, Marvin, a twenty-three-year-old Black data analyst from the Northeast, described himself as "doing pretty well for myself," with a good job, a nice apartment, a good education, and conventional good looks. Yet, he told us, "I've had negative experiences as a Black person trying to date Asian women, and so I don't pursue that anymore." He cited that Asian women often step back out of the fear that, should the relationship continue, they might be "disowned" by their families. Again anti-Blackness is shown as a pervasive U.S. view, not limited to racial binaries.

Apparently, "family" is a universal explanation for choosing not to date Black people. Ana, an Asian woman, was just one of many who pointed out her parents' anti-Black bias:

> My sister and friends wouldn't care at all if I dated a Black guy. My parents, on the other hand, would. It's really sad, but it's always been this way. So let's say it was a Black guy who also grew up in a very White environment.... My parents, I think, would be okay with that. But I just know they would not prefer me dating a Black guy.

Note her parents' *possible* openness to Black men, should they hail from predominantly White environments. This is not surprising: people intimately closed off to Blacks may feel still openness to singular exceptions. Recall that we have also seen this play out in White daters' assessments, whereby they reject most Black daters but note specific celebrities of color they find attractive. The notion that a "Black guy who also grew up in a very White environment" would be a more suitable companion also reflects Ana family's closer identification with Whites in a triracial hierarchy.

While yellow-peril discourses throughout the previous 150 years constructed Asians as forever foreigners and unassimilable, contradictory constructions surfaced during the 1960s, portraying Asian Americans as high achieving, industrious model minorities.[60] Jennifer Lee argues that these conditions created more intergroup contact between Asian Americans and Whites, thus contributing to an increase in White-Asian interracial coupling.[61] Yet, as we have shown, that acceptance process has been uneven because of the continual resurfacing of yellow peril discourse and the gendered racial dynamics that Asian Americans endure in White supremacist U.S. culture. Such racialized gender dynamics are suddenly laid bare in an online-dating context, becoming more universalized as a standard form of digital-sexual racism.

7 "Hey, You're Latin. Do You Like to Dance?"

THE PRIVILEGE AND DISADVANTAGE OF LATINO/A DATERS

They have in their heads that we're passionate and fiery. And willing to have sex and dance well and can cook for them and can clean for them. And we're like the perfect woman that they've always wanted and they don't get here.

Bianca, 2018

I stopped identifying myself as Hispanic on my profile because I thought maybe it would get me more attention. When I didn't list a race at all, I figured that they'll see my skin as White, so they'll assume I'm White. I didn't really notice a change in that. Later on, I was like, "Yeah. You know what. Fuck it. No. I'm not going to posture like that."

Miguel, 2018

To twenty-nine-year-old Bianca, ethnic identity could be an advantage in dating. Many non-Latinos she met on dating sites showed interest, after all, *because she was Latina.* The stereotypes associated with this identity seemed to work in her favor. Yet, Miguel, thirty-two, reported the opposite. Though both Bianca and Miguel lived in the mid-Atlantic states, Miguel suspected he had little success meeting people online *because he was Latino.* He knew he could "pass" as White but wondered whether he should stay true to his identity and proudly proclaim his race on his dating profiles. Their contrasting experiences show that, like Asian and Black daters, Latino/a daters face an intersectionally structured dating world in which race and gender interact to shape their romantic chances. They also demonstrate the role of individual agency in reaffirming, reshaping, or challenging desirability hierarchies.

CONTROLLING IMAGES OF LATINOS/AS

Social scientists generally treat Latinos as a group straddling the categories of White and Black.[1] Others argue that Latinos in the United States have a long history of confronting oppressive racialization, a reality compounded by the anti-Latino and anti-immigrant vitriol of Trumpism.[2] Like Asian Americans, the U.S. Latino population spans many countries of origin. Mexico accounts for the largest portion, 62.2 percent, followed by Puerto Ricans, Salvadorans, and Cubans.[3] About half of Latinos in the United States are foreign-born, and the various ethnic groups differ in their histories and migratory paths. Yet together they have a sense of shared destiny associated with Latino identity.[4]

Popular culture has historically represented this group as "Brown," a category distinct from White, Black, or Indigenous. Partially, this stems from the prevalence of intermarriage and interracial sexual relations in colonial Latin America, which contrasts to the history of antimiscegenation enforcement in the United States. It is also part and parcel of the contrast between the absolute prohibition of the marriage between Blacks and Whites and the commonality of unions between European colonists and Latin Americans in some regions. In the Southwest, for example, many European colonists married light-skinned Mexican women as part of an effort to expand English territories. These women were portrayed as "beautiful," sexually available, and neither fully Indigenous nor Black.[5] These controlling images functioned both to erase a Black or Indigenous Latino identity and to naturalize colonial and patriarchal relations of power.[6] Cultural anthropologist Arlene Dávila argues that even contemporary U.S. media relies on this history of a dichotomy between marginalized Blackness and valorized Whiteness in the current construction of Latina desirability.[7]

The historical antecedents to Latino men's modern controlling images can be traced to representations of dark-skinned Mexican men as exploitable labor, vacillating from "birds of passage" to "illegals" and "deportables."[8] These representations were popularized in the early twentieth century, when the U.S. state aimed to solidify an imaginary territorial and political border after the Spanish-American War. Images of the Mexican "criminal" and "rapist" were circulated vehemently to arouse nativist fear and justify control. Over time the conflation of Mexican masculinity with illegality gained traction because unauthorized entry into the United States was increasingly treated as a criminal, rather than a civil, offense.[9]

The "outlaw" image of Latino men came with sexual connotations. Consider the stereotype of the "Latin lover," perhaps epitomized by Zoro, a fictional character created in the early twentieth century. Zoro is a light-skinned criollo (a "White Spaniard" born in the Americas), a daredevil who seduces women while fighting an endless series of darker Mexican villains. Zoro's image was pendular: he is the exotic and attractive man who seduces, often White, women but also the "macho" chauvinist whose behavior is domineering, aggressive, and rude.[10] This image of machismo was further crystalized in 1961 with the publication of *The Children of Sánchez*, by anthropologist Oscar Lewis. The book portrays a dysfunctional family in Mexico City, confronting "a world of violence and death, of suffering and deprivation, of infidelity and broken homes, of delinquency, corruption, and police brutality, and of the cruelty of the poor to the poor." Lewis attributed the Mexican family's misfortune to their failure to "embrace the egalitarian gender roles of the White, middle-class, nuclear family unit as the pathway to the American dream—that is, a successful occupation, a nuclear marriage, and well-adjusted, successful offspring."[11] While the construct of the *Latino lover* and the *Latino macho* may appear distinct, they send a similar message: Latino men are hypersexual and desirable but also dangerous and dysfunctional. The conflation of Latinness, particularly Mexicanness, and criminality compounds this deleterious representation in the modern era.[12]

Latina women's political and economic marginalization have emerged into a composite image too. In the United States they disproportionately perform low-wage, low-respect care and service work requiring obedience to their customers and employers.[13] The popular television satire *Family Guy*, for instance, includes a character named "Consuela," who plays on the assumed subservience of Latina women. An older, docile domestic servant, Consuela responds to every request with "no"—a response intended to evoke laughter among the show's knowing audience by playing on the contrast between the controlling images of the docile domestic worker and the "fiery" or "hot-headed" Latina. Other examples of this blending in popular media are found in the comedy series *Devious Maids.* As an extension of the history of Latina women playing clichéd roles in mainstream television that reaffirm Latina bodies as unruly, undereducated, hypersexual, and in service of others, the characters here redeploy both servility and feistiness. With so few Latino/a characters in popular media, narrow depictions, however they are played for laughs, limit a diverse community's power for self-definition.

CONTROLLING IMAGES AND ONLINE DATING

Online dating is especially relevant to the Latino/a community in the United States because they are more likely than any other group to meet their partners online.[14] Yet it is also a medium where, given the pervasiveness of digital-sexual racism, *stereotypes* are taken as *knowledge* in deciding whom to contact and how to seduce. The Latino daters we interviewed complained about being boxed in by media portrayals. Andrew, forty-five, had met a White woman just a few months after joining a dating site, and he thought their first date had gone well. But at the end of the night, he said, he was surprised:

> We had just a few drinks, and we're talking. It was going well, as I was walking her home. So, I reached out to hold her hand, and she held it for a second, and then just sort of let it go. Even though we had had this whole date, like a two-hour conversation over drinks, [I] hadn't given her any indication that I was really culturally Latino at all (I was born and raised in the States and all that stuff). Despite all of that she said, "Oh, you Latin guys, you're so physical." I was like, "Oh, okay. That's really not relevant at all to me." Right, like all Latin guys are trying to just jump all over her. I just thought that was interesting that she was still seeing me in that lens, and my behavior in that lens, that I was just trying to be this pushy Latin guy, or whatever. All of a sudden I was put in this category, and a fairly innocent thing, like trying to hold her hand, started being seen from this lens.

Hidden images were nonetheless present in Andrew's encounter, such that his wish to hold a woman's hand became not an expression of individual affection but a suggestion of Latino aggression. The woman never contacted Andrew for another date, though he said he wouldn't have wanted a second date anyway. He had no interest in seeing someone who couldn't see anything but his ethnic identity.

Ricky was another straight Latino who felt he was always contending with a trope: the Latin lover. Some daters, he figured, had lost interest in him because he didn't conform to their racialized and gendered expectations of a Latino man:

> I got a random message from this girl. The only thing she asked was "Hey, you're Latin. Do you like to dance?" I did not reply to that message. Actually, I really wanted to reply, "NOPE," in capital letters in the message. And, you know what, I will say, in my dating experience, that is the stereotype that people always bring up. If you are not good at dancing or you're like, "Yeah, I don't really dance," people get surprised by that. They're like, "But, you're Latin." It's like, "Yeah. So?" I think because there is a stereotype that Latin men are these . . . there's a certain type of Latin lover, I think they assume, who's really smooth and really suave and really good with ladies, and he knows how to dance; that means he's good in bed, kind of thing. That's the stereotype, and I totally do not mesh up with that stereotype.

Like Andrew, Ricky's actions were misinterpreted, but here they did not live up to desired stereotypical traits. Both men were judged in ways that amplified their objectification and depersonalization. Rather than being viewed as whole persons with individual traits, the controlling images of digital-sexual racism funneled emotions, imposing suspicion and leading both men to question their authenticity.

Latinas voiced similar concerns, particularly regarding assumptions around being "sexy," "spicy," and "feisty." Jazmín, who started online dating after she graduated from college, felt the experience had been mostly successful, but she was still convinced that many men racialized their initial interactions:

> Oh my god. The White guy, it was really weird. He kept mentioning that he loved eating at a particular local Latino restaurant. And then he was like, "I love everything about your culture." And, "You're so hot." That experience was

really fetishizing to me, I guess, because I feel that he contacted me because I was Latina, because he kept talking about it. And he just said random things about Latin America and how that was his favorite thing ever. And, yeah, he kept talking about how much he loved Peru and Latin America in general and liked beans. And I'm like, "I'm sorry. I don't eat that much beans." And, yeah, he kept mentioning that Latinas are really sexy and all that kind of stuff.

An array of stereotypes made Jazmín feel fetishized, because controlling images are so pernicious. They give outgroup members the sense of a pseudounderstanding that overwrites attention to individual traits.[15] This man's fixation on her status as a "Latina woman" and evocation of various Latino/a preferences, especially in foods, minimized Jazmín's ability to be seen as a whole person. Sara, a twenty-year-old multiracial White and Latina respondent, railed against this sort of "ceaseless" evaluation in online dating. Particularly frustrating to her was the way White men boxed her into a character type:

They're like, "Oh, you're going to be spicy. You're going to be like a girl from a telenovela. You're going to be curvy like a girl in porn." A lot of it is based on stereotypes. There's a lot of stereotypical expectation that comes from it that is really uncomfortable to navigate. There's definitely a certain body-type expectation. I've definitely had guys be like, "Oh, that Latin ass," like whatever. I'm like, "It's just my body. We don't all have one body type." People expect me to be really loud and angry. It's like, "Yes, I am those things. I'm always loud and angry, but it's not because I'm Latina." Stuff like that comes up a lot.

Given the importance of racial makers on online-dating profiles, such as a presumed "Latina" body type, the operation of digital-sexual racism dehumanizes daters as mere sexual objects of desire. Indeed, men contacting Sara brought up her Dominican background when they evaluated her body and assumed she would be "loud" or "angry." Directly linking her body to her ethnic identity, daters like Sara demonstrated for us that, within the U.S. racial structure, a Latina desirability is rooted in essential, and racist, notions of both gendered and racial *difference.*

Carmen, twenty-seven, described the effects of the nurturer trope. A Dominican American from the Northeast, she said,

A lot of guys are kind of are like, "You'll take care of me and be the caretaker in this situation." They feel like they're more domestic, which I think it's nonsense. Especially if you're actually from that country, not that your family is, like, you were born outside of the United States. They feel like because you were born outside of the United States, you're gonna be some kind of housewife creature that's gonna be okay with being domestic, at home, doing what I'm supposed to do. They've straight up said that to me.

Men assumed Carmen would be a good caretaker not because she is a woman or a Latina but because she was *both*. That intersectional identity, they believed, meant she was not interested in or entitled to an egalitarian relationship. Further, given that Latina women's labor is devalued, she sensed these men believed women like her were suitable for "traditional" domestic work and relationship roles that could no longer be expected from U.S.-born women.[16] Again we see how so-called individual preferences deployed in online dating are often products of structural inequalities and are deployed through digital-sexual racism. In this case the global division of labor between the North and the South translates into the intimate designation of the domestic role to a Latina woman.

Our Latino/a respondents told us that these stereotypes are most summoned by Whites. "I think that stereotype is definitely strong among White girls," said one Latino respondent. "Those are the only people that I have had that brought up with. It's always White girls to bring that up." And another Latina dater estimated, "at least for the negative or sexually related messages, I think I've almost exclusively got that from White men." Indeed, considering these controlling images were constructed largely to serve White political interests and have been circulated to justify White dominance, this is no surprise. Each implicitly assumes White as the unmarked baseline category against which all other forms of racialized femininities and masculinities are judged.

EXCLUSION OF LATINO/A DATERS

Latino men are at times framed as suave, seducing lovers, yet at other times as dangerous criminals. Latina women similarly may be typecast as sexy and feisty, as well as desexualized and docile service workers. This contradictory representation highlights the specific forms of gendered racialization the community has undergone in the United States and is

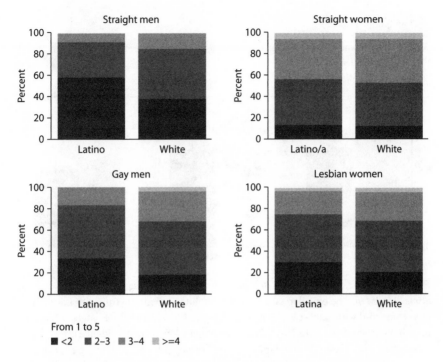

Figure 7.1. Latino/a and White Daters' Website-Based Attractiveness by Sexual Orientation, Gender, and Race. The bars depict the distribution of attractiveness by sexual orientation, gender, and race. Individual users are rated by other users on the website on a scale from one (least attractive) to five (most attractive). Since the ratings are not random and the vast majority of the users are Whites, the distribution is likely skewed due to racial bias.

reflected in their contradictory experiences in the realm of online dating. Daters' deployment of digital-sexual racism sexualizes and rates them as attractive, yet they face racialized and gendered exclusion relative to Whites. Further, since anti-Blackness is central to the measurement of desirability, non-Black Latino/a daters are advantaged over Black Latinos/as. Meanwhile, like other non-Black groups, Latinos/as exclude Blacks when searching for dating partners online.

Figure 7.1 compares the attractiveness ratings of Latino/a and White daters. It shows that, even though most raters are Whites, straight Latina women are considered as attractive as straight White women. Straight Latino men, however, are rated as much less attractive than straight White

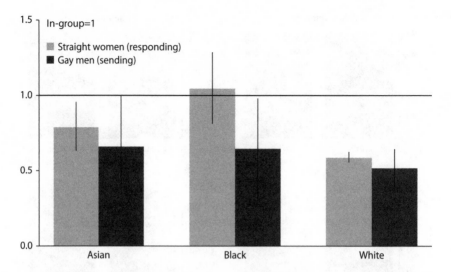

Figure 7.2. Non-Latino/a Daters' Relative Likelihood of Messaging Latino versus Same-Race Men. The bars depict the relative likelihood of interacting with Latino/a men compared with same-race men among Asian, Black, and White daters, adjusted for other observed characteristics. The lines depict 95 percent confidence intervals. Interacting with a same-race dater is indicated by an odds of 1.0. Anything above 1.0 shows a greater relative probability of contacting or responding to a Latino/a dater than a same-race dater; anything below 1.0 indicates a lesser probability. See online tables O.1 and O.2 (at www.ucpress.edu/9780520293458) for full estimates.

men. The ratings received by Latino gays and lesbians are less extreme: although gay Latino men are still rated as less attractive than White men, they are not penalized as much as straight Latino men. Gay Latina women, however, receive more negative ratings than straight Latina women. This may be driven by their deviation from the traditional heteronormative image of Latina women.

The penalty of Latino masculinity is also clear among message patterns (figure 7.2).[17] Compared to men of their own racial group, most straight women and gay men are less enthusiastic about responding or sending messages to Latino men. The only exception is straight Black women, who treat Latino men in the same way they treat Black men.[18]

The Latino/a men and women were well aware that their identity was consequential in their dating experiences. Miguel, whom we met at the opening of this chapter, dithered about how he should list his racial identity in his profile. Finding himself unable to identify as "White," he avoided the penalty associated with identifying as "Latino" by choosing "Other." Women, on the other hand, complained about the ways the messages they received were racially and sexually charged. Mariana, an accountant, saw White men as being far more desirable than men of color. When we asked her if *she* had ever felt discriminated against, she quickly recounted a conversation:

MARIANA: We were talking, and then I think we connected through the phone, and we were texting. I don't know what he said to me, but it was something like, "I would never bring you to my family." I'm like, "Why?" And then he said, "Because you're Latina." . . . He said he wasn't looking for a girlfriend. 'Cause he would never bring me to his family, he wouldn't consider me as a girlfriend.

INTERVIEWER: What did you say to him?

MARIANA: I flipped out and I told him, "What is that supposed to mean?" He didn't currently have a job; he didn't have anything. I'm more educated, prepared. I have a good full-time position, and he pretty much insulted me. I told him to lose my number and never contact me again.

Mariana's anecdote, as much as Miguel's, illustrates the complexity by which many Latinos/as navigate racial hierarchies in online dating. She was shocked that the White man mistreated her because of her ethnicity but still felt comfortable declaring a strong preference for White men over all others. She also echoes some of the comments we heard from Black women in chapter 5 about how some White men saw women of color as appropriate for sex but not for relationships. Nevertheless, this experience did not lead Mariana to further examine her own racialized preferences.

When it comes to in-group interactions, our analysis in figure 7.3 of the website's data suggests that Latinos most prefer Latinas and treat Asian women and White women somewhat equally, messaging them about 40 percent less often than Latina women.[19] They message Black women the least, or approximately 65 percent less often than Latina women. Latinas, on the other hand, are most responsive to White men and, like Latinos, generally ignore Blacks (see figure 7.4). Latinas treat Asians and Latinos as an

For every message Latino men send to Latina women

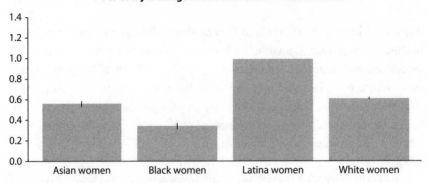

Figure 7.3. Latino Men's Relative Likelihood of Sending to Non-Latina versus Latina Women. The bars depict the relative likelihood of sending a message to non-Latina women compared with Latina women among Latino men, adjusted for other observed characteristics. The lines depict 95 percent confidence intervals. Sending to Latina women is indicated by an odds of 1.0. Anything above 1.0 shows a greater relative probability of sending to a non-Latina dater than a Latina dater; anything below 1.0 indicates a lesser probability. See online table O.1 (at www .ucpress.edu/9780520293458) for full estimates.

For every message Latina women respond to Latino men

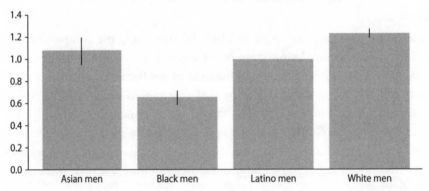

Figure 7.4. Latina Women's Relative Likelihood of Responding to Non-Latino versus Latino Men. The bars depict the relative likelihood of responding to a message from non-Latino men compared with Latino men among Latina women, adjusted for other observed characteristics. The lines depict 95 percent confidence intervals. Responding to Latino men is indicated by an odds of 1.0. Anything above 1.0 shows a greater relative probability of responding to a non-Latino dater than a Latino dater; anything below 1.0 indicates a lesser probability. See online table O.2 for full estimates.

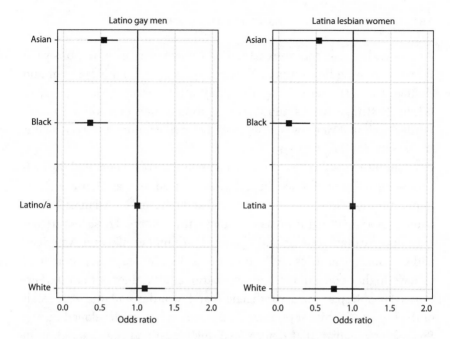

Figure 7.5. Gay Latino/a Daters' Likelihood of Messaging Non-Latino/a versus Latino/a Daters. The estimates depict the relative likelihood of sending a message to non-Latino/a compared with Latino/a daters among Latino/a daters of different sexual orientation, adjusted for other observed characteristics. The lines depict 95 percent confidence intervals. Sending to Latino/a daters is indicated by an odds of 1.0. Anything above 1.0 shows a greater relative probability of sending to a non-Latino/a dater than a Latino/a dater; anything below 1.0 indicates a lesser probability. See online table O.1 for full estimates.

"in-between group," below White desirability but above Black desirability.[20] Gay Latinos also have a strong preference for White men, while lesbian Latinas appear to privilege Latinas over others (see figure 7.5). Despite these differences, pervasive anti-Blackness perseveres: straight or gay, men or women, Latino/a daters avoid Blacks more assiduously than any other group. In other words, even though Latino men and Latina women do face discrimination, particularly from Whites, they seem to conform to the racial hierarchy by excluding daters of lower racial status. For straight daters it's Black men and women. For gay daters it's Black and Asian men and women.

PRIVILEGING WHITENESS THROUGH COLORISM

We saw earlier that heterosexual Latina women were most responsive to White men, a finding supported by past literature.[21] Latino/a men and women are even more likely than any other ethnic group to marry Whites.[22] Unlike Blacks and Asians, Latino/a men and women marry Whites at similar rates, which suggests a shared common preference. But the reasons for the preference differ.

In our interviews we found that such preference often operated through and alongside a preference for lightness. Indeed, just as skin color was important in the hierarchies constructed and followed by Asian and Black daters, colorism is highly present among Latino daters. These hierarchies have historical antecedent and operate in a number of Latin American and Caribbean countries and communities. Lighter-skinned people tend to have higher educational and occupational attainments than darker-skinned people, particularly Indigenous and Afro-descendants—the result of the legacy of White supremacy and *castas*, a system developed during Spanish colonialism that determined one's legal and social standing in society based on ancestry. Lighter skin was often taken as a marker of desired Spanish ancestry and the absence of undesirable Indigenous or African ancestry.[23]

Today and historically some Latin American families participate in the practice often colloquially referred to as *mejorando la raza* (improving the race)—the strategy of choosing lighter-skinned romantic partners in the hopes that they and their future children will gain higher social status by "watering down" African and Indigenous features.[24] Research finds that children of lighter complexions are treated better even *within* their Latin American families than are children with darker skin.[25]

Jazmín had a lot to say on this topic. Being fair skinned, she grew up in a Central American–origin family with wide color variation, and her family was firm that she must date lighter-skinned men. Her Honduran parents and other relatives were, she said, very "biased" in this way:

> White is the ideal. It's brought over from Latin America, from that colonial past, and also that's something that's also very prevalent here as well. When families come from Latin America or even from Europe or whatever, because they also have race issues over there, it's seen as White is better.

There's a saying in Spanish, "mejorando la raza," or bettering the race. If you're a person of color, your family, maybe your mother or something, grandmother, wherever, they'll say that. It means you have to make the race better. If you're of color, you have to make the race better. That means, make it more White. You're going to try to take the Black or the Indigenous out, you're going to mix with somebody who's White. And if you are lighter, maybe they'll say the reverse, that you can't make the race worse; you can't muddy the race, and you can't muddy the blood. They want you to get, obviously, with someone White.

Sending societies' color and race hierarchies can fuse, in this way, with U.S racial schemas such that they reinforce a White ideal. In Jazmín's view the preference for both Whiteness and lightness is gendered, with mothers and other women relatives promoting this preference in policing daughters' dating decisions. She adds, "A man is just expected to get with whoever he wants to get with. A man can get with whoever he wants to exert just his maleness, but he has to choose who he wants to procreate with wisely. There's that kind of distinction." In her view, while color matters for both men and women, Latino men are given more sexual freedom with darker-skinned women, so long as that intimacy does not lead to family formation. As Jazmín and her sisters were being pressured to avoid dark men, the young men in her family openly dated Black American women and dark-skinned Latinas.

This idea that women are especially pressured away from darkness also came up in our interview with Mariana. She viewed herself as "tan and not that light," explaining, "I know it's racist, but growing up [her mother's grandmother] always told you just, because my family's dark, that you have to better the race. Better the hair, all this stuff, which is bad." Mariana was interested in dating mostly "Italian" or "Greek guys" and actively ignored Black men and Latino men of darker complexions if they matched or messaged on dating apps.

Cruz had gotten similar dating advice from her relatives. It started young: "Very close family friends, and family and friends, have said, 'I want to date a Puerto Rican or Italian because they're White. I want to date a White Puerto Rican or just an Italian.' They want Whiter babies." As the child with the darkest complexion in a family that has lighter-skinned Puerto Ricans and darker-skinned Dominicans, she was frequently compared negatively to her lighter-skinned sister, whose hair was straight, rather than like Cruz's curls. Any time she brought White men friends home, her family seemed to revel at the thought of them dating. Now, as an adult, queer Cruz found that the messaging had stopped. "I feel like I entered this other box," she said. "My family stopped asking me if I was dating anybody. They stopped asking me about kids. I don't get the same scripts about marriage. I don't get the same scripts, period." Cruz's queerness attenuated the pressure around skin color: "For me, they also know that I've always just been on my own path. They are just like, 'You're going to do what you're going to do.' I have that freedom, in some ways." Here we see how heteronormative colorism scripts can be. The silence around Cruz assumes that she, because she is queer, will not have children, even though Cruz reported that she was in a long-term relationship with a Black woman with a dark complexion, and they planned to have children in the future.

Despite the seemingly gendered and heteronormative nature of unsolicited parental dating advice, Latino men—straight and even some queer ones—told us that they, too, were conditioned to strive for a light-skinned partner. They were not, however, censured in the ways women were should they not heed the advice. Zenón, a twenty-seven-year-old straight man from a Mexican family with Indigenous roots, said that his grandmother often stressed the importance of dating a *güerita* (a light-skinned or blond person). This grandmother was an Indigenous woman with dark skin, who had married a mestizo land and cattle owner: "My grandma was oddly racist," Zenón said with a chuckle. "She always told every one of her grandkids that they had to date a *güerita* because the very few people that lived over there that were a lighter skin color, they were usually better off." In her view dating and marrying a lighter woman or man ensured class mobility. She wanted that opportunity for her grandchildren.

Javier, a twenty-eight-year-old Brazilian American man, openly preferred to date light-skinned women, particularly Latinas who speak fluent English and could pass for White. Like many others, he attributed his racial preferences to his parents' bias:

> My parents are definitely more aware of race. . . . I don't want to say aware. They're more prejudiced about race than I am. I know I have some residual effect of that. I'm aware of that about myself. My parent always emphasized,

"You should meet a Latin girl." To them, that's the ideal of the kind of person you'd bring back home, is going to be a Latin woman. It can be any Latin woman, but also of a lighter-skin complexion. They would not have an issue with me dating someone who was darker-skinned. But it was always clear to them that they had . . . they see someone with a lighter complexion as being more cultured, more educated. They have a lot of these stereotypes that I like to say, I don't hold, consciously, but I know I've been influenced by.

Interestingly, Javier vacillated between race and color distinctions in trying to make sense of his preference for lightness. Research confirms the coexistence of multiple systems of racial classification and stratification among Latinos in the United States, with immigrants and their offspring adopting a U.S. framework for understanding racial and ethnic distinctions while also borrowing from the earlier racial schemas of their origins.[26] In this sense Javier admitted that his family's pro-light bias impacted his dating preferences for Whiter, lighter, and more "acculturated" Latinas.

PRIVILEGING WHITENESS THROUGH RACE AND GENDER

Whiteness preferences are also created by gender dynamics within Latino/a families.[27] For example, Gabriela, a bisexual woman, explained that her lack of interest in Latino men was because of her assumption that they were what she called "mama boys": demanding men who expected that she would serve their every need. In their immigrant-origin family, Gabriela and her sister had been tasked with a great deal of household work, including doing their brother's laundry and cleaning up after him and the rest of the family:

My dad grew up in our country [Dominican Republic], and he had me. It's just everybody over there has maids and helpers and things like that. Here, me and my sister and my mom pretty much cook, clean. . . . It's just like the way they were raised. My brother was raised like that. He would do yard work and work on the cars. We did everything else. He moved out. Now he's learned he has to do it because he's with an Italian girl, and she travels all the time for work; she's never home. He has to learn how to cook and clean and do his laundry.

Other women in our study told us they had a deep, culturally inflected aversion to the gender conservatism they correlated with Latino men. Gabriela later added, "There's some cultural pieces that I'm trying to avoid. That's why I tend to like White guys." This sentiment is similar to the remarks of some Asian women regarding the "egalitarian knighthood" of White men, and it is documented in sociologist Jessica Vasquez-Tokos's work, in which Latina women prefer White men because they assume that Latino men are domineering and gender conservative like their fathers.[28]

We find it curious, however, that Latina women would view White men as gender progressive, given that sexism operates across racial and ethnic groups. None of our Latina participants indicated that other non-Latino men, such as Asians or Blacks, were suitably gender-egalitarian alternatives. In this sense Latina women's framing of White men as particularly desirable also tacitly reinforces a race-class-gender system that promotes White masculinity and subordinates Latino and other non-White masculinities.[29] Take, for example, how Carmen contrasted the two:

> A lot of people are, like, if you were dating somebody of this race, maybe your relationship would be different; it would be better. I guess because of the values. They're more career driven; they're more family driven. . . . It's like, oh, I feel like when I date a Spanish guy, he just wants to hook up; he just wants to do sexual things, whereas, if I'm dating a White guy, he's talking about how do we take our relationship to the next level? What are we doing?

Carmen, who earlier critiqued the gendered and racialized nurturer trope of the Latina woman, frames Latinos as exclusively interested in sex and hookups, while White men are more serious and relationship-oriented. This belief not only contradicts some experiences we heard from Latina women but also illustrates how minorities may internalize racialized and gendered stereotypes about their own groups as they exalt White masculinity.

Another Latina who used dating apps to find Latino men viewed gender progressiveness as an important quality in a potential partner and understood that many Latina women associated it with Whiteness: "White guys are more educated. At least that's the stereotype, that they're more educated, and they don't have these machista things ingrained in them. I don't want to say that they're easier to control, but they're overall just easier than

Latino men." Character traits such as "educated," "career-driven," or "family driven" are tightly bound to classed conceptualizations of masculinity. Only the most affluent men can achieve high-status careers, the education that is the necessary prerequisite to that career, and the resources to care for a family without relying on supplemental income from their wives, children, and other kin. Yet the hegemony of this masculinity does not extend evenly across all men. It is just as racialized as it is classed. Cultural images, buttressed by other forms of inequality, assign such hegemonic masculinity to White men, while men of color are often framed as deviant or inadequate rather than structurally diverted away from attaining the educational and financial resources accrued by White men, whose privilege is far more self-sustaining. In this way, as an ideal type, White hegemonic forms of masculinity legitimate masculinity hierarchies. We see this in some Latina women's ranking of White masculinity as superior to other subordinated masculinities, including Latino masculinity.[30]

Our Latina women respondents' qualms are not unfounded. Like many other men, heterosexual Latinos certainly possess gender-based power over their partners and may subscribe to misogyny in their own homes. Yet, at the same time, they occupy a contradictory position within a system of male privilege, where they are disadvantaged due to their race, skin color, class, and immigrant status. Compared to affluent, native, and educated White men, Latino men who are working-class, immigrant, and seemingly non-White are less able to attain the masculine ideals coveted by some Latina women.

PAN-CULTURAL AFFINITY AND RACIAL EXCLUSION

Color hierarchies and gender inequality may steer a preference for Whites, yet many Latino/a daters still hope to match with someone with whom they share an ethnic or racial identity. This is an important distinction, given that much demographic research has focused on the prevalence of Latino/a-White unions. Further, preferences *for* Latinos/as are not limited to those who share the same country of origin but include all people who understand what it means to be Latino/a in the United States. Some research has found that Latinos/as, particularly women, may value endogamy to preserve cultural heritage among their children.[31] There is also some evidence that Latina women may seek cross-national Latino marriages because they seek cultural connections but eschew partners from their own specific ethnic subgroup to avoid gendered concerns around their own families' patriarchal structures.[32] Community and family members may also promote endogamy because of cultural similarities.[33]

Our interviews show that Latinos/as who preferred other Latinos/as were nested in a complex web of concerns, ranging from their gendered socialization within families, color hierarchies, and experiences of racialized marginalization. Yesenia, a twenty-eight-year-old U.S.-born Latina woman whose father and mother were from Ecuador, grew up in a predominantly Latino mid-Atlantic city. Because her parents forbade it, she did not date until college. Though her college was only twenty miles away from home, living in a dorm provided her reprieve from her parents' watchful eye. She dated a number of White men in those years, partly because the private college she attended was predominantly White. However, she saw a shift in her preferences after college: today, she told us, she was most likely to respond to messages sent by Latino men. When we asked her why, Yesenia reflected,

> My ideal person would be someone of Latino origin or descent. Hopefully tall, one that could actually preferably speak Spanish as well. It's the shared community type of thing. . . . and then to be able to make food for each other. That's kind of cool. That would be fun. That would be my ideal.

Among ideal cultural similarities Yesenia prioritized speaking Spanish, because her family was primarily monolingual. Like her, some 86 percent of young Latinos/as spoke Spanish at home growing up, and the same percentage of Latino/a parents currently speak Spanish to their children.[34]

Yesenia recognized that her preferences have also been shaped in opposition to her experiences dating White men. They did not treat her as a "long-term girlfriend," she thought, because of her ethnic background:

> When I went to school, I went to a mostly Caucasian university. And it was coming from a lot of White guys that Latino women you really want to fuck, but then no long term thing. Like we're great for fun, quote-unquote, and we're great for cooking and that kind of thing, but we're not great for long

term; we're not the kind of woman that you want to marry because we're crazy. I've heard that we have no control over our emotions, that kind of thing.

Controlling images rear their ugly heads again. Yesenia estimated that, even when she was seen as desirable by White men because she was Latina, that desirability would not translate into equal treatment. Instead, owing to the intersection of her race, ethnicity, and gender, her integration into a White man's social world could not extend beyond sexual intimacy. As stated earlier, part of the toxicity of controlling images is that they strip the marginalized from the power of self-definition. Yesenia added, "Sometimes when you hear it in jest several times, then you start to worry because then it's like there must be a truth to this at this point if I'm hearing it several times from several mouths."

Over time Yesenia began to actively seek Latino men as intimate partners, whether by responding to their messages on dating platforms or by frequenting social venues where there were more Latino men. These changes were part of her transition from a predominantly White college campus back to the neighborhood where she grew up, which coincided with the rise of online dating (and its expansion of ways to search by race and ethnicity). Most important, she realized, she wanted to find someone who sees her as equally qualified rather than less qualified than other women for a serious relationship.

Daters like Yesenia often seek out markers on daters' profiles that hint at cultural affinity. Like the markers of political affiliation noted elsewhere, these markers might take the form of profiles written in Spanish or the presence of a national flag, suggesting a dater's ethnic origin. Zenón, twenty-seven, explained that he frequently encountered other bilingual Mexicans as he browsed dating apps. To demonstrate that he, too, was fluent in English and Spanish, he clarified in his profile that either language worked for him:

> I'm bilingual, so some things are just easier to express in Spanish sometimes than they are in English. If I meet someone and they already speak Spanish, it's pretty good. Actually, right now I live on the border of Mexico. So if I get on the app, there's a good chance I'm meeting someone from Mexicali as well, which is in Mexico, and they mostly, generally, just speak Spanish. So

there has been something that's happened right now, where I have to ask the question, "English or Spanish?" when I first contact someone. Actually, that's on my profile that English or Spanish is cool with me.

Zenón's choice to specify that "English or Spanish is cool" signaled his linguistic and cultural versatility to a diverse community. Though he has resided in the United States for most of his life and was told to date White or light as a kid, as an adult he prioritized the value of shared cultural understanding.

Shared experiences with racial discrimination may also motivate Latinos/as to select Latinos/as and other minority partners.[35] Vasquez-Tokos's work, for example, finds that Latinos/as who married non-White partners such as Native Americans, Asian Americans, and African Americans did so in part because they shared the experience of marginalization.[36] For example, when we asked Cruz about her preference for women of color, she told us it stems not out of hatred for Whites but rather the shared understanding of living in a predominantly White college town. She asked herself: "Will your partner understand what you're going through when you're telling them that you just went to the bar that you go to all the time, you're holding out money, and fifteen other people got served before you?" Cruz, you may recall, was in a long-term relationship with a Black woman she met on a dating app; despite their racial and ethnic differences, Cruz and her partner shared and bonded over the minority experience in the United States.

Another queer dater, Raúl, indicated that he felt a bond with Asian men he met on the app, especially foreign-born men living in the United States:

> When I date someone, I try to relate to him, and someone who is Asian has a background that they came to this country, to a new culture just like me, I guess. They have learned to live here, just as I have. They have another culture that is different to what I know. I guess because just like Latino countries, Asian countries and many other countries, they're not as open-minded as this country, so they kind of like understand how I feel when I was coming to this country, understanding how to behave, kind of like being free here. I think I feel more of a connection that way.

Raúl's sexual identity, immigrant status, and ethnic identity all help him to understand the marginalization faced by other gay men, even when they came from very different countries. However, Raúl did not apply the

same empathy to Black men, who he described as less desirable, less educated, and more criminal than others. Raúl said he was likely to ignore
Black daters when using apps and could make that determination because
he lived in a primarily Black neighborhood:

> I mean, probably, we'll have the racist thought in our mind. . . . You will
> assume that they don't have a high education as other people, most of the
> time, I guess. I am living close to a neighborhood where they are low-income
> neighborhoods, so that's pretty much the ones I see all the time.

Even though a shared immigrant status did seem to allow Raúl to have an
openness for cross-racial desire while using apps, digital-sexual racism
allows for this to occur alongside Raúl's anti-Blackness. Even Raúl evoked
the "parental bias" script as he talked about his racial preferences in dating: "I think if I bring an Asian guy, I don't think they will have any problem with that. I think if I bring anyone but a Black person, to be honest,
they will be okay with it."

Indeed, like many other non-Black but non-White groups in the past
and present, Latinos/as access racial privilege relative to Blacks. To maintain this privilege, they may categorically exclude Black partners.[37] In
chapter 6 we see how Asian daters reproduced anti-Black patterns of
racial exclusion even as they voiced dissatisfaction with their treatment by
White daters. In both cases family plays a prominent role in directing the
younger generations, particularly women, away from dating Blacks.[38] It
also plays a prominent role in daters' racial self-discipline and their identification of reasons behind preferences that could otherwise be seen as
simple racism. Only one straight Latina woman in our sample, Jazmín,
had engaged in extensive correspondence with a Black man on a dating
site. Even she, who found that this handsome man was similarly educated
and had a shared interest in fitness, was reluctant to meet him in person,
explaining that her mother had reacted badly to another Black man she
dated in the past. "We already went through it once, and it was kind of hell
on earth," she described. "Actually, [my mother] made my life a little bit
impossible for a little while." In her view compatibility was not enough,
given the way in which anti-Blackness operated within her family.

As we have discussed in this chapter, Latinos/as are often described as
straddling the U.S. racial hierarchy, but this does not mean they can avoid

racialization.[39] In a racialized and gendered desirability hierarchy, they are prevented from obtaining full acceptance from Whites, but the intersection of transnational color, family, and gendered hierarchies nested within U.S. racial inequality frequently demands that they jockey for position by striving for the upward mobility offered by a prospective partner's proximity to Whiteness. Others retreat to endogamy—a practical defense against misunderstanding and oppression. The pervasiveness of anti-Blackness, however, only reinforces both paths and provides a certainty that reaffirms the desirability hierarchy. Given the way in which social constructions of racial mixedness are inextricably bound to sex, desirability, and interracial intimacy, we now turn our attention to how multiracial daters navigate, resist, and accommodate desirability hierarchies in the era of online dating.

8 Postracial Multiracialism

A CHALLENGE TO THE WHITE RACIAL FRAME?

In a fit of rage, Franky sputtered, "Is it true? Are you Black?" before brutally striking Sarah Jane in a dark alleyway. Sarah, the protagonist of the 1959 U.S. dramatic film *Imitation of Life,* desperately wants to pass for White and attempts to perform Whiteness through her relationship with Franky.[1] In this moment viewers learn that Sarah's acceptance into Whiteness was more precarious than she had thought. In an era of the one-drop rule, the film reflected public concerns around racial impurity, as strong as ever, nearly a century past emancipation.[2]

Controlling images of mixed-race women in the nineteenth and twentieth centuries centered on the so-called tragic mulatto. Sarah Jane is exemplary: a woman of European and African ancestry, the character is simultaneously deemed attractive (she, after all, "passes" and has "White features"); hypersexual (because of her Black sexuality); and psychologically torn because she lives the interstices of race in a divided society. She could never truly fit in, and so she is presented to audiences as an object of pity and scorn.[3] She is also tacitly a warning: miscegenation is a tragedy, and a mixed-race child is a sorry person indeed. Similarly, images of "Eurasian" women and mixed-race Latina "mestizos" have also fallen prey to the judgment of popular culture's "White gaze." Colonial histories of

191

racial domination, war, and conquest underpin "the sexual allure and dissimilarity of exotic otherness" in each case, marking certain women's bodies as ready targets for both valorization and stigma.[4] Their Whiteness comes with an assumed intrinsic superiority, but the presence of otherness, especially Blackness, signals impurity and demands scrutiny and scorn.

Much has changed since *Imitation of Life* flickered on the nation's movie screens. The demise of the one-drop rule went hand in hand with the Supreme Court's invalidation of antimiscegenation laws, and by 2015 interracial and interethnic marriages would account for 17 percent of new marriages in the United States. Of interracial newlyweds, 12 percent are multiracial Whites paired with White Americans.[5] Media portrayals have evolved such that positive and self-affirming representations of mixed-race individuals and families are now fairly commonplace in entertainment and advertising.[6]

The alleyway scene in *Imitation of Life* surely looks hopelessly dated to the United States' younger generations. Compare Sarah Jane with Sam White's character in the popular U.S. satire *Dear White People*. A biracial Black woman who heads an all-Black residence on a prestigious, predominantly White college campus, Sam affirms her Blackness through political activism, critiquing racial transgressions on her campus. While Sarah Jane actively sought out a White partner with whom her association would help her pass as White, Sam seeks to hide her intimate relationship with White classmate Gabe. In one scene, as Sam directs Gabe to be discreet leaving her dorm room, Gabe responds with desperation: he's sick and tired of her "tragic mulatto bullshit." Meanwhile, another Black character, Coco, seethes when a reality TV producer prefers a light-skinned Black woman like Sam rather than her.[7] None of this complexity attended Sarah Jane's story, yet race and identity, pride and social censure, mark both tales.

Movies and TV, of course, cannot be taken at face value. It remains unclear how well modern entertainment reflects multiracials' lived experiences. Scholars have not yet fully addressed, for example, how contemporary folks who identify with more than one race actually treat or perceive Whites and single-race minorities. Nor is it clear how dating and courtship look among multiracials as compared to other racial groups; what distinguishes (or does not distinguish) subgroups of multiracial daters like Asian-White or Latino/a-White heritage people; or, well, much of

anything about multiracial men, who receive less attention than multiracial women in academia and pop culture alike.[8] This chapter seeks to
uncover some of these missing pieces.

WHY MULTIRACIALS, WHY NOW?

Estimates project that, by about 2040 or 2050, non-Latino/a Whites will
become a racial minority in the United States.[9] A fact greeted with some
alarm but also a great deal of excitement, this has led some to speculate
that, with the rise in multiracial individuals and immigration and fertility
trends, the typical future U.S. American will, in fact, be multiracial. To
visualize this dramatic change, *Time* magazine used a computer-generated
cover portrait that fused phenotypical traits of people from various racial
backgrounds.[10] This, *Time* proclaimed, was the future of the United States:
it would be impossible to pin down anyone's racial heritage simply by looking. Media outlets picking up on the idea went further, speculating that, in
this future, racial difference will not only become harder to find but be
socially irrelevant.[11] One heavily circulated piece suggested that these
demographic trends were being accelerated by online-dating websites and
apps: "It's no secret that interracial relationships are trending upward, and
in a matter of years we'll have Tindered, OKCupid-ed and otherwise sexed
ourselves into one giant amalgamated mega-race."[12]

Amid all this optimism about a not-too-distant postracial future, we
have shown throughout this book that race remains a dividing factor in
the world of online dating. Very little of the racial "happy talk" that accompanied some commentators at the time of emancipation or *Loving v.
Virginia* or *Brown v. Board of Education* or the election of Barack Obama
has yet proven wholly true.[13] Can we really expect a near future without
race when every day we see police brutality against the Black population,
the mass incarceration of racial minorities, anti-immigrant sentiment,
blatant White nationalism, and pervasive racial microaggressions? What
about the digital-sexual racism that we have demonstrated to be so very
real and consequential in modern dating right this very moment? In this
chapter we zoom in on the experiences of self-identified multiracials, who
offer a unique window through which to see how racial hierarchies change

and persist over time. But before we can consider how multiracial dating patterns prove protective rather than disruptive when it comes to the racialized and gendered desirability hierarchies we have tracked throughout this book, we must ask a rather squishy question: Who, exactly, is multiracial?

WHO IS MULTIRACIAL?

Racial identities are not biological but social constructs—artificial distinctions created by human beings and legitimated through laws, institutions, and everyday practices.[14] Thus, when entering the terrain of multiraciality, it is important to note that multiracial identities (including variants such as mixed-race, hapa, and biracial) are socially constructed too. We cannot assume that multiracial identification simply reflects mixed-racial parentage. Studies have, in fact, shown the opposite; a 2015 nationally representative survey, for instance, shows that about 61 percent of adults with a reported mixed-racial background do not consider themselves "multiracial." The same survey finds that multiracial identification is fluid and may change over the life course or from one context to the next, in line with shifting social forces and new experiences.[15]

For example, as sociologist Carolyn Liebler finds, children of mixed-racial parentage are not universally reported by their parents as mixed race. Multiracial responses among parents of mixed-race children have been relatively common for part-Asian and part-Black children since the 1980s, whereas part Native Americans are more likely to be identified as monoracial (either White, Black, or Native American).[16] A person's *self-identification* as multiracial may be shaped by additional social identities such as gender, language fluency, religion, or class. In other words, like most social identities, multiraciality is situational.[17] The increasing multiracial population is not only a consequence of intermarriage or interracial sex but also a result of changes in the ways people think about and measure race—including their own.

Indeed, multiracial formation is mediated by how race is conceived in a given sociopolitical context.[18] As our historical survey conveys, ante- and postbellum miscegenation laws and related modes of racial codification reflected how individual states institutionalized boundaries around Whiteness. Racial categories such as *negro, mulatto,* and *quadroon* established who could access the legal and social privileges of Whiteness and who could not. A very different logic was applied to people of mixed-Native ancestry. Aiming to diminish collective land rights among Native Americans, colonists claimed many individuals with both Native and White ancestry were Whites.[19] The ability to affirm a mixed-race identity was restricted to many throughout history, through formal and informal bureaucratic and social measures. Consider Mildred Loving, whom we spoke about in earlier chapters. Though the *Loving v. Virginia* case is typically recast in Black and White—that is, Black Mildred Jeter paired with White Richard Loving—Mildred Loving identified as part Rappahannock Indian in the state of Virginia, where the Racial Integrity Act deemed all non-White persons "colored."[20] Across cases multiraciality was interpreted selectively as states sought to manage, create, diminish, or enforce social difference for all manner of motivations (not least economic and political).[21]

As Melissa Nobles argues, changes to the 2000 U.S. Census were hard-won and reflected a new racial moment in which the collection of data required formalizing the greater social recognition of multiraciality.[22] Now that the "check all that apply" practice has been adopted by the census, surveys, school and job application forms, and many online-dating sites, what have we learned? For one, the U.S. Census Bureau reports that, in 2010, approximately nine million U.S. Americans, or 3 percent of the population, chose two or more racial categories—a 32 percent increase over the 2000 census numbers.[23] A 2015 Pew Research Center study provided further insight into the demographic profile of the self-identified multiracial population, noting that they are younger than the average U.S. American (age nineteen for multiracials compared to thirty-eight for the general population); that the vast majority selects only two categories; and that the majority of those individuals who choose two categories identify as part White. Taking into consideration self-reported race and the racial backgrounds of parents, White multiracials account for over three-quarters of the entire U.S. adult multirace population.[24]

Research also finds significant variation in multiracial groups' identification patterns. Asian groups exhibit strict membership criteria, and, as a result, Asians of mixed-racial parentage are less likely than other groups to identify as solely Asian. Increasing intermarriage rates between Whites and Asians have fueled growth in this population, with 15 percent of the Asian American population reporting a multiracial identification—twice the rate among Black Americans.[25] The multiraciality related to the growing Latino/a population is also complex. It was not until 1980 that the Latino/a category was included on the U.S. Census, and it is considered as an *ethnicity,* not a *race.*[26] Our analysis considers daters who identify as both White and Latino as multiracial to consider whether their dating experiences are distinct from those who identify solely as Latino/a.

REPRESENTING MULTIRACIALS

Multiraciality has received much greater social recognition in today's popular culture. This is in part due to the appreciation for the racial diversity in the United States in the post–civil rights era; to an increased respect for our right to define ourselves; the rise of multiculturalism; and the activism of the mixed-race families who seek understanding, recognition, and pride in their unique situations. Marketing companies, often a bellwether, have clearly begun to feature and target mixed-race individuals and interracial couples, who represent a growing segment of the young middle class and respond positively to a more fluid and progressive view of racial identities.[27] Yet however hard media works to depict a postracial era, social responses to, for instance, General Mills wordlessly showing a loving multiracial family in a Cheerios commercial frequently betray the enduring strength of race and racism. The marriage of biracial American actress Meghan Markle to Britain's Prince Harry was met by a veritable typhoon of media, with some suggesting the incoming Duchess of Essex's Blackness showed the United Kingdom was moving beyond its colonial past. Yet this belief overlooks how multiraciality and claims to colorblindness have been used as political rhetoric, obscuring racial inequalities and protecting both Whiteness and the existing racial order.[28] In this sense, racialized dating and marriage decisions are neither indicative nor reflective of racial politics—they are shunted, instead, into narratives of liberal individualism.

The fashion industry is another domain in which postracial multira-cialism has been foregrounded. Today racially ambiguous bodies are frequently ideal models, "perfect" in the sense that they cultivate a simul-taneously diverse yet still inaccessible look. The most sought-after models are often those with "unique" phenotypical combinations such as light eyes and dark skin or freckles and curly or coiled hair.[29] Here we see that to be both multiracial and beautiful requires exoticism; to be perfectly racially ambiguous means to possess embodied racialized visibility.

Scholars point out that the admiration of multiracial women "functions alongside the denigration of Blackness," in that young, mixed-raced women are often portrayed more positively than Black women with darker skin.[30] This cultural representation vacillates between two polar ends anchored by gendered Whiteness and minority monoraciality. To be mul-tiracial or racially ambiguous is not the same as being White, nor is it the same as being Black. The social picture of multiraciality involves a par-ticular mixture of characteristics from both ends that, when together, cre-ate something distinctive—so long as features associated with Blackness are deemphasized.

Multiracial women also receive far more attention from both scholars and media than do multiracial men.[31] Emergent studies, however, suggest that multiracial men fall under a specific gaze that also imbues their bod-ies with exoticness and desirability.[32] Indeed, in our contemporary cele-bration of racial mixedness and the increasing diversification of the U.S. racial landscape, multiracial men appear poised to join women in their media representation as desirable and unique.

This is evident in the social media storm around Jeremy Meeks, a man whose 2014 mugshot from an arrest on possession of a firearm and grand theft was posted by the Stockton, California, police to Facebook. The photo went viral, and Meeks, later convicted on both charges, was dubbed the "hot felon." With both Black and White heritages, his "unique" and "intriguing" looks, apparently, outshined his criminal record. As soon as he finished his twenty-seven-month sentence, Meeks became a model and rocketed straight into the fashion world. Far from being postracial, Jeremy Meeks's case highlights that *seeing race* is central to contemporary multi-racial formations and racialized desirability.

POSITIONING MULTIRACIALITY IN CYBERSPACE

Our research suggests that, when it comes to dating, fascinations with multiraciality not only carry over but follow the very specific digital-sexual racism patterns we have identified in earlier chapters. The centrality of White preference and anti-Blackness come into clearer focus as we consider the experiences of multiracial daters.

White multiracials, for instance, are treated more favorably by Whites in online dating than are single-race minorities.[33] White straight women—who respond to White men but rarely Black, Asian, and Latino men—demonstrate a greater willingness to date Asian-White, Latino-White, and, to some extent, Black-White multiracial men; that is, White women see White multiracial men as much more desirable than monoracial minorities. This is remarkable, considering White women are most discriminatory in their dating patterns (chapter 4).

The fact that generally exclusionary White women are relatively open to White multiracials could have several drivers. It could be, for instance, that the Whiteness provides a sense of familiarity or that these men's proximity to White masculinity outweighs concerns over their "otherness." If we consider how hegemonic ideologies of "ideal" or "normal" masculinity are often conferred to White heterosexual men, alongside the prevalence of controlling images of Asian men as "effeminate" and "nerdy," it is reasonable to speculate that White multiraciality symbolically Whitens prospective Asian multiracial partners enough for them to be seen as adequately attractive by White women.[34] Amanda, a straight White twenty-one-year-old college student, told us in an interview, "I think [I'm] more open to a White multiracial guy than a non-White guy altogether. I don't know why; I just think I would be." The inclusion of Whiteness seems to provide Amanda a mysterious assurance: they are still at least a little White.

Whiteness also elevates the status of multiracial women among White men. In chapter 4 we show that White men send messages mostly to White women, followed by Latina and Asian women. They rarely contact Black women. Figure 8.1 shows that multiracial women slot in among Asian and Latina women in the desirability rankings. Multiracial women are not as sought after as White women but certainly receive more messages from White men than Black women do. The clear distinction made

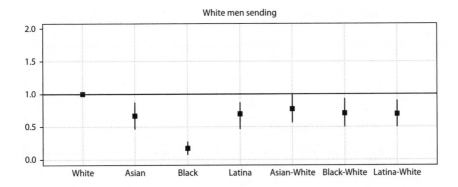

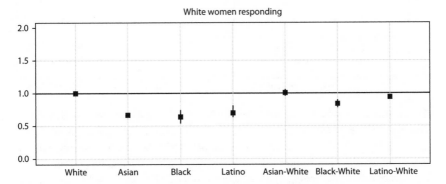

Figure 8.1. White Daters' Relative Likelihood of Messaging Multiracial Daters versus Single Race Daters. The estimates depict the relative likelihood of messaging non-White daters compared with monoracial White daters among White daters, adjusted for other observed characteristics. The lines depict 95 percent confidence intervals. Interacting with monoracial White daters is indicated by an odds of 1.0. Anything above 1.0 shows a greater relative probability of messaging non-White dater than a White dater; anything below 1.0 indicates a lesser probability. See online table O.9 (at www.ucpress.edu/9780520293458) for full estimates.

by White men between Black-White and Black women is striking, show-ing how they privilege Whiteness over Blackness and treat Black-White women as an in-between group.[35] The penalty of being Black seems to be partly canceled out by the premium of being part White.[36]

Thus far, much of the story we have recounted has assumed a White gaze. Looking beyond Whites' preferences, we see that straight minority women also grant White biracial men an elevated status. For Asian, Black,

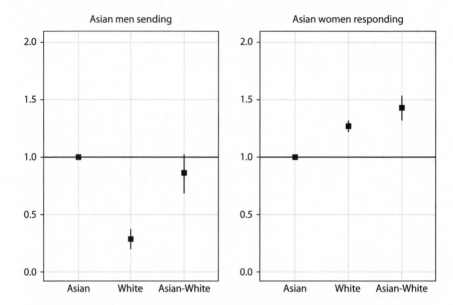

Figure 8.2. Asian Daters' Relative Likelihood of Messaging White or Asian-White Daters versus Asian Daters. The estimates depict the relative likelihood of sending messages to White or Asian-White daters compared with Asian daters among Asian daters, adjusted for other observed characteristics. The lines depict 95 percent confidence intervals. Sending to Asian daters is indicated by an odds of 1.0. Anything above 1.0 shows a greater relative probability of messaging a White or Asian-White dater than an Asian-White dater; anything below 1.0 indicates a lesser probability. See online table O.9 for full estimates.

and Latino/a straight daters, a comparison of interactions with same-race minority daters, Whites, and the multiracial daters who identify with both is instructive. Figure 8.2 shows that Asian men treat Asian-White and Asian women similarly, while sending the fewest messages to White women.[37] In contrast, Asian women respond most frequently to Asian-White multiracial men, followed by Whites, then Asians.

Latino men are similar to Asian men; they contact Latina-White and Latina women at equal rates, while sending messages to White women somewhat less frequently (see figure 8.3).[38] Latinas, like many other minority women, see same-race multiracial men as preferable to both White and same-race monoracial men. They respond to more messages

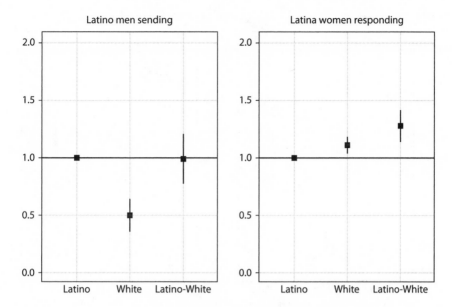

Figure 8.3. Latino/a Daters' Relative Likelihood of Messaging White or Latino/a-White Daters versus Latino/a Daters. The estimates depict the relative likelihood of messaging White or Latino/a-White daters compared with Latino/a daters among Latino/a daters, adjusted for other observed characteristics. The lines depict 95 percent confidence intervals. Messaging Latino/a daters is indicated by an odds of 1.0. Anything above 1.0 shows a greater relative probability of messaging a White or Latino/a-White dater than a Latino/a-White dater; anything below 1.0 indicates a lesser probability. See online table O.9 for full estimates.

sent by Latino-White multiracial men than to those sent by White and Latino men.

Although large confidence intervals prevent definitive conclusions, figure 8.4 also illustrates that Black men appear to send messages more often to Black-White and monoracial Black women, and, like other multiracial men, send the fewest messages to White women.[39] Figure 8.4 suggests that Black women, like other minority women, prefer White and Black-White men to Black monoracial men. Taken together we spot a clear gender difference: minority men afford White multiraciality and minority monoraciality equal prestige in online dating and are less likely to contact White women by comparison. Minority women, on the other

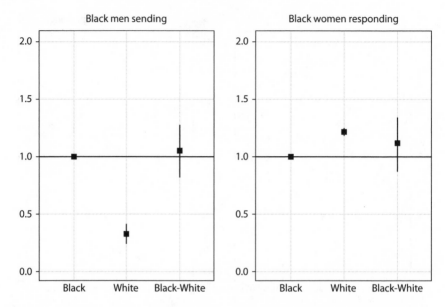

Figure 8.4. Black Daters' Relative Likelihood of Messaging White or Black-White Daters versus Black Daters. The estimates depict the relative likelihood of messaging White or Black-White daters compared with Black daters among Black daters, adjusted for other observed characteristics. The lines depict 95 percent confidence intervals. Messaging Black daters is indicated by an odds of 1.0. Anything above 1.0 shows a greater relative probability of messaging a White or Black-White dater than a Black-White dater; anything below 1.0 indicates a lesser probability. See online table O.9 for full estimates.

hand, generally privilege multiraciality and Whiteness over minority monoracial identities.

Why do minority women privilege Whiteness to a greater extent? As we have discussed throughout, it is certain that the decision of whom to date and marry has been far more consequential historically for women than for men. This may be particularly true among immigrant women, for whom intermarriage with Whites may offer a shorter pathway to cultural assimilation in the United States. Minority women's preference for White-multiracial men over minority monoracial men may be shaped by similar status processes. However, as we argue next, White and minority daters may also find mixed-race people especially desirable in online dating, given the digitized emphasis on racial markers on dating profiles and the cultural stereotypes associated with racial mixedness.

MULTIRACIAL DISSECTION AND EXOTICIZATION

Existing research has illustrated that people assign attractiveness to multiracial women and men because their "looks" disrupt a clean division between the assumed polarity of monoracial identities.[40] The tendency is also observed among our monoracial interviewees, who often sensationalized mixed-race individuals' phenotype as they perused online-dating profiles. As they explained, they feel that mixed-race individuals possessed a "unique" and desirable look, something that they could admire by zeroing in on the electric array of profile pictures that adorned their dating profile.

Derick, a straight Black man, said of mixed-race people,

> For me I think they're getting the best features of both worlds. A lot of times it's with the eyes. . . . It's like one of my friends—he was biracial, and it was always about his eyes. He looked Black, but then he had these piercing green eyes. It's very defined. I think because it's so defined, like a husky, where those blue eyes, they're like really sharp. You can see it. Also, with a mix, a body with a color that's perfect. Very tan, brown skin.

Derick's observation indicates that multiracial individuals are often subjected to a very specific racialized gaze, a detective game assigning features to Blackness or Whiteness. The process obviously objectifies the bodies of multiracial individuals. Derick goes so far as to compare his biracial friend to a carefully bred dog, due to the sharp contrast between his "look" of Blackness and his "piercing green eyes." In her interviews with multiracial boys, Alyssa Newman illuminates similar patterns of "racial dissection" applied to multiracial boys' bodies, as they attempt to name the racial origin of each feature.[41] From Derick's point of view, his friend's attractiveness comes not from his proximity to Whiteness but his disruption of ordinary Blackness. Notably, Derick is heterosexual, yet he subjects his friend to this racial gaze and fascination. The appraisal of multiracial people appears to transcend gender and sexual orientation.

Our multiracial interviewees were well aware of this type of objectification they experienced while using online-dating websites or apps. Some unabashedly confirmed that they believed they possessed "unique" or "interesting" arrays of phenotypic traits, from eye shape to eye color, lip fullness, hair texture, bone structure, breast size, and the size and shape of thighs and buttocks. Sonya identifies as White and Latina, and she seemed proud of the remarks men made about her physical traits when they messaged her:

> I got a lot of comments about my eyes, 'cause I have very light-green, interesting-colored eyes. And so, a lot of people complimented me on that. That was, I would say, the main physical appearance. Yeah. Or sometimes my lips too, because I have pretty big lips, which I think might be a part of my Brazilian heritage. Definitely from my dad's side, but yeah. I feel like White girls tend to have smaller lips.

And Kayla, a bisexual woman with one Black and one White parent, said,

> I think the way I look is what is appealing to men. I'm kind of tan. I don't know. You saw me for five seconds. I have bright-green eyes, and I'm kind of tan, so I think the juxtaposition of my skin color and my eye color. I get a lot of comments about, "You have really beautiful eyes" or "You have really nice eyes."

The narrative of multiracial desirability has the buy-in of some multiracial individuals—in ways that can be deployed as pride, to be sure—and it shows that socially racialized images of mixed bodies have a deep impact on their dating lives. Sonya's and Kayla's accounts both center men's sexual fascination, but they also clearly show that these women play the game when it comes to assigning their phenotypical characteristics to one parental lineage over the other. It is the combination of Sonya's "Brazilian" lips and her "light-green, interesting-colored eyes," and Kayla's juxtaposition of her skin color and eye color that signify their attractive multiraciality. In the process of explaining their uniqueness or exoticness, they unwittingly reified the controlling images that link race and physical features along a continuum of desirability.

Though some of our multiracial participants did not mind exotification when it was dressed in a compliment, some, however, definitely considered it problematic. Stacy, a Taiwanese-White bisexual who identifies as Hapa on her profile, explained that she began to reject being called "exotic" as she aged: "They meant it as just, 'you're beautiful, you don't fit how other people look like around you.' So, when I was younger, I accepted that term. Now as an adult, I don't like that word 'cause I don't want to be labeled as 'exotic,' which means 'the other.'" When her parents called her exotic as a child, it was an innocent gesture, but being labeled exotic made Stacy feel alienated as an adult. Anthony, a multiracial queer man, described his discomfort with the constant racial dissection he experienced, on and offline. The intersection of his Black and Vietnamese American backgrounds often elicited intense erotic interest from monoracial men who, upon learning he was multiracial, made a game of spotting his "Asian" characteristics such as his eyes or hair. Part of their interest in him, Anthony suspected, had to do with the ways in which both Blackness and Asianness are racially objectified within the queer community, often placed at two poles on a spectrum of masculinity. As he explained to us, the hyperfocus on his multiraciality acted as a sort of "veil" between him and others. It felt unavoidable that men would see him through a racialized lens.

Seila, a Black and White twenty-four-year-old multiracial dater, echoed Anthony when it came to the contradictions that accompany the game of multiracial dissection. In her view being seen primarily through the racialized and sexualized "exotic" lens makes her feel others do not truly care to *know her:*

> People I meet on apps will kind of tell me that I look exotic and also further on when we meet up and get to know each other. People kind of think that mixed-race people are more exotic, which is weird, because what is exotic? Foreign? You can be mixed and American. Yeah, I think it's like the mix of my features, but I don't really like the term *exotic,* because I think that being exotic is sort of seductive, because it's like there's so much currency in being so attractive, but so foreign, but you kind of have to sacrifice your genuineness to be exotic. Once you're known, you're no longer exotic, because being exotic is beautiful and far away. I would much rather be genuine and known rather than being exotic.

Seila feels that her U.S. identity is muted as she is cast as foreign and other. These feelings of being unseen yet hyperseen, known and unknown,

U.S. American yet foreign harken back to sociologist W. E. B. Du Bois's theory of double consciousness, or the sensation that one's identity is divided into several parts. In this case the near-constant racial dissection and exotification of their bodies made it difficult for multiracial daters to have one unified identity. They seemed to believe it was inevitable that they would be perceived through others' fragmented racialized and gendered frames.

YOUR CATEGORIES, MY CHOICES

Throughout this book we have shown that White men are most favored in online dating, with Black women and men excluded by non-White and White daters alike. These hierarchies fit fairly neatly with many of the historical racialized and gendered attitudes about courtship we covered in earlier chapters. But at the very beginning of this chapter, we asked whether multiracialism heralds a transcendence, reinforcement, or alteration of racial hierarchies. As much of this book has illustrated, racialized and gendered hierarchies don't exist in the abstract. They are reinforced in interaction and are in many ways amplified in the cyber context of online dating, where digital-sexual racism is naturalized through the ideology of personal preference. If we believe that people have agency in determining whom they wish to date, we cannot ignore how the privileged status afforded to White men and women is created, in part, by the exclusionary preferences groups enact while perusing online-dating profiles. Indeed, though the structure of dating apps may facilitate exclusion, there's a face behind every swipe, like, and ignored message. Multiracials participate in this process by accommodating, internalizing, and sometimes resisting the racialized and gendered desirability hierarchies that are propagated by society as they look for romance.

Many of our multiracial participants espoused liberal or color-blind attitudes about racial preferences, claiming an openness to dating people of most backgrounds, given their own mixed-racial parentage. However, they seemed particularly interested in other multiracials. They described the various strategies they used to highlight their racial and ethnic selves in dating apps and websites. When they use apps that do not allow users to self-identify by race, such as Bumble, multiracial respondents indicated their racial and ethnic background combination to others by stating them in their bios or by including signifiers such as national flags. In this sense online dating may be useful for mixed-race individuals, who may be especially interested in connecting with people who share a mixed-racial background. For example, Kayla, a Black-White woman from the South, felt that multiracial Black men might have a shared understanding around identity and her existence in a racial "liminal space":

> I feel like sometimes I get mixed guys who are similar to me, where they feel like they're in this sort of liminal space between groups. . . . I will say that I'm more attracted to mixed men because I do, I guess, project that they might be able to understand my racial experiences better, and also they might have a more flexible perception of race, where there's not things we can and can't do, because they're prescribed or not endorsed by one racial group. That's really important to me, in terms of the way I interact with the world. I kind of want someone who's also kind of flexible in that way.

Mixed-race daters showed us that others' racial identities could be especially important for people unlikely to meet many matches who are also mixed race. Sociologist Chandra Waring refers to the flexibility Kayla described as "racial capital," or the "repertoire of racial resources (knowledge, experiences, meaning, and language) that biracial Americans draw upon to negotiate or cope with racial boundaries in a highly racialized society."[42] In Kayla's view similar amounts of "racial capital" signal higher compatibility.

Stephen, a queer Latino-Black multiracial dater, met his current partner, who was also mixed race, through online dating. Like Kayla, he explained that their shared background was a sort of shortcut when they first started dating. Specifically, Stephen and his partner both knew what it was like to be racially identified by outsiders while not feeling fully attached to in-group ethnic markers, such as the ability to speak their parents' ethnic language: "He doesn't speak Chinese, similarly with him where I don't speak Spanish. In many ways we're very similar, and maybe that is a very latent influence in why I was attracted to him as a partner, actually now that I think about it."

Multiracial daters also shared a common aversion toward daters who openly espoused racial preferences or "types." Stephen said that when he encountered profiles with such preferences, "I read it as arrogance. I see it as this person deciding that they have this authority or judgment over people in a way that to me is not right. You're equals. You're human as well." Many other mixed-race respondents were dismayed that race should matter so much to some daters. Rodrigo, a heterosexual respondent with a Mexican father and White mother, had issues with explicit racial preferences too, taking pains to explain that was true regardless of whether *his* racial background was favored:

> Either way it's problematic to me, and I see it as red flag when I hear that someone "isn't interested in X"—even if I qualify as X, even if I don't qualify as X. If a woman says, "I'm not interested in Black guys." That's an automatic no for me. Even if they're just saying that because they're just not attracted to Black people in some way, it just raises way too many questions in my mind. It just tells me something I can't help but find kind of ugly about them. Whether their preference is born out of aesthetic preference or actual animus or fear of certain people, it tells me that they're not—at best, they're not open, or familiar enough with other people. That there's a close-mindedness about them. That turns me off.

Rodrigo was not looking for someone who was open to his racial background but one who was open to *all* racial backgrounds. Indeed, while many of our single-race respondents took issue with exclusionary racial preferences, multiracial respondents were different in using "racial openness" as part of their vetting strategy. This was especially true among queer daters who were well versed in an array of pervasive racial codes (no "spice," "rice," or "chicken") as well as explicit racial preferences ("no Blacks") on dating apps.

Anthony, Black and Asian, reflected on anti-Blackness on queer dating apps:

> I think red flags for me are folks that are explicitly discriminatory or list their preferences in their bio. One of the worst things, one of the grievous things I've seen is literally, not the explicit anti-Blackness, but explicit yet implicit anti-Blackness. They'll literally say, "into Whites, Latinos, Asians." So basically no Black, but they're not saying it. I think it's implicit, which is trifling. So there is the argument that you're attracted to what you're attracted to, but to have that in your bio is excessive. Right? I mean, in an ideal world, my idea would be that race isn't a factor as far as attractiveness. I'm kind of being

brought up on Magic School Bus and Power Rangers—the idea that everyone's special in their own way. Nine times out of ten, you're gonna find someone who's attractive that's of the race that you don't immediately care for.

To Anthony, stating racial "preferences" was not just an expression of individuality. It was a way to perpetuate the worldview that some people were less desirable than others. Pro-Black and pro-Asian discourses were, for him, as problematic as anti-Blackness in that they were too narrow-minded for a progressive conversation about race. This attitude was certainly distinct from what we generally heard from some Black women and men, who leveraged pro-Black discourses and "dating Black" as forms of racial resistance.

At face value an affinity toward other multiracial daters and opposition to explicit racial preferences are two sides of the same progressive coin. Yet this does not mean that multiracials operate outside of the dominant racial hierarchies, particularly when it comes to anti-Blackness. Indeed, many of the multiracial daters we interviewed avoided Blacks, despite having experienced racial marginalization themselves. For example, George described himself as very "pro-Black" and indicated that he ignores any White women who appear to less race conscious. As he put it,

> No Beckys, none of that. Any White woman that I can just see right off the bat, if she's wearing a cowboy hat and a USA bikini, I'm like, "You're not going to understand nothing about my life." But if they've got pictures of them hanging out with a multicultural, multiracial group of people . . . well, now I can get to know them and at least know that they're not avoidant of melanin.

Even so George rarely dated Black women. When we asked why he usually dated White and Latina women, he said it likely came from his insecurity in his own multiracial Blackness:

> I feel like because I'm half Black, I feel intimidated sometimes by Black women because I'm like, "Well, shit." I feel like I'm going to be just seen as a fraud or whatever, which is dumb, I know. I'm more, I guess, hesitant because I don't want to provide a watered-down Black person to somebody who I feel is deserving of a strong culture behind them. I don't have any aversion, but I've always been like, "I don't know. I just don't know if I am Black enough." It's easier—I am like the Blackest between me and my girl-friend, who is Latin.

George's explanation was puzzling. He located himself as the product of interracial intimacy between a Black man and a White women, and he rejected racial exclusivity. He carefully examined other daters' responses to one popular dating app's questions, like one that asked whether they were only willing to date someone of the same race. "If they say yes, I hit no," he said, "because that lets me know right off the bat. . . . I want you to see my color, and I want you to not care." Still George did not feel he was adequately Black enough for Black women, who were likely to share similar views about race. George's view that Black women deserve a "truly Black" man seems to resonate with the "pluralistic ignorance" we discussed in chapter 5, whereby White men may assume that Black women have no interest in them.[43] George's own racial status as an intermediary compounded his assumption because he felt like a "fraud" who was not truly Black. Yet George never explained why he was White or Latino enough to date White and Latina women. In that light his reason for not dating Black women sounded more like an "it's not you, it's me" excuse.

Among multiracial women daters, we see similar patterns of digital-sexual racism and reinforcement of the desirability hierarchies we have tracked throughout this book. Just like the Asian and Latina women we interviewed, multiracial women described avoiding dating Blacks to prevent familial dispute. For example, Linda, a Black-White multiracial dater who dated primarily multiracial men and lighter-skinned Black men, said that anti-Blackness permeated her family:

> I think my family is really strange, because we're an interracial family, but I definitely have anxieties about bringing home someone who's not just Black but also darker skinned. Like my mom being from Haiti where colorism is very prevalent, I think she's definitely internalized that. I think she would much prefer me to bring a mixed guy home than someone who's monoracial Black. I've also heard my dad make comments, like, "We don't care who you date, but just don't bring someone home dark as charcoal." I feel like they wouldn't want me to date someone Black. . . . Yeah, I think my parents would prefer me dating someone mixed, White, or foreign.

Linda's mother was a light-skinned Black woman from the Caribbean who told Linda since childhood that she was multiracial and different from other Black kids in the neighborhood.[44] Linda understood that she was different not only because she had a White father but also because she was "upper middle class," and her parents conflated African American's Blackness with lower-class behaviors.

The desirability premium received by multiracial women may also lead them to identify with Whiteness. Helena, a university student who identifies as multiracial, Brazilian, and Jewish, was raised in a diverse city in the western United States, and she remembered vividly how "the hot, popular White girls" were pursued during high school. She and her racially diverse group of friends, on the other hand, were ignored. It wasn't until she entered college that Helena felt more attractive. Dating apps offered her even more confidence. Up until she met her White boyfriend online, she told us, she matched with White men about "60 percent" of the time and rarely dated Asian and Black men. But she had a gnawing sense of guilt that came with all of her left swipes:

> I feel like I sort of defaulted to White, even though I grew up somewhere super diverse. Then every once in a while, I would be like, "Oh, shit. I'm swiping on all these White guys. I should reset my filter." But, yeah, I feel like that was sort of the subconscious default. . . . I have this . . . "I'm not racist" inner monologue, so I should swipe on more Black guys.

Helena didn't provide any real reason for excluding Black men, and later, as if to show that she wasn't anti-Black, she added that she hadn't wanted to date Asian men either. Here she evoked frequent stereotypes, speculating that Asian men on the apps were "the nerdy type of Asian guy who plays video games and is sort of dorky and wears sneakers." She added, "There's kind of a type that you could kind of see and maybe not consciously think, but kind of figure out. So, I don't find myself attracted to that kind." For Helena, the ease by which she could filter out or ignore the "undesirable" groups from her dating universe was not an extension of racial animus but rather a matter of her personal preference—something that the digitized context of dating apps allows her carry out in private.

No one living in a society so saturated with racial hierarchy and distinction is immune to internalizing and reproducing the pervasive controlling images and stereotypes assigned to minority femininity and masculinity. Likewise, though our multiracial respondents described their personal racialized preferences as a private matter of individual choice, many of their narratives reflected the ways personal preferences are shaped by racial hierarchy. For example, Sai, a nineteen-year-old South Asian–White multiracial man who self-identified as politically liberal, indicated that he was most interested in pairing with White women or East Asian women. Sai did not find Indian women like his mother attractive for dating—he wanted to hook up with less conservative women, he said—but they *were* appropriate for marriage. He had little to no interest in Black and Latina women and used "ghetto" stereotypes when he talked about Black women, in particular. "They are loud," he argued. "They tend to do things like drugs, just trashy." Sai lived in a diverse city and admitted that he often matched with Black and Latina women. "Latina women are fifty–fifty," he added. "Half the time they are the most hardworking people I know, but the other half of the time they are trashy or ghetto." Like others we interviewed, Sai claimed a liberal political identity yet drew from a color-blind logic of cultural racism to reconcile his stated public views with the digitized sexual racism of his intimate life.

What do these findings tell us about the future of a multiracial United States? We find it doubtful that even a demographic shift rendering Whites a minority will easily or quickly upend White supremacy. To some extent multiracials with a White racial background enjoy an elevated status in online dating. According to the behavioral data we discussed earlier in this chapter, White multiracial men's association with Whiteness makes them more appealing to White and minority women than are minority men. Multiracial women's minority identity also makes them as attractive as minority monoracial women to minority men. Yet our interview data tell a deeper, more sobering story. Given that single-race respondents' perceptions of multiraciality as attractive often rested on preconceived notions of monoracial bodies with distinct racial characteristics and boundaries, multiracial desirability is systematically linked to monoracial minority stigmatization. Moreover, the exoticization of multiraciality is itself a form of racialization and othering that limits the acknowledgement of multiracials' full personhood.

Even multiracial daters are prey to the desirability hierarchies so pervasive among single-race daters. Relatively more open in *theory*, they may nonetheless consciously or unconsciously avoid dating Blacks in *practice*. Thus, the growth of the multiracial population will not be the "end of race." It may, instead, represent a greater diversification of the racial middle, with even more people distancing from Blackness. These findings are consistent with a triracial system in which multiracials are positioned as an interstitial category.[45] Particularly those with some White ancestry find they possess greater privilege than minority monoracials, especially Blacks, even if they cannot access the complete privilege of Whiteness.[46] And that is, apparently, enough to acquiesce to White supremacy.

Conclusion

ABOLISHING THE DATING DIVIDE

In this book we have traced the history of race and gender's instrumental roles in organizing romance in the United States, showing how the digitalization of courtship has introduced a new manifestation of racism in the form of online racial preference. We took a deep dive into the online-dating experiences of major ethnic-racial groups, seeking to understand the contours of current trends. Everyone has a story to tell, yet one thing was clear as we teased out messaging data from a major online-dating platform and interviewed daters around the country: race cuts across gender and sexual orientation, playing a more fundamental role in our romantic lives than just about any other characteristic. Our decisions about whom we approach and whom we avoid are directed by race, whether we know it or not. Race shades how we are perceived and treated by others. It often predicts the dates we go on and the relationships that might develop. It drives our anxieties about the real reasons others pursue or reject us. It confuses. It angers. It frustrates. And, occasionally, it makes us wonder whether we are as open-minded as we would like to think. The commodification of people in online dating has made it efficient and even convenient to categorize—and exclude—according to someone's race.

It is all too apparent that we are not living in a "postracial" world; in fact, the migration to online courtship so far seems to be remiring us in a new form of romantic apartheid. We make all kinds of romantic judgements based on the intersection of race and gender, some explicit, some implicit. For instance, many people we spoke to are aware that they avoid certain ethnic-racial groups in dating, but they see this as a simple matter of ineffable personal attraction. These same individuals believe race should play no part in selecting friends, colleagues, neighbors, or customers, but their conviction disappears when it comes to intimate partners: racial identity trumps almost everything else known to be important to assortative mating. This is a sobering finding, for racial preferences appear inconsequential only for those who benefit from the status quo.

Aside from an alarming and vocal minority, relatively few U.S. Americans today will openly proclaim a wish to preserve "racial purity," yet centuries of racial division and oppression inescapably shape our notions of sexual desirability. The racial segregation of schools and communities, for example, determine whom we see as foreign and whom we see as familiar. Such discrimination is also hardwired into mainstream cultural media, and so we are saturated with often-negative and inaccurate representations of racial and ethnic minorities and the repeated racialized assignation of beauty to lighter, Whiter people over others.

Above all, people's willingness to uncritically apply racial preferences to dating is perpetuated by a lack of frank public acknowledgement of race as a force in our private lives. Our instincts and "tastes" are supposedly as unique as we are—others should not question them, and many believe we can trust them. Some may ask defensively, Shouldn't we have the right to choose based on our desires? But if intimate preferences are so individualistic and mysterious, why are they so similar and predictable? Our analyses showed over and over that race was crucially important in mate selection, carrying the boundaries of the past into the era of personal choice. White daters are presented with the most options, and minorities the least. Black men and women face the most pronounced exclusion in online dating. The intersection of race and gender is also salient in this setting, earning White men universal acceptance from women, and Black women frequent rejections from everyone but Black men. We are in a new era of digital-sexual racism.

This new form of racial "choice" is pervasive regardless of sexual orientation. Gay men are similar to straight women in their default preference for Whiteness, while lesbians' preferences align with straight men, who prefer to contact daters from their own in-groups first. In other words, Whiteness, at least sexually and romantically, is most valued when it goes hand in hand with masculinity. By contrast, though White women may be the most discriminatory in online dating, White femininity lacks the sexual allure of White masculinity. Furthermore, despite the commonly held belief that gay people are more open-minded racially than straight people, their racial preferences are as strong as their straight counterparts'. Gay and lesbian Americans are not immune to hegemonic White supremacy and anti-Blackness, with the sole exception of Black gay men, who are more open to dating all races and display no apparent special treatment toward Whites.

It would still be foolish to declare that racial discrimination in dating is identical to other forms of discrimination. It can never be addressed in the same ways we try to mitigate unequal access to housing, jobs, and education. Yet it would be equally foolish to declare that this discrimination is unrelated to larger patterns of racial oppression in society. As we have argued, fears around interracial intimacy have always been central to White resistance to the expansion of civil rights. The aversion to interracial sex was so ingrained in White society that antimiscegenation laws were deprioritized in the civil rights agenda. Now, five decades after these laws were deemed unconstitutional, our intimate lives remain segregated. The atomization and informalization of intimate life, from one centered around family and friends to one emphasizing spontaneity and individualism, should set the stage for more inclusive intimacy. Why hasn't it?

We find that dating is a final frontier of race in the United States, where overt racism is still pervasive and largely accepted. Race continues to place constraints, both external and internal, in our searches for partners. We *do* race, borrowing, constructing, and reinforcing boundaries to distinguish certain "racialized strangers" from others whom we might find safer, sexier, or even better conduits to upward mobility. And we often do it without realizing that's what's going on. Dating websites became a laboratory for this book. Combing through their data and talking to their users allowed us to observe the prevalence of racial preferences in the United States. As an extension of the intense commercialization of intimacy and the individual that began in the twentieth century, online dating has introduced a mass dating market marked by pronounced objectification and dehumanization. This new dynamic manifests itself in particularly pernicious ways when it comes to race, forming a new digital-sexual racism.

Yet we can imagine a world in which online-dating sites become powerful agents for social change. In these apps and on the platforms, we find one of the only spaces in the United States where daters have access to millions of others of different racial backgrounds. Online dating has infinitely expanded the options for daters with more inclusive preferences. The screening questions and filtering options available in online dating are also one place that young people begin to contemplate and confront racial preferences in a supposedly "color-blind" country. Their unambiguous selections—to accept or reject all profiles marked with specific racial categories—has led an entire generation of U.S. Americans to confront the poignant racial discrimination they experience and enforce in other domains.[1] Beneath progressive identities, people sifting through hundreds and thousands of profiles find an uncomfortable trove of racial biases.

The U.S. racial hierarchy is poised to undergo an unavoidable and fundamental shift as the non-White population expands and their intermarriage blurs boundaries. We can see as much in the resurgence of White nationalism and anti-immigrant rhetoric: where there is no threat, there is no need for such ugly protectionism. Yet our analysis suggests that the hierarchy is more likely to be restructured than dismantled. Minority women's acceptance of White men over others, combined with pervasive gendered anti-Blackness across demographic groups, indicates that centuries-old polarizing forces may not reverse course quickly, even with dramatic demographic changes.

AN AGENT OF CHANGE

Charlotte is a fifty-year-old White woman in a long-term relationship with Marcos, a Latino man she met on a dating website. Were it not for online dating, Charlotte told us, she would not be in an interethnic relationship—if they'd met out and about in the world, Marco might have seemed too different for them to have anything in common. But chatting online first eased the way:

> Oh, but you know, well, we are different. We're different, but we're similar. So, until you actually get past that initial thinking that you're different, to see, you have to have that avenue to realize that you're not so different. And that's where online, I would think that more, over time, more interethnic relationships will end up happening.

This is social-contact theory at work: people who are not exposed to one another in everyday life assume they are incompatible. People who come into contact with people unlike themselves generally find that's not true.

Sam, a White student, observed how even college settings, known to promote higher interracial contact, still tend to isolate racial groups. Dating apps helped Sam and other students get past these racial boundaries:

> I think most people tend to stick within their groups, and their groups tend to be pretty racially segregated. . . . But, on Tinder, I've actually matched with a bunch of Black women before. I've engaged them in conversation, and we've just conversated. I hadn't conversated with any Black women here. Black men, yeah, but not Black women.

The internet provides an alternative space that disrupts White daters like Sam's and Charlotte's habitual, quotidian segregation.

Likewise, Keisha, a Black woman, had joined the sites specifically looking for a Black partner, but that soon changed: "Through the whole online-dating process I had a chance to see a lot of different cultures, things that I wasn't used to." She ended up dating Indian, Latino, and White men in addition to Black men. Later she reflected that, prior to her online-dating experiences, "I felt like I was doing the same thing, watching the same places, many of the same type of people, whereas with online dating, you get to actually, you know, reach out to different races and cultures that you didn't think about before." By the time of our interview, Keisha was in a relationship with a Black man she met online but said she appreciated how the experience provided her with the opportunity to meet others she might not have ordinarily had the opportunity to connect with.

A recent study confirms that racial exogamy is more prevalent among daters who met online compared to many other meeting contexts.[2] This is the case for both short-term relationships and committed relationships that have lasted at least five years. Another study finds similar results for interracial marriage, with computer simulations based on recent trends revealing that online dating is highly correlated with a sudden recent increase in interracial marriages.[3] The authors optimistically conclude that online dating is likely to promote near-complete racial integration.

These encouraging results may seem inconsistent with the stark racial discrimination presented in this book, but the argument is not that online dating eradicates racial prejudice. Rather, the internet can facilitate interracial relationships for those with preexisting inclusive preferences, and the increase of interracial couples could, perhaps, slowly change the minds of those with more restrictive preferences. Online dating and the behavior it cultivates is not very different from other types of union formation throughout U.S. history. The major difference is that the internet could free individuals from physical boundaries and expand their options—should they be willing to try.

For people of color, mainstream online dating is a more double-edged sword. They are exposed to a greater pool of dating candidates, but that comes with a cost: a high frequency of racist interactions. The trade-off is a difficult one. They either go online and accept the reality that they may be treated as less than their White friends, or they avoid the demoralizing experience by foregoing a resource that has become critical in forming intimate relationships. In other words, as online dating facilitates greater interracial interactions, it also brings to light the deep sexual racism that was less visible in our everyday life. In a way, much like the end of slavery and the rise of Jim Crow, online dating brought U.S. society to a new era of racial and sexual politics by dismantling existing segregation, increasing interracial contacts, and in the process *heightening* racial tension.

But we also know that sexual racism does not come out of nowhere. It is carried out and reinforced in prosaic everyday interactions and reproduced and maintained by popular culture and the media, which has historically elevated Whiteness. We have illustrated how women and men of color find that they date under a White gaze that degrades their bodies.

For many Black people, for example, the goal isn't to match with Whites but to be free from White-produced stereotypes as they search for a mate.

There are always two sides to these racial oppressions. While White hegemonic standards of desirability shape social interaction online as much as offline, marginalized groups resist these standards. Daters may include racial politics in their vetting strategies as they search for a match, such as steering away from profiles that display intolerant symbolism, and they may develop their own "literacy of self-presentation," affirming their own identity and resisting hegemonic White beauty standards in constructing their profiles.[4] For example, the inclusion of natural hairstyles, national flags, Black Lives Matters symbolism, and other cultural markers like "Spanish is cool with me" were ways the daters we spoke with signaled their social identities and alternative values to strangers in the digital context. In other words, marginalized groups actively confront, and at times resist, racial hierarchies of desire by asserting who they *are*, what they *represent*, and what—or whom—they *reject*.

Future scholarship aimed at further understanding online dating as a potential agent of social change will need to compare how race operates differently in online and offline settings. If daters with more racially inclusive preferences are far more likely to date online, our results may actually underestimate the prevalence of racial preferences in U.S. society. It could also be the case, as we see with Charlotte and Keisha, that exposure to more diverse online-dating pools helps daters widen their dating horizons and therefore develop more inclusive preferences. Yet the abundance of potential candidates is overwhelming, and daters may just as easily deploy race as a default filter to narrow down options well before they come into contact with people of other races.

Further, the growing strength of the Black Lives Matter movement that erupted in large-scale protests sweeping the nation in 2020 has brought about increased public recognition of racial oppression. From Nike to NASCAR to the NFL, companies have begun issuing corporate mea culpas and announcing policy changes. Likewise, we agree with legal scholar Sonu Bedi, who pointed out that dating companies should be held responsible for facilitating racial discrimination on their platforms. They have a corporate responsibility to counteract the new digital-sexual racism we document in this book by becoming more intentional about their design and more communicative about race to their clientele. We believe it *is* possible to create an efficient sorting process that decenters rather than fore-grounds the importance of race. For example, websites and apps that emphasize race or ethnicity as a key parameter in the romantic-match proc-ess reinforce existing racial preferences through what Bedi calls "racial steering."[5] Platforms can instead do away altogether with these racial sort-ing and filtering options for mate searches. In fact, some gay-dating compa-nies decided to remove their race filter in the aftermath of the 2020 deaths of George Floyd, Breonna Taylor, Tony McDade, and Ahmaud Arbery.[6]

The prominence of photographs, meanwhile, also affects the extent to which the decision will ride on skin-deep information. Most dating sites, especially phone apps, emphasize images over profile content. Many swip-ing apps provide only a picture and minimal biographical data, which cause daters to factor in the photograph for estimating compatibility more so than they would with an alternative design that emphasized expansive biographical profiles. Allowing daters to connect first over shared inter-ests could set in motion an initial interaction, one otherwise preempted by the inevitable focus on physical features. And platforms that highlight social similarities may counter racial stereotypes and promote greater interaction across all daters.

No dating platform that we know of excludes the opportunity for mem-bers to upload pictures to their profile, although there have been experi-ments. OkCupid ran a short-lived app called Crazy Blind Date, where daters would meet up with a person they had never seen online. Although there was very low user demand for this application, among those who did participate in the experiment, large majorities reported that they had greatly enjoyed the experience. Nevertheless, appearance matters, as we can attest to by the fact that profiles lacking pictures in our own data are all but ignored by others. However, removing pictures until later in the online communication process is one possible approach.

Our ability to understand how behaviors are modulated by platforms is complicated by the invisibility of the proprietary algorithms that secretly shape dater interaction on many such sites.[7] Algorithms take on the veil of scientific objectivity, yet technology is human, and data are social.[8] As Ruha Benjamin's concept of the "New Jim Code" illustrates, new technolo-gies encompass a range of discriminatory designs that encode inequity. Racial and gendered assumptions about whom clients desire or might desire are built into dating-site algorithms, for instance, and that filters which profiles daters see. Such algorithms threaten to disrupt new racial exposure brought about by the internet, reifying preexisting biases by importing historical data and trends and assuming those will hold. Dating app companies should actively participate in the ongoing racial justice work related to AI and algorithmic oppression, such as that of the Algorithmic Justice League and the Auditing Algorithms Initiative.[9]

Other interventions would be to eliminate racial categories altogether on profiles or to consider incorporating profile statistics on how often a given dater responds to those of differing demographics. Though these measures may not totally combat the racial fetishization and demonization that are so commonly experienced by minority daters, they will make it harder for the now-inhibited dater to initiate troubling interactions.

Overall, dating companies hold a tremendous amount of influence in designing how daters approach one another and go about the process of dating. One possibility could be to intentionally incorporate racial and ethnic diversity as a default when displaying search results for matches. Another is for companies to take the lead in educating their users about how individual dating behaviors feed into larger, more systematic trends. As such, companies could regularly publish aggregate trends about racial interactions on their platforms, as well as other types of socially significant consequences emerging through these sites, to keep users aware and sensitive to their own contributing behavior.

RACE IN FUTURE TENSE

We have focused on the past and contemporary significance of race in telling the story of how U.S. Americans form intimate relationships, but these preferences also predict future racial relationships. Intermarriage is rising, and the multiracial population will increase dramatically by midcentury. Yet the long road to racial integration is uneven and highly gendered. Asians and Latinos/as are more likely to marry Whites than their Black counterparts. When Blacks do outmarry other racial groups, particularly Whites, men are more likely than women to cross the intimate color line. Asian women, on the other hand, are more likely than Asian men to marry Whites. Our book shows what national statistics cannot: the lack of Black-White unions appears to be driven by Whites' unease, not Blacks'. Asian men's lower-than-average interracial unions are driven both by White women's rejection and Asian women's ranking of them as second to White men. These patterns are cascading, for Asian men, in turn, are less inclined to contact Black and Latinas, who are actually highly responsive to them. Asian and Latino men respond to as many messages from White women as they do from their coethnics, but White women exclude as often as they exclude Black men.

In previous centuries the multiracial population was absorbed into a polarized Black-White binary. It remains an open question whether today's acknowledged and quickly growing multiracial population will disrupt existing racial hierarchies. Our data suggest that multiracial daters have mixed feelings in their racial preferences and outward identities. The relatively high economic standing of interracial unions means that offspring will generally grow up in predominantly White and middle-class communities, potentially acquiring similar preferences through White socialization. At the same time, our qualitative data show that White and non-White multiracial daters are *both* othered and racialized. They may also reproduce the same patterns of anti-Blackness we have tracked across all groups' dating behaviors. The growth of the multiracial population is not necessarily a harbinger of the profound "postracial" change anticipated by some optimistic social commentators.

Racial dynamics in the United States will inevitably transform as the country becomes increasingly integrated into the global community. A global Black Lives Matter movement is accompanied by a renewed cultural production; after many years of underrepresentation of Black women in beauty competitions, for the first time in history Black women now hold crowns in five major contests.[10] Social media (e.g., #BlackGirlMagic and #BlackTwitter) has opened a space for marginalized communities to "speak back" to hegemonic White-dominated images about their communities. The continuing influx of immigrants from Latin America, Asia, and Africa also imports racial schemas and cultural products that compete with traditional controlling images in the United States. The growth of the continental economy of Asia and its high-skilled Asian migrants, for example, has shifted U.S. stereotypes associated with Asians. Our interviewees pointed to K-pop and anime as cultural materials that have begun to shape younger U.S. Americans' perceptions of Asians, beauty standards, and racial preferences.

These new images, of course, are not necessarily fully representative, and their selective consumption may unwittingly reinforce traditional stereotypes and racial divisions with a false sense of authenticity. Racial ideologies transmitted across national boundaries intersect with new racial discourses and stereotypes in profound and often understudied ways.[11] As evidenced by the continued resurfacing of the model minority/ yellow peril dichotomy in contemporary society, seemingly complementary characterizations contain a pernicious side. Nevertheless, the growth of the immigrant population, racialized social movements, and the increasing immersion of U.S. Americans in globalized popular culture will diversify a cultural regime previously dominated by Whites. We suspect this will work very differently for some racial groups than others, given the pervasiveness of anti-Blackness that winds its way throughout this book.

DOING RACE IN THE TWENTY-FIRST CENTURY

On Reddit, commenters frequently debate whether it's *racist* to have intimate racial preferences. Some are definitive: yes. Any discrimination based on race is a form of racism. Others insist the answer depends on the reasons for such preferences—if it's based in negative cultural stereotypes, the preference is racist. Still others suggest racial preferences are okay, but shouldn't be announced, and some argue that racial preferences have *nothing* to do with racism, end of argument.

Physical attraction is always in the mix when these discussions wear on. Many confess that they find themselves genuinely *not attracted* to men or women of certain racial groups. And most seem to agree that attraction isn't something an individual can control. Thus, it can be seen as less controversial to state that "I tend not to be attracted to women or men from a certain racial background" than "I will not date a person from this racial background." Commenters quickly point out that the elusive concept of attraction is socially constructed by arbitrary and often racist beauty standards, while others defend preferences by insisting that dating is a special or "privileged" domain in which nobody should be shamed for whom they date and don't date. Others emphasize that these preferences *change* and suggest that, in their experience, physical attraction may be "learned" and commonly held beliefs invalidated.

A study of more than two thousand Australian men provides some insight. In this survey only 34 percent agreed that indicating a racial preference in a dating profile was a form of racism; however, analysis showed a positive correlation between indicating a race preference on one's own profile and having lower racial tolerance (measured on the Quick Discrimination Index).[12] In other words, one's racial preference in dating *is* correlated with overall racial attitudes.

Resistance to the notion that racial preferences are racist likely comes from an inability to reconcile these preferences with one's nonracist, or even antiracist, values outside of dating. Such inconsistency is not uncommon. Even the most progressive White Americans often make personal, self-interested decisions that go against the public values they hold. From sending their children to private schools to living in "safe" neighborhoods, paying for college, or passing on their wealth, their "private" decisions sustain racial inequality. What is unique about dating is that racial discrimination is personal and visible. There is a human face associated with every invitation and rejection. As our interviewees told us, dating is a domain where some discover a direct exercise of power, while others are surprised to find how little power they have. For many this power differential is particularly acute because they grew up thinking the world was "postracial" and they were not racist.

We have also illustrated how these preferences mean very different things to Whites and to people of color. For Whites, resistance to outdating takes on particular meaning, given that the privilege of Whiteness shapes cultural notions of beauty and attractiveness. People of color do not have the same power to impose their standards on society as a whole, nor do they have the same influence when they reinforce harmful stereotypes by rejecting entire groups of people. Racially marginalized groups may resist or accommodate these hierarchies in profound ways through their dating choices. To them dating within one's group may signal resistance to a White racial frame. But it can also be an accommodation to the pervasive anti-Blackness that is often used to keep minority women from crossing color lines. In this sense racial preferences are complicated. They are reflective of power dynamics embedded in hierarchies, and their reproduction at the micro, interactional level is profoundly consequential.

This book has argued that whom people date and form unions with is a decision that sits at the root of any racial system. While racial divides can still be maintained even with equal opportunity in housing, education, and employment, greater openness in forming intimate relationships would fundamentally erode existing categories and challenge the crux of the system. This is especially true, given studies showing that preferences in sexual partners turns out to be a *learned, conditioning* process, where the characteristics of one's first sexual partner may powerfully predict future partner preferences.[13]

The fallacy that intimate racial behavior is divorced from the political must be rejected. This will also benefit racially marginalized groups who may self-discipline toward endogamy. Our aim isn't to discount the reasons behind endogamy—whether it's aimed at cultural preservation or resistance to a racially stratified society—but to push us *all* to interrogate and dismantle the constraints that all marginalized groups face when searching for a mate. Racial preferences were historically borne out of domination and perpetuated through law and violence. They are maintained by social and structural inequality made evident in the imbalances we see in housing, workplaces, schools, law enforcement, and cultural representation. Endogamy feels so critical to many marginalized communities, who seek understanding and solace from racial fetishization and demonization via untroubled interactions with same-race daters.

Interacting with others of the same race is simply more comfortable, a default, many daters told us. However, this does not alter the fact that racial avoidance, instead of overt hostility, generates and sustains multiple forms of racial inequality in the contemporary United States. Our unexamined desires and tastes are not benign. Intermarriage between Asian women and U.S. soldiers during the Vietnam War, Black women and Chinese men in the Mississippi Delta, and Mexican women and Black men in colonial Texas indicate that our so-called preferences are plastic and can change when our social context changes. It may not be our intention to have absorbed societal racial preferences, but we *can* be intentional about acknowledging and not cultivating them.

Who we decide to pursue personal relationships with, be it marriage or a brief encounter at a party, is one of the last visible threads sustaining the racial hierarchy now that public racial discrimination is no longer legitimated. The commodifying process of online dating has made the existence of sexual racism undeniable—and our complicity in the process has made it virtually acceptable and commonplace. In this light, searching for a partner is itself a process of remaking race. While it may not be our fault directly if we have a racial preference, it is our responsibility to examine our preferences and decide whether to perpetuate or disrupt them. Are we willing to question why we might have such preferences and what they mean about our relative positions within hierarchies that privilege some and not others? As Antonio Gramsci pointed out about cultural hegemony, systems of power do not solely operate based on force or law but also through our own consent to internalized ideology.[14] The history of antimiscegenation in the United States and its racial logic are a kind of "knowledge" produced by a deeply painful, discriminatory, and cruelly weaponized sentiment, and they continue to infiltrate today's social norms, bureaucratic procedures, and organizational practices. It is up to every one of us to carefully consider how the unique features of online dating are newly reanimating the past in our innermost most private lives.

Acknowledgments

This book was not always an easy one to write, and we found ourselves frequently grappling with the hard truths that emerged from the data. We each came into the project from different perspectives and varying experiences. We often disagreed, engaged in heated discussions, and sometimes called out one another's blind spots. The book is that much stronger for it.

The Dating Divide was written over a number of years and from a number of locations, spanning from Cape Town, Paris, and Lisbon and back to our respective hometowns of Raleigh, Amherst, and Austin. We thank our institutions for the provision of internal funds for the researching of this book. Specifically, we are grateful for course releases and the sabbatical given by North Carolina State University and the University of Massachusetts to Celeste and Jen so that they could undertake the qualitative phase of this project and devote their time to writing this book. Ken thanks Christine Williams for pitching the project to the University of California Press, as well as the University of Texas and Sciences Po for their support.

With the deepest of gratitude, we tip our hats to the many individuals who contributed to this project: Rodrigo Dominguez Villegas, the UMass graduate RA who helped Celeste and Jen conduct interviews; Alyssa

Alexander and Janelle Perez, the NC State RAs who helped code the data; Cilka Bidwell, the UMass undergraduate RA who assisted with reference organization and bibliography building; UC Press and three peer reviewers, who gave us excellent feedback; Chris Lura and Letta Page, whose snappy editing helped us knit together our different writing voices (if you by some chance found this book difficult to read, you should have seen it before they got their hands on it). We are indebted to Janice Irvine, Marc Guillaume, Susan Healey Hickes, and Karina Jamileth Arévalo, all of whom commented on various chapter drafts; to our friends and family members, who have long since given up asking when that damn book would finally be done; to the millions of anonymous online daters, whose digital footprints guided us to this destination; and, most of all, to the many people we interviewed who freely gave their time and unique voices to this work. To all of you, we thank you.

Appendix

DATA AND METHODS

QUANTITATIVE DATA

Unless otherwise specified, the quantitative analysis presented in the book draws on data from one of the largest U.S. dating websites. Our data-sharing agreement does not allow us to disclose the website's name, but it has millions of active users. Like other dating websites, its registered users can set up a profile, view other users' profiles, and contact one another through a site-based instant messaging system. Most profiles contain basic information such as sex, sexual orientation, geographic location, age, race, height, body type, religion, language, lifestyle, and socioeconomic status, as well as photographs and short essays. Because of privacy concerns, we obtained most but not all of the information for these profiles; photographs, written essays, and detailed geographic location information were all withheld. Unlike other websites that require membership fees to view or contact other users, this website allows users to search, view, and contact other users for free. It should also be noted that this website does not select what profiles to show by race. The only criteria used to select which profiles to display are age, sexual orientation, and a matching score derived from personality questions.

There are some clear limitations when using these data. Our sample is not representative of the U.S. population. While we had access to the web of messaging within the platform, we could not access the content of those messages nor photos of the site's users. And these exchanges are obviously not as significant as marital and cohabiting relationships. However, examining the interactions among internet daters gave us several analytic advantages. First, this data set contains actual interactions among daters, which allowed us to observe what people do instead of what people say. Second, since our analysis is limited to a definite population, we could see how race determines the likelihood of interaction in a bounded probability space. Third, because all the variables were extracted from digital records, our data set is largely immune to measurement issues such as social desirability bias and recall errors. Fourth, the large data set enabled us to explore the interaction among minority groups. Importantly, because we had access to almost as much information as the users on the website, we are confident that our estimates are less biased by unobserved variables.

While some may wonder how much we can learn about U.S. society from a dating website, online dating has clearly transformed from a foreign concept to a common practice, as we discuss at the end of chapter 2. Generally speaking, internet daters tend to be younger and of higher socioeconomic status.[1] But the digital divide is rapidly decreasing. Among all U.S. Americans aged eighteen to forty-nine, 91 percent report using the internet.[2] Furthermore, even though dating apps such as Tinder have gained media attention due to their novelty, dating websites remain the main interface used by internet daters.[3]

Compared to other dating sites, our particular site attracts a younger and more educated clientele. If age and education status indicate more liberal attitudes, we expect the daters in our sample to have *more inclusive* racial preferences than the U.S. population in general. Moreover, there is also selection into different websites. Internet daters who use mainstream dating websites are likely to be more open to dating across racial lines than those who use ethnic dating websites exclusively. Taking all this into account, we are likely to *underestimate the significance of racial preferences in the U.S. dating market.*

Our original data set includes approximately nine million registered users worldwide and two hundred million messages sent from November 2003 to October 2010. We filtered users through several steps. First, we focused on those who reside in the twenty largest metropolitan areas in the United States. This allowed us to reconstruct their opportunity structure, bringing the sample size down to about three million daters. Second, we excluded users who did not send or receive at least one message, who did not upload at least one photograph, who listed their birth year later than 1992 or earlier than 1911, or who fit the profile of spammer users (e.g., not answering any personality questions, being flagged by other users, having unusual messaging patterns, and being deleted in less than an hour). As is common on free membership websites, some users did not actively engage with or even return to the website after their initial registration, and other profiles are likely to be fake identities created by spammers. Third, we excluded daters who indicated they were looking only for casual sex or platonic relationships to ensure that the activities we analyzed were related to romantic interests.

We identified users' racial identity with what they reported on their personal profiles. Users have ten options when they create their profiles: Asian, Middle Eastern, Black, Native American, Indian, Pacific Islander, Hispanic/Latino, White, Other, and Undeclared. Users can check as many options as they prefer or skip reporting. We categorized those who checked more than one box as multiracial and those who skipped as undeclared. We analyzed all the initial messages exchanged among these groups: Asian, Black, Latino (labeled as Hispanic/Latino on the website), White, Asian-White, Black-White, and Hispanic-White. Though Americans of East Indian origin are commonly classified as Asian in official statistics, we did not combine Indians with Asian groups because South Asians tend to have very different experiences from East Asians. We didn't examine non-White multiracial groups owing to the small sample size; however, over 80 percent of multiracial Americans report White as part of their ethnic composition, and 93 percent of multiracials report being biracial (as we discuss in chapter 8).

Our main analytic inquiry focused on how dyadic interaction is simultaneously shaped by each individual's demographic and personal characteristics. The variables used in our regression analyses can be viewed in table A.1. We examined how the likelihood of sending and responding to an initial message among daters varies by daters' racial background, while taking all their characteristics into account. To examine the relative likelihood of sending an initial message, we randomly sampled a subset of users and reconstructed their opportunity structure on the website, generating all probable dyads on the website for this subset of users. We then merged these dyads with the initial messages that were actually sent, yielding a binary outcome in which "one" indicates that the probable dyad was realized and "zero" otherwise.

Since interaction decisions are nested within individuals, a dependence structure was expected. We thus modeled both sending and responding behaviors by fitting a series of generalized estimating equations with the logit link function and an exchangeable correlation structure. We controlled for the following confounding factors of these covariate groupings: demographic information, lifestyle, socioeconomic status, degree of online engagement (including total time spent on the website), account lifetime (from registration to the most recent login), number of photographs uploaded, and personality questions answered on the website.

QUALITATIVE DATA

The quantitative analyses elucidate general trends across daters of different backgrounds, but we sought to more fully understand how these outcomes are created through microgenerated and unobservable processes. We drew from

Table A.1 Descriptive Statistics from Online-Dating Website, Men and Women

Characteristic	Men	Women
Sexual Orientation		
Straight	0.89	0.94
Gay	0.11	0.06
Race		
Asian	0.04	0.05
Black	0.04	0.05
Latino/a	0.07	0.07
White	0.80	0.79
White-Black	0.00	0.01
White-Asian	0.01	0.01
White-Latino/a	0.03	0.03
Number of messages sent	8.20	3.81
SD	35.85	13.91
Number of messages received	4.03	8.48
SD	5.82	10.69
Age	30.08	29.37
SD	8.85	9.04
Height (cm)	179.41	165.40
SD	7.46	7.11
Body Type		
Thin	0.09	0.11
Overweight	0.07	0.21
Average	0.22	0.20
Fit	0.31	0.14
Not reported	0.32	0.34
Education		
High school	0.35	0.35
Some college	0.05	0.04
College	0.37	0.38
Professional	0.10	0.12
Not reported	0.12	0.11
Income		
<$20,000	0.07	0.07
$20,000–50,000	0.15	0.10

$50,000–80,000	0.07	0.03
$80,000–150,000	0.04	0.01
>$150,000	0.02	0.01
Not reported	0.64	0.78
Smoking		
Yes	0.25	0.24
No	0.70	0.71
Not reported	0.05	0.05
Drinking		
Often	0.13	0.13
Socially	0.62	0.64
Rarely	0.14	0.14
Not at all	0.08	0.06
Not reported	0.03	0.03
Drug Use		
Sometimes	0.10	0.07
Never	0.75	0.79
Not reported	0.15	0.14
Parental Status		
Has children	0.11	0.15
Likes children	0.49	0.50
Doesn't want children	0.09	0.09
Not reported	0.32	0.26
Region		
Northeast	0.34	0.38
Southeast	0.09	0.09
Midwest	0.14	0.14
West	0.32	0.30
Southwest	0.10	0.09
Online Activity		
Questions answered	252.50	190.91
Time online	141.97	145.90
Photos uploaded	4.33	4.22
Account age	420.06	298.49
N	275292.00	257431.00

NOTE: For specific descriptive breakdowns of the variables by each gender, sexual preference and racial group, link to online tables O12A–D at www.ucpress.edu/9780520293458.

Institutional Review Board–approved interview data to uncover the mechanisms that link important variables in online dating (i.e., gender, sexuality, class, and race) by assessing daters' accounts. Indeed, interviews encourage people to make meaning and sense of the various interactional dynamics nested within their online-dating behaviors. This iterative process reveals the emotional and cultural dimensions of social experience that are otherwise difficult to detect in observational studies.[4] Further, open-ended questions can elicit narratives that enable participants to signal resistance to dominant cultural images or "master narratives" in a way that is socially productive. Participants use and construct stories to engage in identity work that may disrupt widely held dehumanizing and hegemonic stories about marginalized groups. In our research we used the interview as a methodological tool to capture how participants' narratives reflect both of these processes of story making.[5]

Between 2017 and 2019 Celeste Vaughan Curington, Jennifer Lundquist, and research assistant Rodrigo Dominguez Villegas collected seventy-seven interviews with online daters from different regions, races, gender identities, and sexual preferences. These were not the same online daters whose data was analyzed in the quantitative models. Given that some members of the target population are conventionally seen as hard to reach (racial and sexual minorities) and that the research is considered sensitive in that it inquiries about dating behaviors, respondents were recruited through a variety of methods. We initially sent out a general call and flyers for participants through university listservs across states, and we posted flyers on Reddit threads, Facebook pages, and Twitter pages devoted to online dating. We assembled potential leads from these inquiries, and participants referred others. This recruitment material was oriented toward a general population of online daters, but we specified that we were seeking participants from "a variety of racial and ethnic backgrounds and gender identities."

During the initial stages of recruitment, our strategy primarily produced White participants, and women were generally more likely than men to participate. As those who study the intimate experiences of ethnic minorities note, dating is an especially sensitive topic for these groups because of the pervasiveness of gendered and racialized controlling images and stereotypes that demean racialized minorities sexual and dating practices.[6] Thus, we sent out targeted calls and distributed targeted flyers through listservs across the country, advertising our interest in talking to minority online daters, and we posted the materials on social-media pages that served more racially diverse audiences. The combination of these two sampling methods ensured that multiple networks were accessed, to avoid recruiting participants from similar social circles. We offered respondents their choice of interviewers from a set of experienced researchers: a straight Black woman, a straight White woman, and a gay Latino man, ranging in age from late twenties to forties. Since our goal was to augment the large-scale quantitative data to elucidate how the intersection of identity is experienced in the online-dating venue, we aimed at gathering detailed, rather than generalizable, data about the quotidian experience and participant-driven meaning making of online dating across racial, ethnic, and gender status.

On average participants were twenty-seven years old and had online dated for three to five years. Approximately 30 percent of interview respondents were current college students, and 50 percent had completed a bachelor's or master's degree, a reflection of the educated clientele of the online-dating website from which we draw our quantitative data. Twenty-four participants identified as White, eleven as Latino/a, fourteen as Black, eleven as Asian, fifteen as multiracial/mixed-race, and two as Other. As can be seen in table A.2, 28 percent of the sample identified as lesbian, gay, bisexual, pansexual, or queer. Approximately 54 percent of all participants identified as women, 42 percent as men, and 3 percent as gender nonbinary. The numbers were split relatively evenly by gender among racial subgroups.

Interviews lasted between one and two hours and were conducted in person in an interviewer's office, by phone, or via webcast video. We designed a semistructured interview protocol to ensure reliable, comparable data across all three interviewers. The interviewers documented nonverbal cues, such as body language and expressions, as we asked participants to reflect on what led them to online dating, how they make sense of their experiences interacting with others through an online-dating website or application, what preferences they have among potential mates, and how they make sense of those preferences. The inclusion of open-ended questions guided, but did not bind, discussions. Interviews typically began with respondents' demographic characteristics, such as their racial and ethnic background, place of birth, gender identity, and identity claims, then proceeded to participants loosely describing their "online-dating story"; that is, we asked them to "tell us the story of how [they] got involved in online dating." Through this inquiry we adjusted the question order and context by referring to each respondent's nuanced stories. Beginning with an open, overview question emphasizing storytelling was a way to set the tone for the interview such that respondents' own subjective experience and interpretation of those experiences were granted primacy. This alleviated anxiety and strengthened the researcher-respondent relationship. Sometimes daters would show us their online-dating profiles to help drive home a point they wanted to make or read aloud to us from online-dating interactions they had.

Later in the interview we asked how participants navigate, resist, or accommodate behavioral expectations in online dating; how they construct an online-dating persona; whether they ever felt discriminated against or harassed by other online daters; and whether their body, skin color, racial background, or gender identity were ever brought up in conversations with other daters. We asked respondents how they made sense of their own (if any) and others' preferences in

Table A.2	Interview Participant Demographic Characteristics N = 77	

Characteristic	Percent
Race	
Black	18.4
White	31.6
Latino/a	14.5
Asian	13.2
Multiracial	19.7
Other	2.6
Mean age	
18–21	28.0
22–29	42.0
30–39	23.0
40–49	4.0
50–59	3.0
Sexual preference	
Straight/heterosexual	72.0
Lesbian/gay/bisexual/pansexual/queer	28.0
Highest level of education	
Less than high school/GED	1.3
High school/GED	2.0
Some college/associates	4.0
Current college student	34.0
Bachelor's/master's degree	50.7
Advanced degree (PhD, MD, JD)	8.0
Marital status	
Single	90.7
Married	2.7
Divorced	5.3
Widowed	1.3

NOTE: The mean age is 27.3.

online dating, inviting them to describe their searching process, then narrowing the inquiries to respondents' interpretations of others' preferences. These questions invited participants to report their own experiences with regard to identity, racial appearance, and treatment by others, while follow-up probes encouraged participants to provide narratives regarding the ways they interpreted and responded to such experiences. We carefully structured interview questions in a way that did not assume race or gender were the most salient categories but rather allowed participants to reflect on how, if at all, these categories surfaced in any way in online dating.

In most interviews participants rather than interviewers introduced the topic of race organically as they discussed their own or others' preferences or their interactions with other online daters. Still, some participants were reluctant, while others readily discussed racial preferences in online dating—where they come from, why some people (including themselves) have them, and so on. To address this disconnect, toward the end of the interview we asked respondents to share their opinions on previous sociological research findings and some of the narratives we had been hearing throughout interviews, for example, "Some studies have shown that minority daters are less likely than White daters to get interest from other daters. What do you think of this? Do you think many daters have race preferences in whom they would like to date or whom they find most attractive?" These questions helped respondents reflect on the idea of racial preferences and enabled us to sharpen relevant preference-related questions as we finished the interview.

In addition to asking participants to share their own description of how, if at all, they initiated a sorting mechanism in online dating, we also employed a "counter-narrative" methodological approach by asking participants to "speak back" to some of the common race-, gender-, and dating-related narratives we heard throughout interviews: "I'm going to state some common stereotypes about interracial dating, and I'd like you to tell me whether you think they are true or not and why. In responding, I'd like you to think first in terms of dating generally and second about internet dating in particular. If you have never heard the stereotype before or have no opinion, skip."[7] A counternarrative methodology allows for the exploration of the stories people tell that resist dominant cultural narratives, because speakers employ oppositional knowledge to "expose the construction of the dominant story by suggesting how else it could be told."[8]

We audio-recorded all interviews, and all members of the research team wrote field notes after the conclusion of interviews. This allowed the team to document nonverbal cues that would not be captured in transcripts. All interview data was transcribed through professional transcription services, and we utilized pseudonyms in research reporting to protect identities. We obscured or omitted demographic information that could identify participants. Quoted material from sixty-eight participants appear throughout the chapters. In some cases, to protect identities for small N groups, individual respondents who are quoted multiple times appear under different pseudonyms in different chapters of the work.

Celeste Vaughan Curington, along with research assistants Alyssa Alexander and Janelle Perez, entered data from interviews into the software program NVivo and coded the data line by line, analyzing the transcripts iteratively. The research team aggregated codes thematically by grouping material around substantive emergent themes, first at broad levels and then in more specific categories within those broad levels.[9] The research team met regularly throughout data collection and analyses to check for intercoder reliability.

Interviews

Alicia—thirty, cis woman, Black, heterosexual, webcast video interview, South

Amanda—twenty-one, cis woman, White, heterosexual, in-person interview, Northeast

Amber—twenty-five, cis woman, Black, heterosexual, phone interview, mid-Atlantic

Ana—twenty-eight, cis woman, Asian, heterosexual, phone interview, Northeast

Andrew—forty-five, cis man, Latino-White, heterosexual, phone interview, mid-Atlantic

Anthony—twenty-three, cis man, Black-Asian, queer, phone interview, mid-Atlantic

Arthur—twenty-seven, cis man, Asian, heterosexual, phone interview, Northeast

Ben—twenty-five, cis man, Black-Asian, queer, webcast video interview, Northeast

Beth—twenty-seven, cis woman, White, heterosexual, phone interview, mid-Atlantic

Bianca—twenty-nine, cis woman, Latina, heterosexual, in-person interview, Northeast

Carlos—twenty-eight, cis man, Latino, gay, phone interview, mid-Atlantic

Carmen—twenty-seven, cis woman, Latina, heterosexual, webcast video interview, mid-Atlantic

Charlotte—fifty, cis woman, White, heterosexual, phone interview, mid-Atlantic

Clara—twenty-one, cis woman, White, bisexual, in-person interview, Northeast

Connor—twenty-two, cis man, White, heterosexual, webcast video interview, South

Cruz—twenty-nine, cis woman, Latina, lesbian and queer, in-person interview, mid-Atlantic

Damian—twenty-four, cis man, Black, gay, in-person interview, Northeast

Deborah—twenty-six, cis woman, Black, heterosexual, phone interview, Northeast

Derick—twenty-eight, cis man, Black, heterosexual, webcast video interview, Northeast

Gabriela—twenty-nine, cis woman, Latina, bisexual, phone interview, mid-Atlantic

George—thirty-four, cis man, Black-White, heterosexual, webcast video interview, South

Helena—twenty-one, cis woman, Latina-White, heterosexual, in-person interview, Northeast

Henry—twenty-four, cis man, Asian, heterosexual, in-person interview, Northeast

Janice—thirty-one, cis woman, Black, heterosexual, webcast video interview, mid-Atlantic

Jason—twenty-nine, cis man, Asian-White, heterosexual, phone interview, mid-Atlantic

Javier—twenty-eight, cis man, Latino, heterosexual, in-person interview, mid-Atlantic

Jazmín—twenty-seven, cis woman, Latina, heterosexual, in-person interview, Northeast

John—thirty, Asian, cis man, heterosexual, webcast video interview, mid-Atlantic

Jordan—twenty-seven, cis man, Black, heterosexual, webcast video interview, mid-Atlantic

Josie—nineteen, cis woman, White, bisexual, in-person interview, Northeast

J. T. Tran—thirty-nine, cis man, Asian, heterosexual, phone interview, West (not anonymized)

Kayla—twenty-seven, cis woman, Black-White, bisexual, phone interview, South

Keisha—twenty-nine, cis woman, Black, heterosexual, webcast video interview, mid-Atlantic

Kevon—thirty, cis man, Indo-Caribbean, heterosexual, webcast video interview, mid-Atlantic

Levi—twenty, trans man White, bisexual, phone interview, Northeast

Linda—twenty-six, cis woman, Black-White, heterosexual, phone interview, mid-Atlantic

Linh—twenty-two, cis woman, Asian, queer, in-person interview, Northeast

Lisa—eighteen, cis woman, Asian, heterosexual, webcast video interview, West

Lucas—twenty-six, cis man, Black, heterosexual, webcast video interview, Northeast

Mai—thirty, cis woman, Asian, heterosexual, phone interview, Midwest

Mariana—thirty, cis woman, Latina, bisexual, webcast video interview, mid-Atlantic

Marvin—twenty-three, cis man, Black, queer, phone interview, mid-Atlantic

Mary—twenty, cis woman, White, bisexual, in-person interview, Northeast

Mathew—twenty-eight, cis man, Asian-White, queer, webcast video interview, Midwest

Michael—thirty-four, cis man, Black-White, heterosexual, webcast video interview, West

Miguel—thirty-two, cis man, Latino, heterosexual, phone interview, mid-Atlantic

Monica—thirty-three, cis woman, Black, heterosexual, in-person interview, Northeast

Natalie—twenty-two, cis woman, White, heterosexual, in-person interview, Northeast

Nena—thirty-two, cis woman, Black, heterosexual, webcast video interview, Southeast

Paul—thirty, cis man, Latino-White, heterosexual, in-person interview, Northeast

Rae—eighteen, cis woman, Asian, heterosexual, phone interview, West

Raúl—twenty-eight, cis man, Latino, gay and queer, phone interview, Northeast

Raymond—thirty-one, cis man, White, heterosexual, in-person interview, Northeast

Ricky—thirty, Latino, cis man, heterosexual, phone interview, mid-Atlantic

Robert—twenty-two, cis man, Black, heterosexual, in-person interview, South

Rodrigo—forty, cis man, Latino-White, heterosexual, webcast video interview, Northeast

Roger—thirty-one, cis man, Latino, heterosexual, in-person interview, Northeast

Sai—nineteen, cis man, Asian-White, heterosexual, phone interview, mid-Atlantic

Sam—twenty-one, cis man, White, heterosexual, in-person interview, Northeast

Samantha—twenty, cis woman, White, lesbian, webcast video interview, Northeast

Sandra—twenty-six, cis woman, Black, bisexual, webcast video interview, mid-Atlantic

Sanjay—thirty-nine, cis man, Asian, heterosexual, phone interview, Northeast

Sara—twenty, cis woman, Latina-White, heterosexual, phone interview, mid-Atlantic

Seila—twenty-four, cis woman, Black-White, heterosexual, phone interview, mid-Atlantic

Sky—twenty-four, nonbinary, White, queer, phone interview, mid-Atlantic

Sonya—twenty-one, cis woman, Latina-White, heterosexual, in-person interview, Northeast

Stacy—thirty-two, cis woman, Asian-White, bisexual, webcast video interview, West

Stephen—twenty-five, cis man, Latino-Black, queer, phone interview, mid-Atlantic

Sunan—twenty-six, cis man, Asian, heterosexual, phone interview, Northeast

Tim—twenty-three, cis man, Asian, heterosexual, in-person interview, Northeast

Tom—twenty-nine, cis man, White, heterosexual, webcast video interview, West

Tony—twenty-one, cis man, White, heterosexual, phone interview, Northeast

Trevor—twenty-two, cis man, Black, queer, webcast video interview, Northeast

Wei—twenty-nine, cis man, Asian, gay, webcast video interview, Southwest

Wen—twenty-eight, cis woman, Asian, heterosexual, webcast video interview, Midwest

William—twenty-seven, cis man, White, heterosexual, phone interview, mid-Atlantic

Yesenia—twenty-eight, cis woman, Latina, heterosexual, webcast video interview, mid-Atlantic

Zenón—twenty-seven, cis man, Latino, heterosexual, phone interview, West

Notes

INTRODUCTION

1. We capitalize the terms *Black* and *White* in this book in accord with the American Psychological Association's style-manual recommendations.

2. This process has become known as the online disinhibition effect. See Suler, "Online Disinhibition Effect."

3. Goyette, "Cheerios Commercial." Many more comments were positive than negative, but the large minority of bigoted commentary surprised many.

4. E. Kim, "Old Navy Ad."

5. See the vitriolic online reaction to George Yancy's relatively restrained op-ed about White privilege and racism, described in *Backlash*.

6. Collins, *Black Sexual Politics*.

7. Bedi, *Private Racism*, and Benjamin, *Race after Technology*, 6.

8. B. Robinson, "Personal Preference."

9. See Bedi, *Private Racism;* Noble, *Algorithms of Oppression;* and Ruha, *Race after Technology*.

10. An early scale created to quantify prejudice was Emory Bogardus's social distance scale, which placed intermarriage at the end of the spectrum of openness to outgroups; see Bogardus, "Social Distance Scale." Intermarriage also features in Milton Gordon's seven stages of assimilation scale; see Gordon, *Assimilation in American Life*.

11. Gordon, *Assimilation in American Life;* Blau, Beeker, and Fitzpatrick, "Intersecting Social Affiliations."

12. Livingston and Brown, "Intermarriage in the U.S."

13. The fact that the U.S. Census defines Latinos/as as an ethnicity instead of a race is a good example of the social construction of race. More U.S. Latinos/as define themselves as racially White than any other race category; see Humes, Jones, and Ramirez, *Overview of Race.*

14. Blackwell and Lichter, "Homogamy among Dating."

15. Bell and Hartmann, "Diversity in Everyday Discourse."

16. Sharkey, *Stuck in Place;* Massey and Denton, *American Apartheid.*

17. See Acs et al., *Cost of Segregation.*

18. On a hopeful note, a well-known social science theory posits that the lack of social contact with different groups can foster prejudice and bigotry, yet more contact reduces such sentiment; see Allport, *Nature of Prejudice;* and Sigelman and Welch, "Contact Hypothesis Revisited." Recent studies testing this hypothesis have shown that, in fact, sustained social contact improves race relations in a multitude of ways; see Emerson, Kimbro, and Yancey, "Contact Theory Extended"; and Pettigrew and Tropp, "Meta-analytic Test."

19. Dovidio and Gaertner, "Aversive Racism."

20. Omi and Winant, *Racial Formation;* Collins, *Black Sexual Politics;* Nemoto, "Climbing the Hierarchy"; Nemoto, "Intimacy"; Kao, Balistreri, and Joyner, "Asian American Men."

21. Feagin, *White Racial Frame.*

22. Chou, *Asian American Sexual Politics;* Collins, *Black Sexual Politics.*

23. Yet theories on gendered racial formation and the White frame explain largely only the *White* gaze. While other groups may internalize the dominant group's cultural ideologies, there is evidence that different ethnic groups have their own hierarchies of desirability that may differ. This is something that we explicitly examine in this book.

24. Collins, *Black Sexual Politics;* Nagel, "Ethnicity and Sexuality."

25. See Godbeer, *Sexual Revolution;* and Berkhofer, *White Man's Indian.*

26. Hartman, *Scenes of Subjection.*

27. Perea, "Black/White Binary Paradigm."

28. Sexton, "People-of-Color-Blindness," 48.

29. Holland, *Erotic Life of Racism.*

30. "Results from the 1860 Census."

31. Lane, *White Genocide Manifesto.* The White genocide threat movement took on new life in 1995 through a conspiracy theory developed by neo-Nazi David Lane, who argued that state policies around diversity and racial integration, abortion, low-fertility rates, farmland reform, immigration, and so on are promoted with the explicit aim of replacing majority-White populations.

32. Wallenstein, *Tell the Court.*

33. The Nuremburg Laws criminalized marriage and intimate relations between Jewish and non-Jewish Germans, while the Prohibition of Mixed Mar-

riages and the Immorality Acts similarly prohibited cross-racial unions among South Africans. See Whitman, *Hitler's American Model;* and Giliomee, "Making of the Apartheid Plan."

34. It is likely that adoption, foster care, and sperm and egg–donation agencies also solicit their clients' racial preferences in children, another area of society considered to be highly private, but such application data are generally not publicly accessible on the web in the way that online-dating profiles are.

35. Bonilla-Silva, *Racism without Racists.*

36. Bedi, *Private Racism.*

37. Combahee River Collective, "A Black Feminist Statement"; A. Davis, "Rape, Racism"; MacKinnon, *Feminism Unmodified,* 100.

38. Crenshaw, "Mapping the Margins," 1242.

39. Hanisch, "Personal Is Political," in Crow, *Radical Feminism.*

40. Stember, *Sexual Racism.* For internet content, see, for example, B. Robinson, "Personal Preference."

41. Bedi, *Private Racism;* Bedi, "Sexual Racism"; Brooks, *Unequal Desires;* Collins, *Black Sexual Politics;* Cottom, *Thick;* R. Robinson, "Structural Dimensions."

42. Hennessy, *Profit and Pleasure.*

43. Roberts, "Loving v. Virginia."

44. Ibid.

45. Sass, "Mixed Schools," 8.

CHAPTER 1. WHERE HATE TRUMPS LOVE

1. Bailey and Tolnay, *Lynched.*

2. Stampp, *Peculiar Institution;* Bailey and Tolnay, *Lynched.*

3. Jordan, *White over Black.*

4. Pascoe, *What Comes Naturally,* 19, 293.

5. Gutman, *Black Family.*

6. Roediger, *Wages of Whiteness.*

7. Kitch, *Specter of Sex.*

8. Pascoe, *What Comes Naturally.*

9. Pascoe, *What Comes Naturally;* Spillers, "Mama's Baby, Papa's Maybe."

10. Getman, "Sexual Control," 144.

11. Collins, *Black Sexual Politics;* Roberts, *Killing the Black Body.*

12. Sack and Blinder, "Jurors Hear"; Berry and Blassingame, *Long Memory.*

13. Getman, "Sexual Control."

14. Grant, *Passing,* pt. 1, ch. 2.

15. Hodes, *White Women, Black Men.*

16. Wells, *Southern Horrors.*

17. McGuire, *Dark End.*

18. D'Emilio and Freedman, *Intimate Matters.*

19. See Dollard, *Caste and Class,* 93.

20. Hirshman, *Reckoning.*

21. Croly, *Miscegenation.*

22. Pascoe, *What Comes Naturally.*

23. Thomas, "Miscegenation Ball."

24. Elliott, "Telling the Difference."

25. Grant, *Passing,* ch. 4.

26. Spiro, *Defending the Master Race.*

27. Grant, *Passing.*

28. During the nineteenth century the Virginia legislature had defined that a person with one-eighth or less African ancestry was White; see F. Davis, *Who Is Black?*

29. Primary documents of the act can be accessed in Plecker, *New Virginia Law.*

30. As of 1910 non-Whiteness was defined in Virginia as having one-sixteenth or greater non-White heritage; see Wolfe, "Racial Integrity Laws."

31. Pascoe, *What Comes Naturally.*

32. Kitch, *Specter of Sex.*

33. C. Kim, "Racial Triangulation," 109.

34. Moran, "Proper Stranger."

35. Jung, *Coolies and Cane.*

36. Takaki, *Strangers,* 217.

37. "Yellow Terror."

38. Peffer, "Forbidden Families," 28; Le Espiritu, *Asian American Women;* Parreñas and Tam, "Derivative Status," in Salazar Parrenas, *Force of Domesticity,* 110–33.

39. Peffer, "Forbidden Families," 28.

40. Hing, *Making and Remaking.* Because Japan was a rising power and trade partner, it was politically untenable for the United States to treat Japanese immigrants in the way it had treated Chinese immigrants. This legislation's "compromise" resulted in the phenomenon of "picture brides," as discussed in chapter 3.

41. Koshy, *Sexual Naturalization.*

42. Abrams, "Polygamy, Prostitution."

43. Luibhéid, *Entry Denied.*

44. Teng, *Eurasian.*

45. "Our Chinese Colony."

46. Koshy, *Sexual Naturalization.*

47. Treitler, *Ethnic Project,* 92.

48. Loewen, *Mississippi Chinese.*

49. Craver, *Impact of Intimacy*, 27–29.

50. Foley, *White Scourge*.

51. Ibid., 19.

52. Foley, *White Scourge*; Kitch, *Specter of Sex*.

53. Kitch, *Specter of Sex*, 208.

54. Calavita, *Inside the State*.

55. Molina, *How Race Is Made*.

56. Ibid.

57. See Massey, Durand, and Malone, *Beyond Smoke and Mirrors*; and Ngai, "Architecture of Race."

58. See Lukens, *Quiet Victory*. From the 1970 census onward, "Hispanic origin" became an ethnicity, but never again a race; see Cohn, "Census History."

59. It is tempting for White Americans to call on such examples to illustrate how their national origin group overcame racism through hard work and assimilation; however, a brief period of racialized marginalization of coethnic Whites is not equivalent to the systematic and long-term disenfranchisement of African Americans under slavery, Jim Crow, and modern institutionalized anti-Black racism. We employ these examples mainly to demonstrate how race is socially constructed and can shift over time—for some groups more than others.

60. Waters, *Ethnic Options*.

61. Treitler, *Ethnic Project*.

62. Allen, *Invention*.

63. See Borsella, *On Persecution*; and Moses, *Lynching and Vigilantism*. For some time this was believed to be the largest mass lynching in U.S. history, although it appears that the largest mass lynching was actually two decades earlier, with the hanging of seventeen Chinese men and boys in Los Angeles. See Pfaelzer, *Driven Out*.

64. Treitler, *Ethnic Project*, 92.

65. Ngai, *Impossible Subjects*.

66. The origins of this incorporation spanned back to the eighteenth century, when citizenship was reserved only to "Free White persons" under the 1790 Nationality Act. United States Naturalization Law of 1790, 1 Stat. 103. This act was later broadened, after the passage of the Fourteenth Amendment, to include "Persons of African nativity or descent."

67. U.S. War Department, circular 179, June 8, 1942, sec. 1.

68. Pub. L. No. 271, 79th Cong., Ch. 591, 1st Sess. (December 28, 1945); 8 U.S.C. 232 (1945); 8 U.S.C. 204(a) (repealed 1952).

69. See Pub. L. No. 713, 79th Cong., 1st Sess. (August 9, 1945).

70. E. Lee, "Yellow Peril."

71. *Perez v. Sharp*, 32 Cal. 2d 711.

72. Pascoe, *What Comes Naturally*.

73. Myrdal, *American Dilemma*, 60–61.

74. Roberts, "Loving v. Virginia."

75. *Naim v. Naim*, 87 S.E. 2d 749, 756 (Va. 1955), quoted in Roberts, "Loving v. Virginia," 7.

76. Goldberg, *Racial State.*

77. "Alabama Interracial Marriage"; Yancey and Emerson, "Analysis of Resistance."

CHAPTER 2. FROM THE BACK PORCH TO THE
COMPUTER SCREEN

1. Hudson, *Marriage Guide.*

2. Indentured servants often could not marry or have children until after their contract ended, and, as discussed in chapter 1, exclusionary immigration policies and antimiscegenation laws effectively denied marriage and reproduction to Asians within the United States.

3. Roberts, *Killing the Black Body.*

4. Dill, "Our Mothers' Grief"; White, *Ar'n't I a Woman?*

5. A. Davis, *Women, Race, and Class;* Roberts, *Killing the Black Body.*

6. Hamer, "Slavery"; Hunter, *Bound in Wedlock*, 33; White, *Ar'n't I a Woman?*

7. Hunter, *Bound in Wedlock.*

8. Most free Black Americans lived in slave states, where their marriages often weren't legally protected.

9. Coontz, *Marriage, a History.*

10. Addams, *Spirit of Youth*, 43.

11. Cahn, *Sexual Reckonings*, 102.

12. W. Jones, *Recreation and Amusement.*

13. Griffin, "Black Feminists," 35.

14. E. Alexander, "Courtship Season"; Cooper, *Beyond Respectability.*

15. Hill, *Black Intimacies*, 116.

16. Dorce, "American Girl," 2.

17. D'Emilio and Freedman, *Documenting Intimate Matters.*

18. *1880 3Census.*

19. "Infographic."

20. See, for example, *Matrimonial News*, 1870–1901, C. G. Horton and Company, American Antiquarian Society, Historical Periodicals Collection, Chicago.

21. Enss, *Hearts West*, 28.

22. Wang, *Rise of Intermarriage.*

23. Spörlein, Schlueter, and van Tubergen, "Ethnic Intermarriage."

24. Enss, *Hearts West*, 59.

25. "Rachel Calof's Story."

26. Enss, *Hearts West*, 52.

27. Lasch, *Haven.*

28. Branch, *Opportunity Denied;* J. Jones, *Labor of Love.*

29. Glenn, "From Servitude to Service."

30. See D'Emilio and Freedman, *Documenting Intimate Matters.*

31. In *Cold Intimacies* Eva Illouz argues, in contrast to Max Weber and Karl Marx, that capitalism engenders the intertwining, rather than the separation, of the personal and the economic. This is an important distinction between early-stage effects of capitalism on intimacy compared to late-stage effects.

32. Weigel, *Labor of Love.*

33. "Love Is Costly," SM7.

34. D'Emilio, "Capitalism and Gay Identity," in Hansen and Garey, *Families in the U.S.,* 131–41.

35. Ghaziani, *There Goes the Gayborhood?*

36. Peiss, "Charity Girls."

37. See Bell, *White Slave Trade,* 110–11. Anxiety over the prospect of cross-racial sex and dating manifested itself in fears over alleged "White bondage," resulting in the White Slave Traffic Act. Under this act Black heavyweight champion Jack Johnson was arrested for an affair with a White woman in 1913 (posthumously pardoned in 2018).

38. Clement, *Love for Sale.*

39. Modell, *Into One's Own.*

40. Cahn, *Sexual Reckonings.*

41. Carter, "Fragile Blondes," cited in Ngô, *Imperial Blues.*

42. See W. Jones, *Recreation and Amusement,* 148, 122.

43. B. Bailey, *From Front Porch.* Dating practices aren't generally well documented with regard to subgroups. However, based on interviews conducted by E. Franklin Frazier of African American youth, gender norms around who asked and who treated may have been more interchangeable among Black teens, given Black women's greater labor force participation and Black men's systematically lower wages. See *Negro Youth.*

44. Modell, *Into One's Own.*

45. See Weigel, *Labor of Love.*

46. Hope, "Caucasian Female Body Hair."

47. Collins, *Black Sexual Politics,* 193.

48. Bogle, *Toms, Coons, Mulattoes, Mammies.*

49. Carbado, "Colorblind Intersectionality," 822.

50. Cottom, *Thick.*

51. Waller, "Rating and Dating Complex."

52. Herman, "'Going Steady' Complex."

53. Rosenfeld and Thomas, "Searching for a Mate."

54. Cashin, *Loving.*

55. Coontz, *The Way We Never Were.*

56. Gurley Brown, *Single Girl;* Friedan, *Feminine Mystique.*

57. Giddens, *Transformation of Intimacy.*

58. Lamont, *Mating Game.*

59. Wade, *American Hookup.*

60. Fletcher, "Campus Romance"; Greifinger, "What Happened to Dating?"; Levine, "Love on Vacation?"; Matthews Li, "Romance Went the Way"; Eshbaugh and Gute, "Hookups and Sexual Regret"; Stepp, *Unhooked.*

61. Spell, "Not Just Black."

62. See Lundquist and Curington, "Love Me Tinder."

63. See Schor, *Overworked American;* and Kuhn and Lozano, "Expanding Workweek?"

64. For example the video dating service Georgetown Connection cost an annual fee of $450, no small amount in 1983; see Sanoff, "19 Million Singles."

65. L. Newman, "Let's Hear It." Even by 2014 Miss Manners was still describing herself as "no advocate of dating services"; however, she had accepted by then that a large portion of her readership had a real need for her input on online-dating etiquette.

66. Grubman, "Cyberspace Date," C5.

67. McVicar, "Ivy Valentines," A-01.

68. See Nussbaum, "Are We a Match?"

69. S. Lee, "History of Online Dating."

70. Hindell, "Lurking Lovers."

71. A "family values" dating service that excludes LGBTQ daters, eHarmony was the first to do this. According to the founder, he was motivated by rising divorce rates in the United States and sought to use science to preventatively match compatible couples. See Slater, *Love in the Time.*

72. See Smith and Duggan, "Online Dating and Relationships."

73. See Aaron Smith, "15% of American Adults."

74. Bagell, qtd. in Brinkerhoff, "Dateless?"

75. Woodley, "91% of Surveyed."

76. See Rosenfeld and Thomas, "Searching for a Mate."

77. Cacioppo et al., "Marital Satisfaction"; "Only 1 in 3."

78. See Rosenfeld and Thomas, "Searching for a Mate."

79. Rosenfeld, Thomas, and Hausen, "Disintermediating Your Friends."

80. See Illouz, *Cold Intimacies.*

81. See Waller, "Rating and Dating Complex."

82. For example, see McKinlay, *Optimal Cupid;* and Webb, *Data, a Love Story.*

83. Rudder, *Dataclysm.*

84. eHarmony, home page; OkCupid, home page; Match, home page.

85. Feliciano, Robnett, and Komaie, "Gendered Racial Exclusion."

86. Massey, "Residential Segregation."

87. Foucault, *Foucault Effect.*

88. Fields and Fields, *Racecraft.*

CHAPTER 3. NEW RULES?

1. Coontz, *Marriage, a History.*

2. Lamont, *Mating Game.*

3. The persistence of gendered norms in courtship is often explained by theories ranging in title from the beauty status–exchange hypothesis to social role theory to evolutionary mate-selection theory; see Buss, "Sex Differences"; Chappetta and Barth, "Gender Role Stereotypes"; Eagly, "Sex Differences"; Elder, "Appearance and Education"; and Fales et al., "Mating Markets." In short, the premise of such theories is that—whether due to sociobiological conditions that promote reproductive fitness or to socially constructed gender norms that reflect a power hierarchy, or both—heterosexual men will prioritize physical characteristics, such as youth and attractiveness, in selecting a mate, while women will prioritize economic status.

4. For desired education levels, see Abramova et al., "Gender Differences," in *49th Hawaii International Conference,* 3858–67. For age preferences, see Alterovitz and Mendelsohn, "Partner Preferences"; Burrows, "Age Preferences"; and Hitsch, Hortaçsu, and Ariely, "Matching and Sorting." For physical markers, see Fales et al., "Mating Markets"; Fisman et al., "Gender Differences"; Glasser, Robnett, and Feliciano, "Internet Daters' Body Type"; Hitsch, Hortaçsu, and Ariely, "Matching and Sorting"; Hitsch, Hortaçsu, and Ariely, "What Makes You Click?"; Li et al., "Necessities and Luxuries"; Li and Kenrick, "Sex Similarities"; and Sritharan et al., "I Think I Like." For income factors, see Hitsch, Hortaçsu, and Ariely, "Matching and Sorting"; and Hitsch, Hortaçsu, and Ariely, "What Makes You Click?"

5. "Why Does It Seem?"

6. We are prohibited legally from identifying the data, but see the appendix for a full description of the data.

7. Our appendix details how we identify inauthentic profiles.

8. Collins, *Black Feminist Thought.*

9. Eng, *Racial Castration.*

10. Collins, *Black Feminist Thought.*

11. Waller, "Rating and Dating Complex," 729, 728.

12. Klinenberg and Ansari, *Modern Romance.*

13. Lamont, "We Can Write."

CHAPTER 4. A PRIVILEGE ENDURES

1. Case and Deaton, "Rising Morbidity"; Case and Deaton, "Mortality and Morbidity," 398. Part of what contributed to the sense of Whites losing at the expense of Black gain is figure 1 from Case and Deaton, "Mortality and Morbidity," 402,

showing a crossover of White mortality rates becoming higher than Black mortality rates from 2008 forward. However, the White rates depicted in the crossover were limited to less educated Whites (no high school diploma or college degree), whereas the Black rates depicted were for all people, which included college graduates, who have lower mortality rates compared to less educated people. Though the authors note this nonequivalent comparison in the text, it was widely overlooked in the public attention to these findings.

2. Donnan, "Deaths of Despair"; Kurtz, "White Middle Class Americans"; Belluz, "White Middle Class."

3. Centers for Disease Control and Prevention, "Health, United States."

4. Kimmel, *Angry White Men*.

5. Anderson, qtd. in Glasser and Thrush, "America's White People," 6.

6. Since few heterosexual women sent first messages, men's responding and women's sending patterns are likely to be driven by great selectivity. We therefore focus on men's sending and women's responding patterns. Because gay and lesbian daters do not follow this norm, we report initial sending patterns for both groups and note their responding patterns. For background information on our data sample and the analytic methods behind the models, see the appendix.

7. When assessing sending patterns (rather than response behaviors) in the more rare case where heterosexual minority women initiate first, each group is more likely to contact their own in-group before they contact White men.

8. In sending patterns White women are over twice as likely to contact White men than minority men.

9. Eng, *Racial Castration*; Fanon, *Black Skin, White Masks*.

10. Robnett and Feliciano, "Racial-Ethnic Exclusion"; Tsunokai, Kposowa, and Adams, "Racial Preferences."

11. Rafalow, Feliciano, and Robnett, "Racialized Femininity."

12. Rudder, "How Your Race Affects."

13. Connell and Messerschmidt, "Hegemonic Masculinity."

14. In fact, Asian men are the only group (of men or women) who now earn higher wages than White men. Patten, "Racial, Gender Wage Gaps."

15. See Massey, "Racial Formation"; and Mirandé, *Hombres y Machos*.

16. Roderique, "Dating While Black."

17. Trubey, "Race."

18. See Feagin, *White Racial Frame*.

19. Le Espiritu, "We Don't Sleep Around"; Tuan, *Forever Foreigners*.

20. See Cheryan and Monin, "Where Are You?"

21. Tuan, *Forever Foreigners*.

22. Nemoto, "Intimacy"; Vasquez-Tokos, *Marriage Vows*.

23. N. Kim, "So Third World."

24. Pascoe, "Intercultural Relations."

25. This is likely to be the case more for non-Black women than for Black women.

26. Collins, *Black Sexual Politics.*

27. Chasin, *Selling Out.*

28. Many of our interviewees spoke to these terms, and they are documented around the internet. A video series released by Grindr focuses on how the racial climate differs drastically for White men on the dating app compared to minority men.

29. G. Gates, *Same-Sex Couples;* Jepsen and Jepsen, "Empirical Analysis"; Ellingson et al., "Theory of Sex Markets," in Laumann et al., *Sexual Organization;* Kurdek, "Gay and Lesbian Cohabiting."

30. Bailey, "21 Things."

31. Ouiser, "Nice Guys"; Weiss, "Nice Guy Syndrome"; Bailey, "21 Things."

32. Nagle, "New Man of 4Chan."

33. See F. Garcia, "White Men Radicalised"; and Wilkinson, "We Need to Talk."

34. Glasstetter, "Elliot Rodger."

35. Other examples are Scott Bierle and Alek Minassian; see "Male Supremacy."

36. Blakely, "Virgin Killer"; Janik, "Laugh at the Death"; Selk, "Man Who Had Been."

37. "Male Supremacy."

38. Bederman, *Manliness and Civilization.*

39. "Mass Shootings."

40. Bruch and Newman, "Aspirational Pursuit."

41. When assessing response patterns (rather than initial sending behaviors), we find that Asian and Black daters are equally likely to respond to initial messages from White women as they are from their own in-groups. Latinos are still less likely to respond to White women than they are to Latinas. When assessing response patterns of White men (rather than initial sending behaviors), we find that they are equally likely to respond to White women as they are non-White women.

42. Cottom, *Thick.*

43. Collins, *Black Sexual Politics.*

44. See Le Espiritu, "We Don't Sleep Around."

45. Wilkins, "Becoming Black Women."

46. Ibid.; Childs, "Looking behind the Stereotypes."

47. Note how different the responses about personal preferences are from answers to a similar question we asked in the introduction regarding generic approval of *other* people's behaviors, about which U.S. Americans are much more approving (see figure I.1). The difference is that here daters are asked about *their own* racial preference, and the stakes are higher—it helps them meet their dating goals.

48. Women's sending behaviors show that they are even less likely to send to minorities (versus Whites) as they are to respond, at only 43 percent of the time to Latinos, 31 percent of the time to Black men, and 20 percent of the time to Asians. Although we do not have space here to devote to the messaging behaviors of White gay daters, our results show that both lesbian and gay daters also show a preference for other White daters over minority groups, but with lesbians' boundaries being more open than gays' boundaries. For more on this, see our paper: Lundquist and Lin, "Is Love (Color) Blind?"

49. Rich, "Compulsory Heterosexuality"; Deliovsky, *White Femininity*.

50. Moon, "White Enculturation," in Nakayama and Martin, *Whiteness*, 182.

51. Men's response behaviors (as opposed to sending behaviors) show that they respond about equally to all daters—except Black women.

52. Bonilla-Silva, "From Bi-racial to Tri-racial"; Feagin, *Racist America*.

53. Obviously, personal characteristics beyond race are important factors in daters' attraction to others, which is why the figures we have shown throughout this chapter show the probability of contact *after* controlling for many other characteristics across the two daters. The following models interact race and specific variables with each other directly so that we can get a sense for the relative importance of race.

54. Kalmijn, "Status Homogamy."

55. Skopek, Schulz, and Blossfeld, "Who Contacts Whom?"

CHAPTER 5. THE UNIQUE DISADVANTAGE

1. Feliciano, Lee, and Robnett, "Racial Boundaries"; Feliciano, Robnett, and Komaie, "Gendered Racial Exclusion"; Lin and Lundquist, "Mate Selection"; Lundquist and Lin, "Is Love (Color) Blind?"; Rudder, *Dataclysm*.

2. Interestingly, even though we know that men are more likely than women to use attractiveness as a primary motivation for whom they contact, the figures here indicate that they are more generous than women in whom they rate as attractive. Despite this, they still tend to largely contact only the most attractive of the women, whereas women's messaging is less tightly tied to men's attractiveness scores.

3. "Online Dating Is Horrible"; "Online Dating While Black"; Morpheus-Man, "If You Are Black, Don't Bother Using Tinder."

4. Fu, Tora, and Kendall, "Marital Happiness"; Herskovits, *American Negro*; Kalmijn, "Spouse Selection"; Qian, "Breaking the Racial Barriers"; Tucker and Mitchell-Kernan, "New Trends."

5. Collins, *Black Feminist Thought*; Collins, *Black Sexual Politics*.

6. Nagel, *Race, Ethnicity, and Sexuality*.

7. Roberts, *Killing the Black Body*; White, *Ar'n't I a Woman?*

8. Collins, *Black Sexual Politics*, 72.

9. South Carolina General Assembly, *Reports and Resolutions,* 236.

10. Additionally, the mammy character justified the ongoing exploitation of Black women, as the controlling image implied that Black women were particularly suited for service work, such as domestic work. See "Mammy."

11. Hodes, "Sexualization."

12. Foster, "Sexual Abuse."

13. Collins, *Black Sexual Politics.*

14. Collins, *Black Feminist Thought.*

15. M. Alexander, *New Jim Crow;* Pettit and Western, "Mass Imprisonment."

16. Dow, "Deadly Challenges."

17. Kipnis, *Bound and Gagged,* 167.

18. Dines, "White Man's Burden."

19. Miller-Young, *Taste for Brown Sugar.*

20. While straight Asian, Latino, and White men are least likely to send messages to Black women, response models also illustrate that they are least likely to respond to messages sent to them by Black women.

21. As in the previous chapter, this model predicts women's response behavior, since heterosexual gender standards in online dating tilt toward men initiating first and women responding. For gay daters we show results from sending models, since the same dynamics are not at play, and sending models tend to have larger sample sizes.

22. Though we do find that anti-Blackness is acutely gendered when considering the treatment of straight Black women, our quantitative findings are conservative estimates of the discrimination faced by all respondents because we are unable to gauge, for example, the potential discrimination enacted via message content. The interactional data show only the relative likelihood of messaging or response compared to other same-gender daters. While Black women are clearly disadvantaged relative to other women's popularity, Black women still receive more messages overall than even White men do (because women also generally receive twice as many messages as men owing to gendered messaging dynamics). And they receive twice as many messages as Black men do.

23. Essed, *Understanding Everyday Racism.*

24. Du Bois, *Souls of Black Folk.*

25. Collins, *Black Sexual Politics.*

26. H. Gates, *Black in Latin America;* J. Kim, "Yellow over Black"; N. Kim, *Imperial Citizens.*

27. Vasquez, "Disciplined Preferences."

28. Buggs, "Dating in the Time."

29. In response models of straight Black men, they respond somewhat similarly to all groups, though they appear to be slightly more likely to respond to messages sent by Latina and White women than to Black women, and they show slightly less preference to Asian women.

30. Banks, *Marriage for White People?*

31. Among the small pool of heterosexual minority women who do initiate first (sending models), all women are more likely to initiate contact with their same race counterparts. Women's sending models, however, indicate that, when Black women initiate, they send messages primarily to Black men and rarely send to any other racial group. We focus primarily on response since Black women are about three times more likely to engage in responding behaviors over initiating behaviors (as are all other non-Black women). Nevertheless, it's instructive that Black women who do take the initiative show a tendency toward homophily, in contrast to their responses, which are to all men equally with a slight preference for White men.

32. Bialik, "Key Facts."

33. Joseph, *Transcending Blackness;* Sexton, *Amalgamation Schemes.*

34. Conrad, Dixon, and Zhang, "Controversial Rap Themes."

35. Bialik, "Key Facts."

36. Collins, *Black Sexual Politics;* Wilson and Russell, *Divided Sisters.*

37. Childs, "Looking behind the Stereotypes."

38. Ibid.

39. Banks, *Marriage for White People?*

40. Thompson and Keith, "Blacker the Berry."

41. Monk, "Skin Tone Stratification."

42. Thompson and Keith, "Blacker the Berry."

43. Collins, *Black Feminist Thought;* Griffin, "Black Feminists"; Higginbotham, *Righteous Discontent.*

44. Collins, *Black Feminist Thought,* 157; Griffin, "Black Feminists"; White, *Too Heavy a Load.*

45. "Serena Williams."

46. Coontz, *Marriage, a History;* Gullickson, "Black/White Interracial Marriage"; Spickard, *Mixed Blood.*

47. DuMonthier, Childers, and Milli, *Status of Black Women.*

48. R. Garcia, "Normative Ideals"; see also Childs, "Looking behind the Stereotypes."

49. Torche and Rich, "Declining Racial Stratification."

50. Hill, *Black Intimacies,* 116.

51. Bonilla-Silva, "From Bi-racial to Tri-racial"; O'Brien, *Racial Middle.*

CHAPTER 6. THE ASIAN EXPERIENCE

1. Chan et al., *Big Aiiieeeee!*

2. For example, the literature chafes at Asian men being compared to that of an "efficient housewife" at best and disrespected because they are seen as "wom-

anly, effeminate, devoid of all the traditionally masculine qualities of originality, daring, physical courage, creativity" as well as the fact that "four of the five American-born Chinese-American writers are women." See Chin and Chan, "Racist Love," in Kostelanetz, *Seeing through Shuck*, 68. Other work lauds the resurrection of the male-centered heroic tradition of Asian military prowess and martial artistry. See Chan et al., *Big Aiiieeeee!*

3. Luna, "Reconciliasian."

4. Chin and Chan, "Racist Love," in Kostelanetz, *Seeing through Shuck*, 68.

5. Note the dualistic relationship of this dynamic to the previous chapter's depiction of what Black women and men contend with in such a regime of "racist hate," which unwinds into just the reverse dynamic—the erasure of Black women's femininity and the hypermasculinization of Black men.

6. See Chou, *Asian American Sexual Politics*.

7. Ngai, *Impossible Subjects*, 26. Although anti-Asian policy started specifically against the Chinese, as the largest Asian population in the United States, it came to exclude all Asian people by 1917 with the Asiatic Barred Zone Act.

8. Eng, David L. *Racial Castration*.

9. There was already a long-standing association between Asia and feminization by colonial Western Europe, according to Edward Said (see *Orientalism*), and, although it was primarily about the Middle East, it has salience for cultural values that have seeped into the U.S. imaginary about the East generally.

10. Yuh, *Beyond the Shadow*.

11. Parreñas Shimizu, *Hypersexuality of Race*.

12. Prasso, *Asian Mystique*, 87, 96, 334.

13. See Lowe, *Immigrant Acts*, 16.

14. J. Lee, "From Undesirable to Marriageable."

15. There is immense income heterogeneity among Asian Americans, with Asians having the most income inequality of all racial groups; see Kochhar and Cilluffo, "Income Inequality."

16. See "Rise of Asian Americans." Some of the difference is due to the larger population size of the other three groups compared to Asian Americans, who compose close to 6 percent of the U.S. population. Nevertheless, it is a big difference from historical concentrations of Asians in enclaves when the population was much smaller.

17. Chou and Feagin, *Model Minority*.

18. See Zhang, "Asian Americans"; and Okihiro, *Margins and Mainstreams*.

19. Lan, Pei-Chia. *Raising Global Families*.

20. See Chou and Feagin, *Model Minority;* and S. Hwang, "New White Flight." For college-admissions discrimination against Asian Americans, see Benner's discussion of the Harvard University case, in "Justice Dept." Although the case has documented what appears to be real bias in admissions, it is also a good

example of how model minorities are pitted against other minorities in efforts to roll back affirmative action admissions, for example.

21. Tuan, *Forever Foreigners.*

22. Yang and Liu, "China Threat."

23. "Discrimination in America."

24. Karabel, *Chosen.*

25. Viala-Gaudefroy and Lindaman, "Donald Trump's 'Chinese Virus.'"

26. E. Park, "Confronting Anti-Asian Discrimination."

27. Wylie and Eardley, "Penile Size"; Chou, *Asian American Sexual Politics;* Eng, *Racial Castration.*

28. Shen, "Asian American Man Study."

29. M. Park, "Race, Hegemonic Masculinity."

30. Systematic Asian marginalization in the larger gay community has been well documented in the scholarly literature as well. For example, see Han, "Geisha"; Han, "Sexy Like a Girl"; and Han, "They Don't Want."

31. See Chou, *Asian American Sexual Politics;* and Glenn, "Yearning for Lightness."

32. Natalie Tran's YouTube documentary, subtitled "White Male Asian Female," effectively captures what is a large social debate among the Asian diaspora living in the West; see "YouTube Creators."

33. See Kondō, "Deeper Roots."

34. Chiu, "Asian, Ew Gross."

35. Among the small pool of heterosexual minority women who do initiate first (sending models), all women are more likely to initiate contact with their same race counterparts over Asian men. And in assessing response models among gay men, it appears that Black and Latino men are as likely to respond to Asian men's messages as they are their same race in-groups, which contrasts to the results from the sending models in the text where gay Latinos were unlikely to initiate contact. It appears that, when gay Asian men contact them first, they, like Black men, are more interested in responding. But White gay men, even when Asian men initiate first, are still less likely to respond to Asian men.

36. The commonly repeated finding that Asian men are the most penalized group of men is largely due to data from two studies that analyzed 2004–5 Yahoo personal profiles. While many of their other reported findings are groundbreaking, their claims that "many more white women prefer black or Latino men than are open to dating Asian men" and "Asian men are also much more excluded than white men (.31), Latinos (.63) or black men (.68)" have not been well understood by the public. See Feliciano, Robnett, and Komaie, "Gendered Racial Exclusion," 50; and Robnett and Feliciano, "Racial-Ethnic Exclusion," 819. What their data actually show are within-race gender differences in the likelihood of excluding Asians in people's dating profile preference statements—thus, the difference they allege is the *gender gap* in Asian exclusion within each racial group. So, for

example, the coefficient showing the contrast between White men who exclude Asian women and White women who exclude Asian men is going to be much larger than the coefficient showing White men's exclusion of Black women versus White women's exclusion of Black men simply because White men and White women are more similar in their anti-Black exclusion. Comparing stated exclusions of Black men to Asian men directly in their data indicates that, in fact, Asian men are as likely to be excluded as Black men. Furthermore, their models analyze only daters who express racial preferences, and the 40-plus percent of men and 25-plus percent of women who are race-open in their sample are not analyzed. The study findings are often interpreted by the public as though they represent the entire sample of daters, and thus the degree of racial bias has been inflated.

37. Women's sending models, however, indicate that, when Asian women initiate, they send to Asian men first and White men second. We focus primarily on response since Asian women are three times more likely to engage in responding behaviors over initiating behaviors. Nevertheless, it's instructive that Asian women who do take the initiative show a tendency toward homophily. The response results for gay daters are similar to the models shown in figure 6.2.

38. W. Hwang, "People Willing to Date"; Robnett and Feliciano, "Racial-Ethnic Exclusion."

39. Phua and Kaufman, "Crossroads."

40. It is also possible that Asian American adoptee women more often grow up in White families because of gendered transnational adoption patterns from many Asian countries, and that Asian American children in mixed-race families will be more socialized toward a Asian woman–White man family model since that is currently the most common interracial pairing among Asian Americans. However, these trends are not large enough to explain the entire phenomenon.

41. Vasquez-Tokos, *Marriage Vows.*

42. Lamont, *Mating Game;* Wang, *Rise of Intermarriage.*

43. See Kelsky, *Women on the Verge;* Nemoto, "Intimacy"; and Pyke, "Intersectional Approach."

44. Ku, "White Men."

45. Nemoto, "Intimacy," 43.

46. Hondagneu-Sotelo, *Gendered Transitions.*

47. Yang, *Souls of Yellow Folk,* introd.

48. Chua and Fujino, "New Asian-American Masculinities."

49. Asian perpetrators of sexual violence are combined into the "other" category in the Bureau of Justice's crime statistics because the numbers are so much lower than other groups. Victimization statistics show that Asian women also report the lowest rates of intimate partner homicide, violence, sexual assault, rape, and stalking among all women, although there may be underreporting. See Smith et al., *National Intimate Partner;* and Petrosky et al., "Racial and Ethnic Differences."

50. Chou, *Asian American Sexual Politics;* Pyke and Johnson, "Asian American Women."

51. Gluszek and Dovidio, "Way *They* Speak."

52. Zheng, "Yellow Fever."

53. Nemoto, "Intimacy."

54. Ibid., 49.

55. While lesbians are generally even *less* likely to send messages to Asian women than are Black, White, and Latino men, confidence intervals are too large to indicate statistical significance in the case of Latina women's sending. In separate models that examine response patterns of straight men to the small pool of Asian women who initiate first contact, the results do not attain statistically significant differences.

56. K. Kreider, "Jeremy Lin."

57. Robnett and Feliciano, "Racial-Ethnic Exclusion," 819.

58. Connell and Messerschmidt, "Hegemonic Masculinity."

59. Bonilla-Silva, *Racism without Racists.*

60. Kawai, "Stereotyping Asian Americans."

61. J. Lee, "From Undesirable to Marriageable."

CHAPTER 7. "HEY, YOU'RE LATIN. DO YOU LIKE TO DANCE?"

1. Bonilla-Silva, "From Bi-racial to Tri-racial."

2. Aranda and Vaquera, "Immigration Enforcement Regime"; Flores-González, *Citizens but Not Americans;* Massey, "Racialization of Latinos," in Bucerius and Tonry, *Oxford Handbook*, 21–40.

3. Noe-Bustamante, "Key Facts."

4. Flores, "Facts on U.S. Latinos."

5. Molina-Guzmán, *Dangerous Curves.*

6. Castañeda, "Sexual Violence," in Torre and Pesquera, *Building with Our Hands*, 15–33.

7. Dávila, *Latinos, Inc.*

8. Ngai, *Impossible Subjects.*

9. Vasquez-Tokos and Norton-Smith, "Talking Back."

10. Rodríguez, *Heroes, Lovers, and Others;* Mirandé, *Hombres y Machos.*

11. Lewis, *Children of Sánchez*, xi, 115. See also Hurtado and Sinha, *Beyond Machismo.*

12. Vasquez-Tokos and Norton-Smith, "Talking Back."

13. Hondagneu-Sotelo, *Doméstica.*

14. Cacioppo et al., "Marital Satisfaction."

15. Collins, *Black Feminist Thought.*

16. Glenn, "From Servitude to Service."

17. This model predicts women's response behavior, since heterosexual gender standards in online dating still tilt toward men initiating first and women responding. For gay daters we show results from sending models, since the same dynamics are not at play, and sending models tend to have larger sample sizes.

18. In assessing sending models among straight women, it appears that Asian, Black, and White women are less likely to send messages to Latinos than to people of their own racial group.

19. Responding models among Latino men illustrate that they are slightly more likely to respond to messages sent by Asian women than to Latina and White women, whom they respond to about equally, and they are relatively less likely to respond to Black women.

20. Among the small pool of heterosexual minority women who do initiate first (sending models), all women are more likely to initiate contact with their same race counterparts. Women's sending models, however, indicate that, when Latina women initiate, they primarily send messages to Latino men first and to White men second. They similarly ignore inquiries from Black and Asian men. We focus primarily on responses since Latinas are three times more likely to engage in responding behaviors over initiating behaviors (as are other non-Latina women). Nevertheless, it's instructive that Latina women who do take the initiative show a tendency toward homophily, in contrast to their responses, which are most frequently to White men.

21. Lin and Lundquist, "Mate Selection."

22. Bialik, "Key Facts."

23. Burton et al., "Critical Race Theories."

24. Tharps, *Same Family;* Stephens, Fernandez, and Richman, "Ni Pardo, Ni Prieto," in Kawahara and Espin, *Feminist Therapy,* 15–29; Osuji, "Confronting Whitening."

25. Hordge-Freeman, *Color of Love.*

26. Roth, *Race Migrations.*

27. Le Espiritu, "We Don't Sleep Around"; Raffaelli and Ontai, "Gender Socialization."

28. Vasquez-Tokos, *Marriage Vows.*

29. Pyke, "Class-Based Masculinities."

30. Connell and Messerschmidt, "Hegemonic Masculinity."

31. R. Garcia, "Normative Ideals."

32. Vasquez-Tokos, *Marriage Vows.*

33. Vasquez, "Disciplined Preferences."

34. Lopez, Krogstad, and Flores, "Key Facts."

35. Garcia et al., "Latinos' Perceptions."

36. Vasquez-Tokos, *Marriage Vows.*

37. Muro and Martinez, "Is Love Color-Blind?"

38. Morales, "Parental Messages."

39. O'Brien, *Racial Middle.*

CHAPTER 8. POSTRACIAL MULTIRACIALISM

1. Freya, "Harrowing Scene."

2. Kitch, *Specter of Sex,* 109.

3. Curington, "Rethinking Multiracial Formation."

4. Matthews, "Eurasian Persuasions," 50.

5. Livingston and Brown, "Intermarriage in the U.S."

6. DaCosta, *Making Multiracials.*

7. Simien, *Dear White People.*

8. See Buggs, "Color, Culture, or Cousin?"; and Littlejohn, "Race and Social Boundaries."

9. Frey, "Minority White."

10. Thai, "New Face of America."

11. Cadet, "Striking Photos."

12. Cheney-Rice, "National Geographic," 1.

13. Bell and Hartman, "Diversity in Everyday Discourse," 895.

14. Omi and Winant, *Racial Formation.*

15. Parker et al., "Multiracial in America," 8.

16. Liebler, "Boundaries of Race."

17. For example, Lauren Davenport finds that gender is the single best predictor of a multiracial identification. See "Role of Gender"; see also Liebler, "Ties on the Fringes."

18. Daniel, *More Than Black?;* Curington, "Rethinking Multiracial Formation."

19. Andrea Smith, "Settler Colonialism," in Martinez HoSang, LaBennett, and Pulido, *Racial Formation,* 66–90.

20. Coleman, *Blood Stay Pure.*

21. DaCosta, *Making Multiracials.*

22. Nobles, *Shades of Citizenship;* see also Williams, *Mark One or More.*

23. Jones and Bullock, *Two or More Races.*

24. Parker et al., "Multiracial in America."

25. J. Lee, "From Undesirable to Marriageable."

26. The census finds that 12.1 percent of Latino/a adults have multiracial backgrounds. Of this group 79 percent identify as White and Latino/a. Parker et al., "Multiracial in America."

27. DaCosta, *Making Multiracials;* Ellis, Holloway, and Wright, *Marrying Out;* Jones and Bullock, *Two or More Races;* Taylor, Passel, and Wang, *Marrying Out.*

28. Bonilla-Silva, *Racism without Racists;* Sexton, *Amalgamation Schemes;* Strmic-Pawl, *Multiracialism.*

29. Sengupta, "Fashion's Newfound 'Inclusivity.'"

30. Joseph, *Transcending Blackness,* 168.

31. Joseph-Salisbury, *Black Mixed-Race Men;* A. Newman, "Standard Light Skin."

32. Curington, Lin, and Lundquist, "Positioning Multiraciality"; A. Newman, "Standard Light Skin"; Waring, "They See Me."

33. Even though our original data set consists of a large number of users, non-White multiracial users are much more rare and therefore do not have much opportunity to interact with other daters of the same racial background. As such, we focus only on White biracial daters.

34. Eng, *Racial Castration;* Ono and Pham, *Asian Americans.*

35. Because of the small sample size of the various multiracial populations in our data, we are unable to run analyses for gay and lesbian multiracials.

36. Separate models that examine response patterns to the small pool of messages sent by multiracial and monoracial women illustrate that straight White men are slightly more likely to respond to messages sent to them by Asian-White and Latina-White women than to those sent by White women. They respond slightly less frequently to messages sent by Black-White women, through they still exclude Black monoracial women the most.

37. While it appears that Asian men send most frequently to Asian women and send second most frequently to multiracial Asian-White women, the confidence interval indicates that the difference is not statistically significant. Their responding patterns also appear to indicate that they are most responsive to Asian-White multiracial women, but the overlapping confidence intervals similarly indicates that the difference is not significant.

38. Separate models that examine straight Latino men's responding patterns illustrate that Latino men are most responsive to Latina women. While it appears that their responsiveness toward Latina-White and White women is less than that of Latina monoracial women, the confidence interval indicates that the difference is not statistically significant.

39. Although large confidence intervals in separate models for Black men's responsiveness leave the precise sorting mechanism unclear, it appears, however, they are most responsive to messages sent by Black-White and White monoracial women and respond less to Black monoracial women.

40. Haritaworn, "Caucasian and Thai"; Waring, "They See Me."

41. A. Newman, "Standard Light Skin."

42. Waring, "It's Like We Have," 150.

43. Banks, *Marriage for White People?*

44. This parallels past work on Caribbean immigrants, which highlights how Black immigrants may strategically distance themselves and their children from being associated with native-born Blacks; see Rumbaut and Portes, *Ethnicities.*

45. Bonilla-Silva, "We Are All Americans!"

46. Bonilla-Silva, "From Bi-racial to Tri-racial."

CONCLUSION

1. Bonilla-Silva, Goar, and Embrick, "When Whites Flock Together."

2. Potarca, "Does the Internet Affect?"

3. Hergovich and Ortega, "Strength of Absent Ties."

4. Fullick "'Gendering' the Self," 545.

5. Bedi, *Private Racism,* 8.

6. Thomson, Carville, and Lanxon, "Match Opts."

7. To our best knowledge one's racial identity is not used in our source data to determine which profiles are displayed to the users. This does not rule out the possibility, however, that racial identity is correlated with the parameters used in the algorithm.

8. Noble, *Algorithms of Oppression.*

9. https://www.ajl.org/, http://auditingalgorithms.science/.

10. Zavery, "Black Women Now Hold."

11. Kim, *Imperial Citizens;* Roth, *Race Migrations;* Zamora, "Racial Remittances."

12. Callander, Newman, and Holt, "Sexual Racism."

13. Hoffmann, "Situating Human Sexual Conditioning."

14. Gramsci, *Prison Notebooks.*

APPENDIX

1. Sautter, Tippett, and Morgan, "Social Demography."

2. Zickuhr and Smith, *Digital Differences.*

3. Aaron Smith, "15% of American Adults."

4. Pugh, "What Good Are Interviews?"

5. Childs, "Looking behind the Stereotypes"; Le Espiritu, "We Don't Sleep Around"; Rose, *Longing to Tell.*

6. Collins, *Black Sexual Politics.*

7. Solórzano and Yosso, "Critical Race Methodology."

8. Harris, Carney, and Fine, "Counter Work." 13.

9. Saldaña, *Coding Manual.*

Bibliography

1880 3Census. Vol. 1, *Statistics of the Population of the United States.* Accessed May 9, 2020. www2.census.gov/library/publications/decennial/1880 /vol-01-population/1880_v1-map-13.pdf?#.

ABCs of Attraction. Home page. Accessed June 4, 2020. www.abcsofattraction .com.

Abramova, Olga, Annika Baumann, Hanna Krasnova, and Peter Buxmann. "Gender Differences in Online Dating: What Do We Know So Far? A Systematic Literature Review." In *2016 49th Hawaii International Conference on System Sciences*, 3858–67. Koloa, HI, 2016. https://core.ac.uk /download/pdf/33089117.pdf.

Abrams, Kerry. "Polygamy, Prostitution, and the Federalization of Immigration Law." *Columbia Law Review* 105, no. 3 (2005): 641–716.

Acs, Gregory, Rolf Pendall, Mark Treskon, and Amy Khare. *The Cost of Segregation: National Trends and the Case of Chicago, 1990–2010.* Urban Institute. March 2017. www.urban.org/sites/default/files/publication/89201/the_cost_ of_segregation_final_0.pdf.

Addams, Jane. *The Spirit of Youth and the City Streets.* Vol. 80. New York: Macmillan, 1930.

"Alabama Interracial Marriage, Amendment 2 (2000)." Ballotpedia. Accessed February 16, 2019. https://ballotpedia.org/Alabama_Interracial_Marriage,_ Amendment_2_(2000).

Alexander, Eleanor. "The Courtship Season: Love, Race, and Elite African American Women at the Turn of the Twentieth Century." *OAH Magazine of History* 18, no. 4 (2004): 17–19.

Alexander, Michelle. *The New Jim Crow: Mass Incarceration in the Age of Colorblindness.* New York: New Press, 2012.

Allen, Theodore W. *The Invention of the White Race: The Origin of Racial Oppression in Anglo-America.* Vol. 2. New York: Verso, 1994.

Allport, Gordon W. *The Nature of Prejudice.* New York: Doubleday Anchor Books, 1954.

Alterovitz, Sheyna Sears-Roberts, and Gerald A. Mendelsohn. "Partner Preferences across the Life Span: Online Dating by Older Adults." *Psychology and Aging* 24, no. 2 (2009): 513–17.

Aranda, Elizabeth, and Elizabeth Vaquera. "Racism, the Immigration Enforcement Regime, and the Implications for Racial Inequality in the Lives of Undocumented Young Adults." *Sociology of Race and Ethnicity* 1, no. 1 (2015): 88–104.

Bailey, Amy Kate, and Stewart E. Tolnay. *Lynched: The Victims of Southern Mob Violence.* Chapel Hill: University of North Carolina Press, 2015.

Bailey, Beth L. *From Front Porch to Back Seat: Courtship in Twentieth-Century America.* Baltimore: Johns Hopkins University Press, 1989.

Bailey, Luke. "21 Things That Prove Nice Guys Are the Absolute Worst." Buzzfeed. October 1, 2015. www.buzzfeed.com/lukebailey/nice-guys?utm_term=.wmBp20yL5#.xyBXQkNLB.

Baldwin, James. Notes of a Native Son. Boston: Beacon, 1955.

Banks, Ralph Richard. *Is Marriage for White People? How the African American Marriage Decline Affects Everyone.* New York: Penguin, 2011.

Bederman, Gail. *Manliness and Civilization: A Cultural History of Gender and Race in the United States, 1880–1917.* Chicago: University of Chicago Press, 1995.

Bedi, Sonu. *Private Racism.* Cambridge: Cambridge University Press, 2019.

———. "Sexual Racism: Intimacy as a Matter of Justice." *Journal of Politics* 77, no. 4 (2015): 998–1011.

Bell, Ernest Albert, ed. *War on the White Slave Trade: A Book Designed to Awaken the Sleeping and to Protect the Innocent.* Chicago: Thompson, 1909.

Bell, Joyce M., and Douglas Hartmann. "Diversity in Everyday Discourse: The Cultural Ambiguities and Consequences of 'Happy Talk.'" *American Sociological Review* 72, no. 6 (2007): 895–914.

Belluz, Julia. "Why the White Middle Class Is Dying Faster, Explained in 6 Charts: The Complicated Collapse of Middle-Aged White Americans." Vox. March 23, 2017. www.vox.com/science-and-health/2017/3/23/14988084/white-middle-class-dying-faster-explained-case-deaton.

Benjamin, Ruha. *Race after Technology: Abolitionist Tools for the New Jim Code.* Oxford: Cambridge, UK; Polity, 2019.

Benner, Katie. "Justice Dept. Backs Suit Accusing Harvard of Discriminating against Asian-American Applicants." *New York Times,* August 30, 2018. www.nytimes.com/2018/08/30/us/politics/asian-students-affirmative-action-harvard.html.

Berkhofer, Robert F., Jr. *The White Man's Indian: Images of the American Indian from Columbus to the Present.* New York: Knopf, 1978.

Berry, Mary Frances, and John W. Blassingame. *Long Memory: The Black Experience in America.* Vol. 124. New York: Oxford University Press, 1982.

Bialik, Kristen. "Key Facts about Race and Marriage, 50 Years after Loving v. Virginia." Pew Research Center. June 12, 2017. www.pewresearch.org /fact-tank/2017/06/12/key-facts-about-race-and-marriage-50-years-after-loving-v-virginia/.

Blackwell, Debra L., and Daniel T. Lichter. "Homogamy among Dating, Cohabiting, and Married Couples." *Sociological Quarterly* 45, no. 4 (2004): 719–37.

Blakely, Rhys. "Virgin Killer Was Member of 'Male Supremacist' Website." *Times,* May 28, 2014. www.thetimes.co.uk/article/virgin-killer-was-member-of-male-supremacist-website-t7ffv982clt.

Blau, Peter M., Carolyn Beeker, and Kevin M. Fitzpatrick. "Intersecting Social Affiliations and Intermarriage." *Social Forces* 62, no. 3 (1984): 585–606.

Bogardus, Emory S. "A Social Distance Scale." *Sociology and Social Research* 17 (1933): 265–71.

Bogle, Donald. *Toms, Coons, Mulattoes, Mammies, and Bucks: An Interpretive History of Blacks in American Films.* London: Bloomsbury, 2001.

Bonilla-Silva, Eduardo. "From Bi-racial to Tri-racial: Towards a New System of Racial Stratification in the USA." *Ethnic and Racial Studies* 27, no. 6 (2004): 931–50.

———. *Racism without Racists: Color-Blind Racism and the Persistence of Racial Inequality in America.* Lanham, MD: Rowman and Littlefield, 2017.

———. "We Are All Americans! The Latin Americanization of Racial Stratification in the USA." *Race and Society* 5, no. 1 (2002): 3–16.

Bonilla-Silva, Eduardo, Carla Goar, and David G. Embrick. "When Whites Flock Together: The Social Psychology of White Habitus." *Critical Sociology* 32, nos. 2–3 (2006): 229–53.

Borsella, Cristogianni. *On Persecution, Identity and Activism: Aspects of the Italian-American Experience from the Late 19th Century to Today.* Boston: Dante University Press, 2005.

Branch, Enobong. 2011. *Opportunity Denied: Limiting Black Women to Devalued Work.* New Brunswick, NJ: Rutgers University Press.

Brinkerhoff, Elizabeth. "Dateless? Might Want to Try Online Service." *Daily Targum,* February 14, 2001.

Brooks, Siobhan. 2010. *Unequal Desires: Race and Erotic Capital in the Stripping Industry*. Albany: State University of New York Press.

Bruch, Elizabeth E., and M. E. J. Newman. "Aspirational Pursuit of Mates in Online Dating Markets." *Science Advances* 4, no. 8 (2018): 1–6.

Buggs, Shantel Gabrieal. "Color, Culture, or Cousin? Multiracial Americans and Framing Boundaries in Interracial Relationships." *Journal of Marriage and Family* 81, no. 5 (2019): 1221–36.

———. "Dating in the Time of #BlackLivesMatter: Exploring Mixed-Race Women's Discourses of Race and Racism." *Sociology of Race and Ethnicity* 3, no. 4 (2017): 538–51.

Burrows, Kathryn. "Age Preferences in Dating Advertisements by Homosexuals and Heterosexuals: From Sociobiological to Sociological Explanations." *Archives of Sexual Behavior* 42, no. 2 (2013): 203–11.

Burton, Linda M., Eduardo Bonilla-Silva, Victor Ray, Rose Buckelew, and Elizabeth Hordge Freeman. "Critical Race Theories, Colorism, and the Decade's Research on Families of Color." *Journal of Marriage and Family* 72, no. 3 (2010): 440–59.

Buss, David M. "Sex Differences in Human Mate Preferences: Evolutionary Hypotheses Tested in 37 Cultures." *Behavioral and Brain Sciences* 12, no. 1 (1989): 1–14.

Cacioppo, John T., Stephanie Cacioppo, Gian C. Gonzaga, Elizabeth L. Ogburn, and Tyler J. VanderWeele. "Marital Satisfaction and Break-Ups Differ across On-Line and Off-Line Meeting Venues." *Proceedings of the National Academy of Sciences* 110, no. 25 (2013): 10135–40.

Cadet, Danielle. "Striking Photos Will Change the Way You See the Average American." HuffPost. Last modified December 6, 2017. www.huffpost.com/entry/national-geographic-changing-face-of-america-photos_n_4024415?guccounter=1.

Cahn, Susan K. *Sexual Reckonings*. Cambridge, MA: Harvard University Press, 2012.

Calavita, Kitty. *Inside the State: The Bracero Program, Immigration, and the INS*. New Orleans: Quid Pro Books, 2010.

Callander, Denton, Christy E. Newman, and Martin Holt. "Is Sexual Racism *Really* Racism? Distinguishing Attitudes toward Sexual Racism and Generic Racism among Gay and Bisexual Men." *Archives of Sexual Behavior* 44, no. 7 (2015): 1991–2000.

Carbado, Devon W. "Colorblind Intersectionality." *Signs: Journal of Women in Culture and Society* 38, no. 4 (2013): 811–45.

Carter, Marion. "Fragile Blondes Float over Dance Floor in Arms of Filipino Partners." *New York Evening Journal*, January 28, 1930.

Case, Anne, and Angus Deaton. "Mortality and Morbidity in the 21st Century." *Brookings Papers on Economic Activity*, 2017, 397–476. www.brookings.edu/wp-content/uploads/2017/08/casetextsp17bpea.pdf.

———. "Rising Morbidity and Mortality in Midlife among White Non-Hispanic Americans in the 21st Century." *Proceedings of the National Academy of Sciences* 112, no. 49 (2015): 15078–83.

Cashin, Sheryll. *Loving: Interracial Intimacy in America and the Threat to White Supremacy.* Boston: Beacon, 2017.

Castañeda, Antonia I. "Sexual Violence in the Politics and Policies of Conquest: Amerindian Women and the Spanish Conquest of Alta California." In *Building with Our Hands: New Directions in Chicana Studies,* edited by Adela de la Torre and Beatríz M. Pesquera, 15–33. Berkeley: University of California Press, 1993.

Centers for Disease Control and Prevention. "Health, United States, 2016: Individual Charts and Tables." Table 15. National Center for Health Statistics. Accessed March 9, 2019. www.cdc.gov/nchs/hus/contents2016 .htm#015.

Chan, Jeffery Paul, Frank Chin, Lawson Fusao Inada, and Shawn Wong, eds. *The Big Aiiieeeee! An Anthology of Chinese American and Japanese American Literature.* New York: Meridian, 1991.

Chappetta, Kelsey C., and Joan M. Barth. "How Gender Role Stereotypes Affect Attraction in an Online Dating Scenario." *Computers in Human Behavior* 63 (2016): 738–46.

Chasin, Alexandra. *Selling Out: The Gay and Lesbian Movement Goes to Market.* Basingstoke, UK: Palgrave Macmillan, 2001.

Cheney-Rice, Zak. "National Geographic Determined What Americans Will Look Like in 2050, and It's Beautiful." Mic. April 10, 2014. www.mic.com /articles/87359/national-geographic-determined-what-americans-will-look-like-in-2050-and-it-s-beautiful#.eOxANxqKY.

Cheryan, Sapna, and Benoît Monin. "Where Are You *Really* From? Asian Americans and Identity Denial." *Journal of Personality and Social Psychology* 89, no. 5 (2005): 717–30.

Childs, Erica Chito. "Looking behind the Stereotypes of the 'Angry Black Woman': An Exploration of Black Women's Responses to Interracial Relationships." *Gender and Society* 19, no. 4 (2005): 544–61.

Chin, Frank, and Jeffery Paul Chan. "Racist Love." In *Seeing through Shuck,* edited by Richard Kostelanetz, 65–79. New York: Ballantine Books, 1972.

Chiu, Allyson. "'Asian, Ew Gross': How the 'Crazy Rich Asians' Movie Could Help Change Stereotypes about Asian Men." *Washington Post,* August 3, 2018. www.washingtonpost.com/news/morning-mix/wp/2018/08/03 /asian-ew-gross-how-the-crazy-rich-asians-movie-could-help-change-stereotypes-about-asian-men/?noredirect=on&utm_term=.504283113cbd.

Chou, Rosalind S. *Asian American Sexual Politics: The Construction of Race, Gender, and Sexuality.* Lanham, MD: Rowman and Littlefield, 2012.

Chou, Rosalind S., and Joe R. Feagin. *Myth of the Model Minority: Asian Americans Facing Racism*. New York: Routledge, 2015.

Chua, Peter, and Diane C. Fujino. "Negotiating New Asian-American Masculinities: Attitudes and Gender Expectations." *Journal of Men's Studies* 7, no. 3 (1999): 391–413.

Clement, Elizabeth Alice. *Love for Sale: Courting, Treating, and Prostitution in New York City, 1900–1945*. Chapel Hill: University of North Carolina Press, 2006.

Cohn, D'Vera. "Census History: Counting Hispanics." Pew Research Center. March 3, 2010. www.pewsocialtrends.org/2010/03/03/census-history-counting-hispanics-2/.

Coleman, Arica L. 2013. *That the Blood Stay Pure: African Americans, Native Americans, and the Predicament of Race and Identity in Virginia*. Bloomington: Indiana University Press.

Collins, Patricia Hill. *Black Feminist Thought: Knowledge, Consciousness, and the Politics of Empowerment*. New York: Routledge, 2002.

———. *Black Sexual Politics: African Americans, Gender, and the New Racism*. New York: Routledge, 2004.

Combahee River Collective. "A Black Feminist Statement." 1977. *Women's Studies Quarterly* 42, nos. 3–4 (2014): 271–80.

Connell, Robert W., and James W. Messerschmidt. "Hegemonic Masculinity: Rethinking the Concept." *Gender and Society* 19, no. 6 (2005): 829–59.

Conrad, Kate, Travis L. Dixon, and Yuanyuan Zhang. "Controversial Rap Themes, Gender Portrayals and Skin Tone Distortion: A Content Analysis of Rap Music Videos." *Journal of Broadcasting and Electronic Media* 53, no. 1 (2009): 134–56.

Coontz, Stephanie. *Marriage, a History: How Love Conquered Marriage*. New York: Penguin, 2006.

———. *The Way We Never Were: American Families and the Nostalgia Trap*. New York: Basic Books, 1992.

Cooper, Brittney C. *Beyond Respectability: The Intellectual Thought of Race Women*. Urbana: University of Illinois Press, 2017.

Cottom, Tressie McMillan. *Thick: And Other Essays*. New York: New Press, 2018.

Craver, Rebecca McDowell. *The Impact of Intimacy: Mexican-Anglo Intermarriage in New Mexico, 1821–1846*. El Paso: Texas Western Press, University of Texas at El Paso, 1982.

Crenshaw, Kimberle. "Mapping the Margins: Intersectionality, Identity Politics, and Violence against Women of Color." *Stanford Law Review* 43 (1990): 1241–99.

Croly, David Goodman. *Miscegenation: The Theory of the Blending of the Races, Applied to the American White Man and Negro*. New York: Dexter, Hamilton, 1864.

Curington, Celeste Vaughan. "Rethinking Multiracial Formation in the United States: Toward an Intersectional Approach." *Sociology of Race and Ethnicity* 2, no. 1 (2016): 27–41.

Curington, Celeste Vaughan, Ken-Hou Lin, and Jennifer Hickes Lundquist. "Positioning Multiraciality in Cyberspace: Treatment of Multiracial Daters in an Online Dating Website." *American Sociological Review* 80, no. 4 (2015): 764–88.

DaCosta, Kimberly McClain. *Making Multiracials: State, Family, and Market in the Redrawing of the Color Line.* Stanford: Stanford University Press, 2007.

Daniel, G. Reginald. *More Than Black? Multiracial Identity and the New Racial Order.* Philadelphia: Temple University Press, 2010.

Davenport, Lauren D. "The Role of Gender, Class, and Religion in Biracial Americans' Racial Labeling Decisions." *American Sociological Review* 81, no 1 (2016): 57–84.

Dávila, Arlene. *Latinos, Inc.: The Marketing and Making of a People.* Berkeley: University of California Press, 2012.

Davis, Angela Y. "Rape, Racism and the Capitalist Setting." *Black Scholar* 12, no 6 (1981): 39–45.

———. *Women, Race, and Class.* New York: Vintage, 1983.

Davis, F. James. *Who Is Black? One Nation's Definition.* University Park, PA: Penn State University Press, 2010.

Deliovsky, Katerina. *White Femininity: Race, Gender and Power.* Black Point, NS: Fernwood, 2010.

D'Emilio, John. "Capitalism and Gay Identity." In *Families in the U.S.: Kinship and Domestic Politics,* edited by Karen V. Hansen and Anita Ilta Garey, 131–41. Philadelphia: Temple University Press, 1998.

D'Emilio, John, and Estelle B. Freedman. *Documenting Intimate Matters: Primary Sources for a History of Sexuality in America.* Chicago: University of Chicago Press, 2012.

———. *Intimate Matters: A History of Sexuality in America.* Chicago: University of Chicago Press, 1997.

Dines, Gail. "The White Man's Burden: Gonzo Pornography and the Construction of Black Masculinity." *Yale Journal of Law and Feminism* 18 (2006): 283.

Dill, Bonnie Thornton. "Our Mothers' Grief: Racial Ethnic Women and the Maintenance of Families." *Journal of Family History* 13, no. 4 (1988): 415–431.

"Discrimination in America." *Grand Haven Tribune.* Accessed May 19, 2019. www.grandhaventribune.com/mediaFiles?type=image&url=/image/2015 /03/24/20150223-Discrimination.jpg&caption=Poll%20showing%20 who%20Americans%20feel%20are%20the%20most%20discriminated% 20against.

Dollard, John. *Caste and Class in a Southern Town*. Vol. 6. Madison: University of Wisconsin Press, 1937.

Donnan, Shawn. "'Deaths of Despair' Surge among US White Working Class." *Financial Times*, March 23, 2017. www.ft.com/content/34637e1a-0f41-11e7-b030-768954394623.

Dorce, Belle B. "The American Girl." *Christian Recorder* (Philadelphia), December 15, 1887.

Dovidio, John F., and Samuel L. Gaertner. "Aversive Racism." *Advances in Experimental Social Psychology* 36 (2004): 4–56.

Dow, Dawn Marie. "The Deadly Challenges of Raising African American Boys: Navigating the Controlling Image of the 'Thug.'" *Gender and Society* 30, no. 2 (2016): 161–88.

Du Bois, W. E. B. *The Souls of Black Folk*. 1903. Reprint, London: Longmans, Green, 1965.

———. *The Philadelphia Negro: A Social Study*. Philadelphia: University of Pennsylvania, 1899.

DuMonthier, Asha, Chandra Childers, and Jessica Milli. *The Status of Black Women in the United States*. Washington, DC: Institute for Women's Policy Research, 2017. https://iwpr.org/wp-content/uploads/2017/06/The-Status-of-Black-Women-6.26.17.pdf.

Eagly, Alice H. "Sex Differences in Social Behavior: Comparing Social Role Theory and Evolutionary Psychology." *American Psychologist* 52, no. 12 (1997): 1380–83.

eHarmony. Home page. Accessed July 9, 2020. www.eharmony.com/.

Elder, Glen H., Jr. "Appearance and Education in Marriage Mobility." *American Sociological Review* (1969): 519–33.

Ellingson, Stephen, Edward O. Laumann, Anthony Paik, and Jenna Mahay. "The Theory of Sex Markets." In *The Sexual Organization of the City*, edited by Edward O. Laumann, Stephen Ellingson, Jenna Mahay, Anthony Paik, and Yoosik Youm, 3–38. Chicago: University of Chicago Press, 2004.

Elliott, Michael A. "Telling the Difference: Nineteenth-Century Legal Narratives of Racial Taxonomy." *Law and Social Inquiry* 24, no. 3 (1999): 611–36.

Ellis, Mark, S. Holloway, and Richard Wright. *Marrying Out and Fitting In: Interracial Households, Residential Segregation, and the Identity of Multiracial Children*. London: Sage Foundation, 2001.

Emerson, Michael O., Rachel Tolbert Kimbro, and George Yancey. "Contact Theory Extended: The Effects of Prior Racial Contact on Current Social Ties." *Social Science Quarterly* 83, no. 3 (2002): 745–61.

Eng, David L. *Racial Castration: Managing Masculinity in Asian America*. Durham, NC: Duke University Press, 2001.

Enss, Chris. *Hearts West: True Stories of Mail-Order Brides on the Frontier*. Guilford, CT: Globe Pequot, 2005.

Eshbaugh, Elaine M., and Gary Gute. "Hookups and Sexual Regret among College Women." *Journal of Social Psychology* 148, no. 1 (2008): 77–90.

Essed, Philomena. *Understanding Everyday Racism: An Interdisciplinary Theory.* Vol. 2. Newbury Park, CA: Sage, 1991.

Fales, Melissa R., David A. Frederick, Justin R. Garcia, Kelly A. Gildersleeve, Martie G. Haselton, and Helen E. Fisher. "Mating Markets and Bargaining Hands: Mate Preferences for Attractiveness and Resources in Two National US Studies." *Personality and Individual Differences* 88 (2016): 78–87.

Fanon, Frantz. *Black Skin, White Masks.* New York: Grove, 2008.

Feagin, Joe R. *Racist America: Roots, Current Realities, and Future Reparations.* London: Routledge, 2000.

———. *The White Racial Frame: Centuries of Racial Framing and Counter-Framing.* New York: Routledge, 2010.

Feliciano, Cynthia, Rennie Lee, and Belinda Robnett. "Racial Boundaries among Latinos: Evidence from Internet Daters' Racial Preferences." *Social Problems* 58, no. 2 (2011): 189–212.

Feliciano, Cynthia, Belinda Robnett, and Golnaz Komaie. "Gendered Racial Exclusion among White Internet Daters." *Social Science Research* 38, no. 1 (2009): 39–54.

Fields, Karen E., and Barbara Jeanne Fields. *Racecraft: The Soul of Inequality in American Life.* Brooklyn: Verso Trade, 2014.

Fisman, Raymond, Sheena S. Iyengar, Emir Kamenica, and Itamar Simonson. "Gender Differences in Mate Selection: Evidence from a Speed Dating Experiment." *Quarterly Journal of Economics* 121, no. 2 (2006): 673–97.

Fletcher, Michael A. "Campus Romance, Unrequited: Dating Scene Fails Women, Study Says." *Washington Post*, July 26, 2001.

Flores, Antonio. "Facts on U.S. Latinos, 2015." *Hispanic Trends.* Pew Research Center. Last modified September 18, 2017. www.pewhispanic.org/2017/09/18/facts-on-u-s-latinos/.

———. "How the U.S. Hispanic Population Is Changing." Pew Research Center. September 18, 2017. www.pewresearch.org/fact-tank/2017/09/18/how-the-u-s-hispanic-population-is-changing/.

Flores-González, Nilda. *Citizens but Not Americans: Race and Belonging among Latino Millennials.* New York: New York University Press, 2017.

Foley, Neil. *The White Scourge: Mexicans, Blacks, and Poor Whites in Texas Cotton Culture.* Vol. 2. Berkeley: University of California Press, 1998.

Foster, Thomas. "The Sexual Abuse of Black Men under American Slavery." *Journal of the History of Sexuality* 20, no. 3 (2011): 445–64.

Foucault, Michel. *The Foucault Effect: Studies in Governmentality.* Chicago: University of Chicago Press, 1991.

Frazier, E. Franklin. *Negro Youth at the Crossways: Their Personality Development in the Middle States.* New York: Schocken Books, 1940.

Frey, William H. "The U.S. Will Become 'Minority White' in 2045, Census Projects." Brookings. March 14, 2018. Accessed February, 24, 2019. www .brookings.edu/blog/the-avenue/2018/03/14/the-us-will-become-minority-white-in-2045-census-projects/.

Freya. "Harrowing Scene from Imitation of Life." YouTube video, 1:42. November 29, 2013. www.youtube.com/watch?v=0WgenwfYmwk.

Friedan, Betty. *The Feminine Mystique*. New York: Norton, 1963.

Fu, Xuanning, Jessika Tora, and Heather Kendall. "Marital Happiness and Inter-racial Marriage: A Study in a Multi-ethnic Community in Hawaii." *Journal of Comparative Family Studies* (2001): 47–60.

Fullick, Melonie. "'Gendering' the Self in Online Dating Discourse." *Canadian Journal of Communication* 38, no. 4 (2013): 545–62.

Garcia, Amber L., Heidi R. Riggio, Subha Palavinelu, and Lane Locher Culpepper. "Latinos' Perceptions of Interethnic Couples." *Hispanic Journal of Behavioral Sciences* 34, no. 2 (2012): 349–62.

Garcia, Feliks. "White Men Radicalised Online Were amongst the 'Silent Majority' Who Chose Donald Trump." *Independent*, November 14, 2016. www.independent.co.uk/news/world/americas/us-elections/donald-trump-white-men-online-radicalization-reddit-twitter-alt-right-latest-a7417296 .html.

Garcia, Rocio. "Normative Ideals, 'Alternative' Realities: Perceptions of Inter-racial Dating among Professional Latinas and Black Women." *Societies* 5, no. 4 (2015): 807–30.

Gates, Gary J. *Same-Sex Couples in Census 2010: Race and Ethnicity*. Los Angeles: Williams Institute, UCLA School of Law, 2012.

Gates, Henry Louis. *Black in Latin America*. New York: New York University Press, 2011.

Getman, Karen A. "Sexual Control in the Slaveholding South: The Implementation and Maintenance of a Racial Caste System." *Harvard Women's Law Journal* 7 (1984): 115–52.

Ghaziani, Amin. *There Goes the Gayborhood?* Princeton, NJ: Princeton University Press, 2015.

Giddens, Anthony. *The Transformation of Intimacy: Sexuality, Love and Eroticism in Modern Societies*. Oxford: Cambridge, UK: Polity, 1992.

Giliomee, Hermann. "The Making of the Apartheid Plan, 1929–1948." *Journal of Southern African Studies* 29, no. 2 (2003): 373–92.

Glasser, Carol L., Belinda Robnett, and Cynthia Feliciano. "Internet Daters' Body Type Preferences: Race-Ethnic and Gender Differences." *Sex Roles* 61, nos. 1–2 (2009): 14–33.

Glasser, Susan B., and Glenn Thrush. "What's Going on with America's White People?" *Politico Magazine*, September–October 2016. www.politico.com

/magazine/story/2016/09/problems-white-people-america-society-class-race-214227.

Glasstetter, Josh. "Elliot Rodger, Isla Vista Shooting Suspect, Posted Racist Messages on Misogynistic Website." Southern Poverty Law Center. May 23, 2014.www.splcenter.org/hatewatch/2014/05/23/elliot-rodger-isla-vista-shooting-suspect-posted-racist-messages-misogynistic-website.

Glenn, Evelyn Nakano. "From Servitude to Service Work: Historical Continuities in the Racial Division of Paid Reproductive Labor." *Signs: Journal of Women in Culture and Society* 18, no. 1 (1992): 1–43.

———. "Yearning for Lightness: Transnational Circuits in the Marketing and Consumption of Skin Lighteners." *Gender and Society* 22, no. 3 (2008): 281–302.

Gluszek, Agata, and John F. Dovidio. "The Way *They* Speak: A Social Psychological Perspective on the Stigma of Nonnative Accents in Communication." *Personality and Social Psychology Review* 14, no. 2 (2010): 214–37.

Godbeer, Richard. *Sexual Revolution in Early America*. Baltimore: Johns Hopkins University Press, 2002.

Goldberg, David Theo. *The Racial State*. Vol. 8. Malden, MA: Blackwell, 2002.

Gordon, Milton M. *Assimilation in American Life: The Role of Race, Religion, and National Origins*. New York: Oxford University Press, 1964.

Goyette, Braden. "Cheerios Commercial Featuring Mixed Race Family Gets Racist Backlash." HuffPost. Last modified June 15, 2013. www.huffingtonpost.com/2013/05/31/cheerios-commercial-racist-backlash_n_3363507.html.

Gramsci, Antonio. *Selections from the Prison Notebooks*. Edited and translated by Quintin Hoare and Geoffrey Nowell Smith. New York: International, 1971.

Grant, Madison. *The Passing of the Great Race, or The Racial Basis of European History*. New York: Scribner's Sons, 1916.

Greifinger, Rena. "What Happened to Dating?" *Michigan Daily*, November 21, 2002.

Griffin, Farah Jasmine. "Black Feminists and Du Bois: Respectability, Protection, and Beyond." *Annals of the American Academy of Political and Social Science* 568, no. 1 (2004): 28–40.

Grubman, Cathy. "The Cyberspace Date: Better Connections through Technology." *Washington Post*, August 23, 1994. www.washingtonpost.com/archive/lifestyle/1994/08/23/the-cyberspace-date/a610dd4d-8cb9-4f96-8b4b-746b57adb2ce/.

Gullickson, Aaron. "Black/White Interracial Marriage Trends, 1850–2000." *Journal of Family History* 31, no. 3 (2006): 289–312.

Gurley Brown, Helen. *Sex and the Single Girl*. New York: Geis Associates, 1962.

Gutman, Herbert George. *The Black Family in Slavery and Freedom, 1750–1925*. New York: Pantheon Books, 1976.

Hamer, Jennifer. "Slavery, Civil War, and Reconstruction: Creating a Context for Black Live-Away Fatherhood." In *What It Means to Be a Daddy: Fatherhood for Black Men Living Away from Their Children*, 33–52. New York: Columbia University Press, 2001.

Han, Chong-suk. "Geisha of a Different Kind: Gay Asian Men and the Gendering of Sexual Identity." *Sexuality and Culture* 10, no. 3 (2006): 3–28.

———. "Sexy Like a Girl and Horny Like a Boy: Contemporary Gay 'Western' Narratives about Gay Asian Men." *Critical Sociology* 34, no. 6 (2008): 829–50.

———. "They Don't Want to Cruise Your Type: Gay Men of Color and the Racial Politics of Exclusion." *Social Identities* 13, no. 1 (2007): 51–67.

Hanisch, Carol. "The Personal Is Political." 1970. In *Radical Feminism: A Documentary Reader*, edited by Barbara A. Crow. New York University Press, 2000.

Haritaworn, Jin. "'Caucasian and Thai Make a Good Mix': Gender, Ambivalence and the 'Mixed-Race' Body." *European Journal of Cultural Studies* 12, no. 1 (2009): 59–78.

Harris, Anita, Sarah Carney, and Michelle Fine. "Counter Work: Theorising the Politics of Counter Stories." *International Journal of Critical Psychology* 4, no. 2 (2000): 6–18.

Hartman, Saidiya V. *Scenes of Subjection: Terror, Slavery, and Self-Making in Nineteenth-Century America*. New York: Oxford University Press, 1997.

Hennessy, Rosemary. *Profit and Pleasure: Sexual Identities in Late Capitalism*. 2nd ed. London: Routledge, 2017.

Hergovich, Philipp, and Josué Ortega. "The Strength of Absent Ties: Social Integration via Online Dating." arXiv. 2017. https://arxiv.org/pdf/1709.10478.pdf.

Herman, Robert D. "The 'Going Steady' Complex: A Re-examination." *Marriage and Family Living* 17, no. 1 (1955): 36–40.

Herskovits, Melville Jean. *The American Negro: A Study in Racial Crossing*. New York: Knopf, 1928.

Higginbotham, Evelyn Brooks. *Righteous Discontent: The Women's Movement in the Black Baptist Church, 1880–1920*. Cambridge, MA: Harvard University Press, 1993.

Hill, Shirley Ann. *Black Intimacies: A Gender Perspective on Families and Relationships*. Lanham, MD: Rowman Altamira, 2005.

Hindell, Juliet. "Lurking Lovers Get Green Light in Japan." *Ottawa Citizen*, May 9, 1998.

Hing, Bill Ong. *Making and Remaking Asian America through Immigration Policy: 1850–1990*. Stanford: Stanford University Press, 1993.

Hirshman, Linda. *Reckoning: The Epic Battle against Sexual Abuse and Harassment*. New York: Houghton Mifflin Harcourt, 2019

Hitsch, Günter J., Ali Hortaçsu, and Dan Ariely. "Matching and Sorting in Online Dating." *American Economic Review* 100, no. 1 (2010): 130–63.

———. "What Makes You Click? Mate Preferences in Online Dating." *Quantitative Marketing and Economics* 8, no. 4 (2010): 393–427.

Hodes, Martha. "The Sexualization of Reconstruction Politics: White Women and Black Men in the South after the Civil War." *Journal of the History of Sexuality* 3, no. 3 (1993): 402–17.

———. *White Women, Black Men: Illicit Sex in the Nineteenth-Century South.* New Haven: Yale University Press. 1997.

Hoffmann, Heather. "Situating Human Sexual Conditioning." *Archives of Sexual Behavior* 46, no. 8 (2017): 2213–29.

Holland, Sharon Patricia. *The Erotic Life of Racism.* Durham, NC: Duke University Press, 2012.

Hondagneu-Sotelo, Pierrette. *Doméstica: Immigrant Workers Cleaning and Caring in the Shadows of Affluence.* Berkeley: University of California Press, 2007.

———. *Gendered Transitions: Mexican Experiences of Immigration.* Berkeley: University of California Press, 1994.

Hope, Christine. "Caucasian Female Body Hair and American Culture." *Journal of American Culture* 5, no. 1 (1982): 93–99.

Hordge-Freeman, Elizabeth. *The Color of Love: Racial Features, Stigma, and Socialization in Black Brazilian Families.* Austin: University of Texas Press, 2015.

Hudson, George W. *The Marriage Guide for Young Men: A Manual of Courtship and Marriage.* Ellsworth, ME: Hudson, 1883.

Humes, Karen R., Nicholas A. Jones, and Roberto R. Ramirez. *Overview of Race and Hispanic Origin: 2010.* Suitland, MD: U.S. Census Bureau, 2010. www.census.gov/prod/cen2010/briefs/c2010br-02.pdf.

Hunter, Tera W. *Bound in Wedlock: Slave and Free Black Marriage in the Nineteenth Century.* Cambridge, MA: Harvard University Press, 2017.

Hurtado, Aída, and Mrinal Sinha. *Beyond Machismo: Intersectional Latino Masculinities.* Austin: University of Texas Press, 2016.

Hwang, Suein. "The New White Flight." *Wall Street Journal,* November 19, 2005. http://pgbovine.net/NewWhiteFlight.pdf.

Hwang, Wei-Chin. "Who Are People Willing to Date? Ethnic and Gender Patterns in Online Dating." *Race and Social Problems* 5, no. 1 (2013): 28–40.

Illouz, Eva. *Cold Intimacies: The Making of Emotional Capitalism.* Cambridge, UK: Polity, 2007.

"Infographic: A History of Love and Technology." POV. Accessed April 10, 2019. http://archive.pov.org/xoxosms/infographic-technology-dating/.

Janik, Rachel. "'I Laugh at the Death of Normies': How Incels are Celebrating the Toronto Mass Killing." Southern Poverty Law Center. April 24, 2018.

www.splcenter.org/hatewatch/2018/04/24/i-laugh-death-normies-how-incels-are-celebrating-toronto-mass-killing.

Jepsen, Lisa K., and Christopher A. Jepsen. "An Empirical Analysis of the Matching Patterns of Same-Sex and Opposite-Sex Couples." *Demography* 39, no. 3 (2002): 435–53.

Jones, Jacqueline. *Labor of Love, Labor of Sorrow: Black Women, Work, and the Family, from Slavery to the Present.* New York: Basic Books, 2009.

Jones, Jeff, and Lydia Saad. "Gallup Poll Social Series: Minority Rights and Relations." Gallup News Service. June 13–July 5, 2013. www.gallup.com/file/poll/163703/Interracial_marriage_130725.pdf.

Jones, Nicholas A., and Jungmiwha Bullock. *The Two or More Races Population: 2010.* U.S. Census Bureau. September 2012. www.census.gov/prod/cen2010/briefs/c2010br-13.pdf.

Jones, William Henry. *Recreation and Amusement among Negroes in Washington, DC: A Sociological Analysis of the Negro in an Urban Environment.* Washington, DC: Howard University Press, 1927.

Jordan, Winthrop D. *White over Black: American Attitudes toward the Negro, 1550–1812.* Chapel Hill: University of North Carolina Press, 1968.

Joseph, Ralina L. *Transcending Blackness: From the New Millennium Mulatta to the Exceptional Multiracial.* Durham, NC: Duke University Press, 2013.

Joseph-Salisbury, Remi. *Black Mixed-Race Men: Transatlanticity, Hybridity and "Post-Racial" Resilience.* Bingley, UK: Emerald, 2018.

Jung, Moon-Ho. *Coolies and Cane: Race, Labor, and Sugar in the Age of Emancipation.* Baltimore: Johns Hopkins University Press, 2006.

Kalmijn, Matthijs. "Spouse Selection among the Children of European Immigrants: A Comparison of Marriage Cohorts in the 1960 Census." *International Migration Review* 27, no. 1 (1993): 51–78.

———. "Status Homogamy in the United States." *American Journal of Sociology* 97, no. 2 (1991): 496–523.

Kao, Grace, Kelly S. Balistreri, and Kara Joyner. "Asian American Men in Romantic Dating Markets." *Contexts* 17, no. 4 (2018): 48–53.

Karabel, Jerome. *The Chosen: The Hidden History of Admission and Exclusion at Harvard, Yale, and Princeton.* Boston: Houghton Mifflin Harcourt, 2006.

Kawai, Yuko. "Stereotyping Asian Americans: The Dialectic of the Model Minority and the Yellow Peril." *Howard Journal of Communications* 16, no. 2 (2005): 109–30.

Kelsky, Karen. *Women on the Verge: Japanese Women, Western Dreams.* Durham, NC: Duke University Press, 2001.

Kim, Claire Jean. "The Racial Triangulation of Asian Americans." *Politics and Society* 27, no. 1 (1999): 105–38.

Kim, Eun K. "Old Navy Ad with Interracial Family Prompts Social Media Outrage—and Support." *Today,* May 3, 2016. www.today.com/style

/old-navy-ad-interracial-family-prompts-social-media-outrage-support-
t90226.

Kim, Jae Kyun. "Yellow over Black: History of Race in Korea and the New Study
of Race and Empire." *Critical Sociology* 41, no. 2 (2015): 205–17.

Kim, Nadia Y. *Imperial Citizens: Koreans and Race from Seoul to LA*. Stanford:
Stanford University Press, 2008.

———. "'Patriarchy Is So Third World': Korean Immigrant Women and
'Migrating' White Western Masculinity." *Social Problems* 53, no. 4 (2006):
519–36.

Kimmel, Michael. *Angry White Men: American Masculinity at the End of an
Era*. New York: Nation Books, 2017.

Kingston, Maxine Hong. *China Men*. New York: Vintage, 1989.

Kipnis, Laura. *Bound and Gagged: Pornography and the Politics of Fantasy in
America*. Durham, NC: Duke University Press, 1999.

Kitch, Sally L. *The Specter of Sex: Gendered Foundations of Racial Formation
in the United States*. Albany: State University of New York Press, 2009.

Klinenberg, Eric, and Aziz Ansari. *Modern Romance*. New York: Penguin
Books, 2015.

Kochhar, Rakesh, and Anthony Cilluffo. "Income Inequality in the U.S. Is
Rising Most Rapidly among Asians." Pew Research Center. July 12, 2018.
www.pewsocialtrends.org/2018/07/12/income-inequality-in-the-u-s-is-rising-
most-rapidly-among-asians/.

Kondō, Oxford. "The Deeper Roots of the Celeste Ng Controversy." *Plan A
Magazine,* October 12, 2018. https://planamag.com/celeste-ng-controversy-
deeper-roots-167717287ba1.

Koshy, Susan. *Sexual Naturalization: Asian Americans and Miscegenation*.
Stanford: Stanford University Press, 2004.

Kreider, Kevin. "Jeremy Lin: Breaking Stereotypes and Asian Masculinity."
YouTube video, 2:12. April 20, 2017. www.youtube.com/watch?time_
continue=6&v=paSH0Ip9pcU.

Kreider, Rose M. "A Look at Interracial and Interethnic Married Couple
Households in the U.S. in 2010." U.S. Census Bureau. April 26, 2012. www
.census.gov/newsroom/blogs/random-samplings/2012/04/a-look-at-
interracial-and-interethnic-married-couple-households-in-the-u-s-in-
2010.html.

Ku, Esther. "White men shouldn't have to be made to feel bad about their
attraction to AF's [Asian females]. They make nicer partners than wife
beating Asian men." Twitter, January 8, 2016. https://twitter.com
/EstherKuKu/status/685553670654685188?s=20.

Kuhn, Peter, and Fernando Lozano. "The Expanding Workweek? Understanding Trends in Long Work Hours among U.S. Men, 1979–2006." *Journal of
Labor Economics* 26, no. 2 (2008): 311–43.

Kurdek, Lawrence A. "Are Gay and Lesbian Cohabiting Couples Really Different from Heterosexual Married Couples?" *Journal of Marriage and Family* 66, no. 4 (2004): 880–900.

Kurtz, Annalyn. "Why White Middle Class Americans Are Dying at an Alarming Rate." *Fortune,* March 23, 2017.

Lan, Pei-Chia. *Raising Global Families: Parenting, Immigration, and Class in Taiwan and the US.* Stanford: Stanford University Press, 2018.

Lane, David. *White Genocide Manifesto.* Saint Maries, ID: 14 Word Press, 1988.

Lamont, Ellen. *The Mating Game: How Gender Still Shapes How We Date.* Berkeley: University of California Press, 2020

———. "'We Can Write the Scripts Ourselves': Queer Challenges to Heteronormative Courtship Practices." *Gender and Society* 31, no. 5 (2017): 624–46.

Lasch, Christopher. *Haven in a Heartless World: The Family Besieged.* New York: Basic Books, 1977.

Lee, Erika. "The 'Yellow Peril' and Asian Exclusion in the Americas." *Pacific Historical Review* 76, no. 4 (2007): 537–62. doi:10.1525/phr.2007.76.4 .537.

Lee, Jennifer. "From Undesirable to Marriageable: Hyper-selectivity and the Racial Mobility of Asian Americans." *Annals of the American Academy of Political and Social Science* 662, no. 1 (2015): 79–93.

Lee, Susie. "The History of Online Dating from 1695 to Now." HuffPost. Last modified December 6, 2017. www.huffpost.com/entry/timeline-online-dating-fr_b_9228040.

Le Espiritu, Yen. *Asian American Women and Men: Labor, Laws, and Love.* Lanham, MD: Rowman and Littlefield, 2008.

———. "'We Don't Sleep Around Like White Girls Do': Family, Culture, and Gender in Filipina American Lives." *Signs: Journal of Women in Culture and Society* 26, no. 2 (2001): 415–40.

Levine, Rory. "Love on Vacation? Romance Displaced by Flings on Modern College Campus." *Daily Pennsylvanian,* September 18, 2003.

Lewis, Oscar. *The Children of Sánchez: Autobiography of a Mexican Family.* 1961. Reprint, New York: Vintage, 2011.

Li, Norman P., J. Michael Bailey, Douglas T. Kenrick, and Joan A. W. Linsenmeier. "The Necessities and Luxuries of Mate Preferences: Testing the Tradeoffs." *Journal of Personality and Social Psychology* 82, no. 6 (2002): 947.

Li, Norman P., and Douglas T. Kenrick. "Sex Similarities and Differences in Preferences for Short-Term Mates: What, Whether, and Why." *Journal of Personality and Social Psychology* 90, no. 3 (2006): 468.

Liebler, Carolyn A. "On the Boundaries of Race: Identification of Mixed-Heritage Children in the United States, 1960 to 2010." *Sociology of Race and Ethnicity* 2, no. 4 (2016): 548–68.

———. "Ties on the Fringes of Identity." *Social Science Research* 33 (2004): 702–23.

Littlejohn, Krystale E. "Race and Social Boundaries: How Multiracial Identification Matters for Intimate Relationships." *Social Currents* 6, no. 2 (2019): 177–94.

Lin, Ken-Hou, and Jennifer Lundquist. "Mate Selection in Cyberspace: The Intersection of Race, Gender, and Education." *American Journal of Sociology* 119, no. 1 (2013): 183–215.

Livingston, Gretchen, and Anna Brown. "Intermarriage in the U.S. 50 Years after Loving v. Virginia." Pew Research Center. May 18, 2017. www.pewsocialtrends.org/2017/05/18/intermarriage-in-the-u-s-50-years-after-loving-v-virginia/.

Loewen, James W. *The Mississippi Chinese: Between Black and White.* 2nd ed. Long Grove, IL: Waveland, 1988.

Lopez, Mark Hugo, Jens Manuel Krogstad, and Antonio Flores. "Key Facts about Young Latinos, One of the Nation's Fastest-Growing Populations." Pew Research Center. September 13, 2018. www.pewresearch.org/fact-tank/2018/09/13/key-facts-about-young-latinos/.

"Love Is Costly." *Boston Daily Globe,* February 24, 1907.

Lowe, Lisa. *Immigrant Acts: On Asian American Cultural Politics.* Durham, NC: Duke University Press, 1996.

Luibhéid, Eithne. *Entry Denied: Controlling Sexuality at the Border.* Minneapolis: University of Minnesota Press, 2002.

Lukens, Patrick D. *A Quiet Victory for Latino Rights: FDR and the Controversy over "Whiteness."* Tucson: University of Arizona Press, 2012.

Luna, Joshua. "Reconciliasian." *Tumblr.* April 10, 2018. https://joshualunacreations.tumblr.com/post/172800530329/please-dont-repost-or-edit-my-work-reblogs-are.

Lundquist, Jennifer Hickes, and Celeste Vaughan Curington. "Love Me Tinder, Love Me Sweet." *Contexts* 18, no. 4 (2019): 22–27.

Lundquist, Jennifer H., and Ken-Hou Lin. "Is Love (Color) Blind? The Economy of Race among Gay and Straight Daters." *Social Forces* 93, no. 4 (2015): 1–27.

MacKinnon, Catharine A. *Feminism Unmodified: Discourses on Life and Law.* Cambridge, MA: Harvard University Press, 1987.

"Male Supremacy." Southern Poverty Law Center. Accessed February 28, 2019. www.splcenter.org/fighting-hate/extremist-files/ideology/male-supremacy.

"The 'Mammy.'" *Black Women in Film.* Accessed May 4, 2019. https://blackwomeninfilm.weebly.com/the-mammy.html.

Manners, Miss. "Dismissing Online Date Takes the Right Timing." *Washington Post,* March 9, 2014. www.washingtonpost.com/lifestyle/style/miss-manners-dismissing-online-date-takes-the-right-timing/2014/02/25/88abe528-9b3d-11e3-975d-107dfef7b668_story.html.

Massey, Douglas S. "Racial Formation in Theory and Practice: The Case of Mexicans in the United States." *Race and Social Problems* 1, no. 1 (2009): 12–26.

———. "The Racialization of Latinos in the United States." In *The Oxford Handbook of Ethnicity, Crime, and Immigration,* edited by Sandra Bucerius and Michael Tonry, 21–40. Oxford: Oxford University Press, 2014.

———. "Residential Segregation Is the Linchpin of Racial Stratification." *City and Community* 15, no. 1 (2016): 4.

Massey, Douglas S., and Nancy A. Denton. *American Apartheid: Segregation and the Making of the Underclass.* Cambridge, MA: Harvard University Press, 1993.

Massey, Douglas S., Jorge Durand, and Nolan J. Malone. *Beyond Smoke and Mirrors: Mexican Immigration in an Era of Economic Integration.* New York: Sage Foundation, 2002.

"Mass Shootings in the United States: 2009–2017." Everytown for Gun Safety Support Fund. Last modified December 6, 2018. https://everytownresearch .org/reports/mass-shootings-analysis/.

Match. Home page. Accessed July 9, 2020. www.match.com.

Matthews, Julie. "Eurasian Persuasions: Mixed Race, Performativity and Cosmopolitanism." *Journal of Intercultural Studies* 28, no. 1 (2007): 41–54.

Matthews Li, Mike. "Romance Went the Way of the Dodo." *Vanderbilt Hustler,* November 2, 2004.

McGuire, Danielle L. *At the Dark End of the Street: Black Women, Rape, and Resistance; A New History of the Civil Rights Movement from Rosa Parks to the Rise of Black Power.* New York: Vintage, 2010.

McVicar, D. Morgan. "Ivy Valentines: Brown Students Now Meet Their Matches Online; 1,500 Buy into a Computer Dating Service." *Providence Journal,* February 8, 1996.

Miller-Young, Mireille. *A Taste for Brown Sugar: Black Women in Pornography.* Durham, NC: Duke University Press, 2014.

Mirandé, Alfredo. *Hombres y Machos: Masculinity and Latino Culture.* New York: Routledge, 2018.

Modell, John. *Into One's Own: From Youth to Adulthood in the United States, 1920–1975.* Berkeley: University of California Press, 1989.

Molina, Natalia. *How Race Is Made in America: Immigration, Citizenship, and the Historical Power of Racial Scripts.* Vol. 38. Berkeley: University of California Press, 2014.

Molina-Guzmán, Isabel. *Dangerous Curves: Latina Bodies in the Media.* New York: New York University Press, 2010.

Monk, Ellis P., Jr. "Skin Tone Stratification among Black Americans, 2001–2003." *Social Forces* 92, no. 4 (2014): 1313–37.

Moon, Dreama. "White Enculturation and Bourgeois Ideology." In *Whiteness: The Communication of Social Identity*, edited by Thomas K. Nakayama and Judith N. Martin, 177–97. Thousand Oaks, CA: Sage, 1999.

Morales, Erica. "Parental Messages concerning Latino/Black Interracial Dating: An Exploratory Study among Latina/o Young Adults." *Latino Studies* 10, no. 3 (2012): 314–33.

Moran, Rachel F. "Love with a Proper Stranger: What Anti-miscegenation Laws Can Tell Us about the Meaning of Race, Sex, and Marriage." *Hofstra Law Review* 32, no. 4 (2004): 22.

Morpheus-Man. "If You Are Black, Don't Bother Using Tinder." Red Pill. Accessed July 10, 2020. www.forums.red/p/TheRedPill/72330/if_you_re_black_don_t_bother_using_tinder/2226957/?timeframe=&userid=&search=&sort=6.

Moses, Norton H. *Lynching and Vigilantism in the United States: An Annotated Bibliography*. Westport, CT: Greenwood, 1997.

Muro, Jazmin A., and Lisa M. Martinez. "Is Love Color-Blind? Racial Blind Spots and Latinas' Romantic Relationships." *Sociology of Race and Ethnicity* 4, no. 4 (2018): 527–40.

Myrdal, Gunnar. *An American Dilemma: The Negro Problem and Modern Democracy*. Vol. 1. 2nd ed. New York: Harper and Bros., 1944.

Nagel, Joane. "Ethnicity and Sexuality." *Annual Review of Sociology* 26 (2000): 107–33. www.jstor.org/stable/223439.

———. *Race, Ethnicity, and Sexuality: Intimate Intersections, Forbidden Frontiers*. New York: Oxford University Press, 2003.

Nagle, Angela. "The New Man of 4Chan." Baffler. March 2016. https://thebaffler.com/salvos/new-man-4chan-nagle.

Naim v. Naim. 87 S.E. 2d 749, 756 (Va. 1955). Leagle. Accessed May 17, 2020. www.leagle.com/decision/195583687se2d7491826.

Nemoto, Kumiko. "Climbing the Hierarchy of Masculinity: Asian American Men's Cross-racial Competition for Intimacy with White Women." *Gender Issues* 25, no. 2 (2008): 80–100.

———. "Intimacy, Desire, and the Construction of Self in Relationships between Asian American Women and White American Men." *Journal of Asian American Studies* 9, no. 1 (2006): 27–54.

Newman, Alyssa M. "Desiring the Standard Light Skin: Black Multiracial Boys, Masculinity and Exotification." *Identities* 26, no. 1 (2019): 107–25.

Newman, Lisa. "Let's Hear It for Cupid!" *Washington Post*, February 6, 1998. www.washingtonpost.com/archive/lifestyle/1998/02/06/lets-hear-it-for-cupid/0c298e28-88d2-4c3e-933d-8a314298b8f6/.

Ngai, Mae M. "The Architecture of Race in American Immigration Law: A Reexamination of the Immigration Act of 1924." *Journal of American History* 86, no. 1 (1999): 67–92.

————. *Impossible Subjects: Illegal Aliens and the Making of Modern America.* Princeton, NJ: Princeton University Press, 2014.

Ngô, Fiona I. B. *Imperial Blues: Geographies of Race and Sex in Jazz Age New York.* Durham, NC: Duke University Press, 2014.

Noble, Safiya Umoja. *Algorithms of Oppression: How Search Engines Reinforce Racism.* New York: New York University Press, 2018.

Nobles, Melissa. *Shades of Citizenship: Race and the Census in Modern Politics.* Stanford: Stanford University Press, 2000.

Noe-Bustamante, Luis. "Key Facts about U.S. Hispanics and Their Diverse Heritage." September 16, 2019. www.pewresearch.org/fact-tank/2019/09/16/key-facts-about-u-s-hispanics/.

Nussbaum, Emily. "Are We a Match?" *New York Times,* April 25, 2004. www.nytimes.com/2004/04/25/education/are-we-a-match.html.

O'Brien, Eileen. *The Racial Middle: Latinos and Asian Americans Living beyond the Racial Divide.* New York: New York University Press, 2008.

OkCupid. Home page. Accessed July 9, 2020. www.okcupid.com/.

Okihiro, Gary Y. *Margins and Mainstreams: Asians in American History and Culture.* Seattle: University of Washington Press, 1994.

Omi, Michael, and Howard Winant. *Racial Formation in the United States: From the 1960s to the 1990s.* 2nd ed. New York: Routledge, 1994.

"Online Dating Is Horrible If You Are a Young and Black Woman." Reddit. Accessed July 10, 2020. www.reddit.com/r/OkCupid/comments/28tmbh/online_dating_is_horrible_if_you_are_a_young/.

"Online Dating While Black, It Sucks." Reddit. Accessed July 10, 2020. www.reddit.com/r/OkCupid/comments/3qbgwv/online_dating_while_black_21f_it_sucks/.

"Only 1 in 3 US Marriage Proposals Are a Surprise; Engagement Ring Spend Rises, according to the Knot 2017 Jewelry and Engagement Study." *Knot.* Last modified November 9, 2017. www.prnewswire.com/news-releases/only-1-in-3-us-marriage-proposals-are-a-surprise-engagement-ring-spend-rises-according-to-the-knot-2017-jewelry--engagement-study-300552669.html.

Ono, Kent A., and Vincent Pham. *Asian Americans and the Media.* Vol. 2. Cambridge, UK: Polity, 2009.

Osuji, Chinyere. 2013. "Confronting Whitening in an Era of Black Consciousness: Racial Ideology and Black-White Interracial Marriages in Rio de Janeiro." *Ethnic and Racial Studies* 36 (10): 1490–506.

Ouiser, Boudreaux. "The Not-So-Nice 'Nice Guys' of Online Dating." *Buzzfeed,* May 15, 2012.

"Our Chinese Colony." *Harper's Weekly* 34, no. 1770 (1890): 910.

Park, Ed. "Confronting Anti-Asian Discrimination during the Coronavirus Crisis." *New Yorker,* March 17, 2020. www.newyorker.com/culture/culture-desk/confronting-anti-asian-discrimination-during-the-coronavirus-crisis.

Park, Michael K. "Race, Hegemonic Masculinity, and the 'Linpossible'! An Analysis of Media Representations of Jeremy Lin." *Communication and Sport* 3, no. 4 (2015): 367–89.

Parker, Kim, Juliana Menasce Horowitz, Rich Morin, and Mark Hugo Lopez. "Multiracial in America: Proud, Diverse and Growing in Numbers." Pew Research Center. June 11, 2015. www.pewsocialtrends.org/2015/06/11/multiracial-in-america/.

Parreñas, Rhacel Salazar, and Winnie Tam. "The Derivative Status of Asian American Women." In *The Force of Domesticity: Filipina Migrants and Globalization*, edited by Rhacel Salazar Parreñas, 110–33. New York: New York University Press, 2008.

Parreñas Shimizu, Celine. *The Hypersexuality of Race: Performing Asian /American Women on Screen and Scene.* Durham, NC: Duke University Press, 2007.

Pascoe, Peggy. "Race, Gender, and Intercultural Relations: The Case of Interracial Marriage." *Frontiers: A Journal of Women Studies* 12, no. 1 (1991): 5–18.

———. *What Comes Naturally: Miscegenation Law and the Making of Race in America.* Oxford: Oxford University Press, 2009.

Patten, Eileen. "Racial, Gender Wage Gaps Persist in U.S. Despite Some Progress." Pew Research Center. July 1, 2016. www.pewresearch.org/fact-tank/2016/07/01/racial-gender-wage-gaps-persist-in-u-s-despite-some-progress/.

Peffer, George Anthony. "Forbidden Families: Emigration Experiences of Chinese Women under the Page Law, 1875–1882." *Journal of American Ethnic History* 6, no. 1 (1986): 28–46.

Peiss, Kathy. "Charity Girls and City Pleasures." *OAH Magazine of History* 18, no. 4 (2004): 14–16.

Perea, Juan F. "The Black/White Binary Paradigm of Race: The 'Normal Science' of American Racial Thought." *California Law Review* 85, no. 5 (1997): 1213–58. doi:10.2307/3481059.

Perez v. Sharp. 32 Cal. 2d 711. SCOCAL: Supreme Court of California Resources. Stanford Law School. Accessed March 27, 2019. https://scocal.stanford.edu/opinion/perez-v-sharp-26107.

Petrosky, Emiko, Janet M. Blair, Carter J. Betz, Katherine A. Fowler, Shane P. D. Jack, and Bridget H. Lyons. "Racial and Ethnic Differences in Homicides of Adult Women and the Role of Intimate Partner Violence: United States, 2003–2014." *Morbidity and Mortality Weekly Report* 66, no. 28 (2017): 741–46.

Pettigrew, Thomas F., and Linda R. Tropp. "A Meta-analytic Test of Intergroup Contact Theory." *Journal of Personality and Social Psychology* 90, no. 5 (2006): 751–83.

Pettit, Becky, and Bruce Western. "Mass Imprisonment and the Life Course: Race and Class Inequality in U.S. Incarceration." *American Sociological Review* 69, no. 2 (2004): 151–69.

Pfaelzer, Jean. *Driven Out: The Forgotten War against Chinese Americans.* New York: Random House, 2007.

Phua, Voon Chin, and Gayle Kaufman. "The Crossroads of Race and Sexuality: Date Selection among Men in Internet 'Personal' Ads." *Journal of Family Issues* 24, no. 8 (2003): 981–94.

Plecker, Walter A. *The New Virginia Law to Preserve Racial Integrity.* Richmond: Virginia Department of Health, 1924. https://lva.omeka.net/exhibits /show/law_and_justice/item/62.

Poinier, Arthur. "Statue of Liberty Welcoming Her Children." *Detroit Free Press,* 1941.

Potarca, Gina. "Does the Internet Affect Assortative Mating? Evidence from the U.S. and Germany." *Social Science Research* 61 (2017): 278–97.

Prasso, Sheridan. *The Asian Mystique: Dragon Ladies, Geisha Girls and Our Fantasies of the Exotic Orient.* New York: Public Affairs, 2005.

Pub. L. No. 271, 79th Cong., Ch. 591, 1st Sess. (December 28, 1945). Library of Congress. Accessed May 17, 2020. www.loc.gov/law/help/statutes-at-large /79th-congress.php.

Pugh, Allison J. "What Good Are Interviews for Thinking about Culture? Demystifying Interpretive Analysis." *American Journal of Cultural Sociology* 1, no. 1 (2013): 42–68.

Pyke, Karen D. "Class-Based Masculinities: The Interdependence of Gender, Class, and Interpersonal Power." *Gender and Society* 10, no. 5 (1996): 527–49.

———. "An Intersectional Approach to Resistance and Complicity: The Case of Racialised Desire among Asian American Women." *Journal of Intercultural Studies* 31, no. 1 (2010): 81–94.

Pyke, Karen D., and Denise L. Johnson. "Asian American Women and Racialized Femininities: 'Doing' Gender across Cultural Worlds." *Gender and Society* 17, no. 1 (2003): 33–53.

Qian, Zhenchao. "Breaking the Racial Barriers: Variations in Interracial Marriage between 1980 and 1990." *Demography* 34, no. 2 (1997): 263–76.

"Rachel Calof's Story: Jewish Homesteader on the Northern Plains." Jewish Women's Archive. Accessed April 20, 2019 https://jwa.org/discover /inthepast/readingseries/calof.

Rafalow, Matthew H., Cynthia Feliciano, and Belinda Robnett. "Racialized Femininity and Masculinity in the Preferences of Online Same-Sex Daters." *Social Currents* 4, no. 4 (2017): 306–21.

Raffaelli, Marcela, and Lenna L. Ontai. "Gender Socialization in Latino/a Families: Results from Two Retrospective Studies." *Sex Roles* 50, nos. 5–6 (2004): 287–99.

"Results from the 1860 Census." *Civil War*. Accessed February 15, 2019. www
.census.gov/library/publications/1864/dec/1860a.html.

Rich, Adrienne. "Compulsory Heterosexuality and Lesbian Existence." *Signs: Journal of Women in Culture and Society* 5, no. 4 (1980): 631–60.

"The Rise of Asian Americans." Pew Research Center. June 19, 2012. www
.pewsocialtrends.org/2012/06/19/the-rise-of-asian-americans/.

Roberts, Dorothy E. *Killing the Black Body: Race, Reproduction, and the Meaning of Liberty*. New York: Vintage Books, 1999.

———. "Loving v. Virginia as a Civil Rights Decision." *New York Law School Law Review* 59 (2014): 175.

Robinson, Brandon Andrew. "'Personal Preference' as the New Racism: Gay Desire and Racial Cleansing in Cyberspace." *Sociology of Race and Ethnicity* 1, no. 2 (2015): 317–30.

Robinson, Russell, K. "Structural Dimensions of Romantic Preferences." *Fordham Law Review* 76 (2007): 2787.

Robnett, Belinda, and Cynthia Feliciano. "Patterns of Racial-Ethnic Exclusion by Internet Daters." *Social Forces* 89, no. 3 (2011): 807–28.

Roderique, Hadiya. "Dating While Black." Walrus. Last modified April 2, 2020. https://thewalrus.ca/dating-while-black/.

Rodríguez, Clara E. *Heroes, Lovers, and Others: The Story of Latinos in Hollywood*. Oxford: Oxford University Press, 2008.

Roediger, David R. *The Wages of Whiteness: Race and the Making of the American Working Class*. New York: Verso, 1999.

Rose, Tricia. *Longing to Tell: Black Women Talk about Sexuality and Intimacy*. New York: Farrar, Straus and Giroux, 2004.

Rosenfeld, Michael J., and Reuben J. Thomas. "Searching for a Mate: The Rise of the Internet as a Social Intermediary." *American Sociological Review* 77, no. 4 (2012): 523–47.

Rosenfeld, Michael J., Reuben J. Thomas, and Sonia Hausen. "Disintermediating Your Friends: How Online Dating in the United States Displaces Other Ways of Meeting." *Proceedings of the National Academy of Sciences* 116, no. 36 (2019). https://doi.org/10.1073/pnas.1908630116.

Roth, Wendy. *Race Migrations: Latinos and the Cultural Transformation of Race*. Stanford: Stanford University Press, 2012.

Rudder, Christian. *Dataclysm: Love, Sex, Race, and Identity; What Our Online Lives Tell Us about Our Offline Selves*. New York: Broadway Books, 2014.

———. "How Your Race Affects the Messages You Get." OkTrends. Last modified October 5, 2009. www.gwern.net/docs/psychology/okcupid /howyourraceaffectsthemessagesyouget.html.

Rumbaut, Rubén G., and Alejandro Portes, eds. *Ethnicities: Children of Immigrants in America*. Berkeley: University of California Press, 2001.

Sack, Kevin, and Alan Blinder. "Jurors Hear Dylann Roof Explain Shooting in Video; 'I Had to Do It.'" *New York Times,* December 9, 2016. www.nytimes .com/2016/12/09/us/dylann-roof-shooting-charleston-south-carolina-church-video.html.

Said, Edward W. *Orientalism.* New York: Vintage, 1979.

Saldaña, Johnny. *The Coding Manual for Qualitative Researchers.* Los Angeles: Sage, 2015.

Sanoff, Alvin P. "19 Million Singles: Their Joys and Frustrations." *U.S. News and World Report,* February 21, 1983.

Sass, Herbert Ravenel. "Mixed Schools and Mixed Blood." Folder 42P. Box 3. M393 McCain (William D.) Pamphlet Collection. University of Southern Mississippi, Hattiesburg, 1–12. Reprinted in *Atlantic Monthly,* November 1956, 45–49.

Sautter, Jessica M., Rebecca M. Tippett, and S. Philip Morgan. "The Social Demography of Internet Dating in the United States." Social Science Quarterly 91, no. 2 (2010): 554–75. www.jstor.org/stable/42956416.

Schor, Juliet. *The Overworked American: The Unexpected Decline of Leisure.* New York: Basic Books, 2008.

Selk, Avi. "Man Who Had Been Accused of Groping Opens Fire on Tallahassee Yoga Class, Killing Two, Police Say." *Washington Post,* November 3, 2018. www.washingtonpost.com/nation/2018/11/03/man-with-groping-history-opens-fire-tallahassee-yoga-class-killing-two-police-say/?noredirect= on&utm_term=.2f5bfbdbf347.

Sengupta, Anita. "Is Fashion's Newfound 'Inclusivity' Only Skin Deep?" Refinery29. Last modified May 9, 2018. www.refinery29.com/en-us /multiracial-women-fetishized-in-fashion-industry-controversy.

"Serena Williams Owes Black Men Nothing for Her White Fiancé." Grio. December 30, 2016. https://thegrio.com/2016/12/30/serena-williams-owes-you-nothing-for-her-White-fiance/.

Sexton, Jared. *Amalgamation Schemes: Antiblackness and the Critique of Multiracialism.* Minneapolis: University of Minnesota Press, 2008.

———. "People-of-Color-Blindness: Notes on the Afterlife of Slavery." *Social Text* 28, no. 2 (103) (2010): 31–56.

Sharkey, Patrick. *Stuck in Place: Urban Neighborhoods and the End of Progress toward Racial Equality.* Chicago: University of Chicago Press, 2013.

Shen, Jason. "The Asian American Man Study: 2015 Results." Medium. January 22, 2016. https://medium.com/@JasonShen/what-it-s-like-to-live-work-and-date-as-an-asian-man-in-america-f1371d3770ee.

Sigelman, Lee, and Susan Welch. "The Contact Hypothesis Revisited: Black-White Interaction and Positive Racial Attitudes." *Social Forces* 71, no. 3 (1993): 781–95.

Simien, Justin, dir. *Dear White People*. Los Angeles: Lionsgate/Roadside Attractions, 2014.

Skopek, Jan, Florian Schulz, and Hans-Peter Blossfeld. "Who Contacts Whom? Educational Homophily in Online Mate Selection." *European Sociological Review* 27, no. 2 (2010): 180–95.

Slater, Dan. *Love in the Time of Algorithms: What Technology Does to Meeting and Mating*. New York: Penguin, 2013.

Smith, Aaron. "15% of American Adults Have Used Online Dating Sites or Mobile Dating Apps." Pew Research Center. February 11, 2016. www .pewinternet.org/2016/02/11/15-percent-of-american-adults-have-used-online-dating-sites-or-mobile-dating-apps/.

Smith, Aaron, and Maeve Duggan. "Online Dating and Relationships." Pew Research Center. October 21, 2013. www.pewinternet.org/2013/10/21 /online-dating-relationships/.

Smith, Andrea. "Indigeneity, Settler Colonialism, White Supremacy." In *Racial Formation in the Twenty-First Century*, edited by Daniel Martinez HoSang, Oneka LaBennett, and Laura Pulido, 66–90. Berkeley: University of California Press, 2012.

Smith, Sharon G., Jieru Chen, Kathleen C. Basile, Leah K. Gilbert, Melissa T. Merrick, Nimesh Patel, Margie Walling, and Anurag Jain. *The National Intimate Partner and Sexual Violence Survey: 2010–2012 3State Report*. Atlanta: National Center for Injury Prevention/Control Centers for Disease Control and Prevention, 2017. www.cdc.gov/violenceprevention/pdf/NISVS-StateReportBook.pdf.

Solórzano, Daniel G., and Tara J. Yosso. "Critical Race Methodology: Counter-Storytelling as an Analytical Framework for Education Research." *Qualitative Inquiry* 8, no. 1 (2002): 23–44.

South Carolina General Assembly. *Reports and Resolutions of South Carolina to the General Assembly*. Vol. 3. Columbia, SC: Gonzales and Bryan, 1914.

Spell, Sarah A. "Not Just Black and White: How Race/Ethnicity and Gender Intersect in Hookup Culture." *Sociology of Race and Ethnicity* 3, no. 2 (2017): 172–87.

Spickard, Paul R. *Mixed Blood: Intermarriage and Ethnic Identity in Twentieth-Century America*. Madison: University of Wisconsin Press, 1991.

Spillers, Hortense J. "Mama's Baby, Papa's Maybe: An American Grammar Book." *Diacritics* 17, no. 2 (1987): 65–81.

Spiro, Jonathan P. *Defending the Master Race: Conservation, Eugenics, and the Legacy of Madison Grant*. Hanover, NH: University Press of New England, 2009.

Spörlein, Christoph, Elmar Schlueter, and Frank van Tubergen. "Ethnic Intermarriage in Longitudinal Perspective: Testing Structural and Cultural

Explanations in the United States, 1880–2011." *Social Science Research* 43 (2014): 1–15.

Sritharan, Rajees, Kimberly Heilpern, Christopher J. Wilbur, and Bertram Gawronski. "I Think I Like You: Spontaneous and Deliberate Evaluations of Potential Romantic Partners in an Online Dating Context." *European Journal of Social Psychology* 40, no. 6 (2010): 1062–77.

Stampp, Kenneth M. *The Peculiar Institution: Negro Slavery in the American South.* London: Eyre and Spottiswoode, 1964.

Stember, Charles Herbert. *Sexual Racism: The Emotional Barrier to an Integrated Society.* New York: Elsevier, 1976.

Stephens, Dionne P., Paula B. Fernandez, and Erin L. Richman. "Ni Pardo, Ni Prieto: The Influence of Parental Skin Color Messaging on Heterosexual Emerging Adult White-Hispanic Women's Dating Beliefs." In *Feminist Therapy with Latina Women*, edited by Debra M. Kawahara and Oliva M. Espin, 15–29. London: Routledge, 2013.

Stepp, Laura Sessions. *Unhooked: How Young Women Pursue Sex, Delay Love and Lose at Both.* New York: Penguin, 2007.

Strmic-Pawl, Hephzibah V. *Multiracialism and Its Discontents: A Comparative Analysis of Asian-White and Black-White Multiracials.* Lanham, MD: Lexington Books, 2016.

Suler, John. "The Online Disinhibition Effect." *Cyberpsychology and Behavior* 7, no. 3 (2004): 321–26.

Takaki, Ronald. *Strangers from a Different Shore: A History of Asian Americans.* Rev. ed. New York: Little, Brown, 1998.

Taylor, Paul, Jeffrey S. Passel, and Wendy Wang. *Marrying Out: One-in-Seven New U.S. Marriages Is Interracial or Interethnic.* Washington, DC: Pew Research Center, 2010. www.pewresearch.org/wp-content/uploads/sites/3/2010/10/755-marrying-out.pdf.

Teng, Emma Jinhua. *Eurasian: Mixed Identities in the United States, China, and Hong Kong, 1842–1943.* Berkeley: University of California Press, 2013.

Thai, Ted. "The New Face of America: How Immigrants Are Shaping the World's First Multicultural Society." *Time*, November 18, 1993. http://content.time.com/time/covers/0,16641,19931118,00.html.

Tharps, Lori L. *Same Family, Different Colors: Confronting Colorism in America's Diverse Families.* Boston: Beacon, 2016.

Thomas, Henry Atwell. "The Miscegenation Ball." Smithsonian. Accessed July 8, 2020. www.si.edu/object/nmah_325557.

Thompson, Maxine S., and Verna M. Keith. "The Blacker the Berry: Gender, Skin Tone, Self-Esteem, and Self-Efficacy." *Gender and Society* 15, no. 3 (2001): 336–57.

Thomson, Amy, Olivia Carville, and Nate Lanxon. "Match Opts to Keep Race Filter for Dating as Other Sites Drop It." Bloomberg. June 8, 2020, www

.bloomberg.com/news/articles/2020-06-08/dating-apps-debate-race-filters-as-empowering-or-discriminating.

Torche, Florencia, and Peter Rich. "Declining Racial Stratification in Marriage Choices? Trends in Black/White Status Exchange in the United States, 1980 to 2010." *Sociology of Race and Ethnicity* 3, no. 1 (2017): 31–49.

Tran, Natalie. "YouTube Creators for Change: Natalie Tran/White Male Asian Female." YouTube video, 39:44. December 1, 2017. www.youtube.com/watch?time_continue=1&v=chFKDaZns6w.

Treitler, Vilna Bashi. *The Ethnic Project: Transforming Racial Fiction into Ethnic Factions.* Stanford University Press, 2013.

Trubey, Corbett. "Race." Episode 1 of *What the Flip?* Vimeo video, 3:20. Accessed March 9, 2019. https://vimeo.com/252068918.

Tsunokai, Glenn T., Augustine J. Kposowa, and Michele A. Adams. "Racial Preferences in Internet Dating: A Comparison of Four Birth Cohorts." *Western Journal of Black Studies* 33, no. 1 (2009): 1–15.

Tuan, Mia. *Forever Foreigners or Honorary Whites? The Asian Ethnic Experience Today.* New Brunswick, NJ: Rutgers University Press, 1998.

Tucker, M. Belinda, and Claudia Mitchell-Kernan. "New Trends in Black American Interracial Marriage: The Social Structural Context." *Journal of Marriage and the Family* 52, no. 1 (1990): 209–18.

U.S. Census Bureau. *Decennial Census Datasets: 2010.* 2010. www.census.gov/programs-surveys/decennial-census/data/datasets.2010.html.

Vasquez, Jessica M. "Disciplined Preferences: Explaining the (Re)production of Latino Endogamy." *Social Problems* 62, no. 3 (2015): 455–75.

Vasquez-Tokos, Jessica. *Marriage Vows and Racial Choices.* New York: Sage Foundation, 2017.

Vasquez-Tokos, Jessica, and Kathryn Norton-Smith. "Talking Back to Controlling Images: Latinos' Changing Responses to Racism over the Life Course." *Ethnic and Racial Studies* 40, no. 6 (2017): 912–30.

Viala-Gaudefroy, Jérôme, and Dana Lindaman. "Donald Trump's 'Chinese Virus': The Politics of Naming," *Conversation*, April 21, 2020. https://theconversation.com/donald-trumps-chinese-virus-the-politics-of-naming-136796.

Wade, Lisa. *American Hookup: The New Culture of Sex on Campus.* New York: Norton, 2017.

Wallenstein, Peter. *Tell the Court I Love My Wife: Race, Marriage, and Law; An American History.* New York: Palgrave Macmillan, 2004.

Waller, Willard. "The Rating and Dating Complex." *American Sociological Review* 2, no. 5 (1937): 727–34.

Wang, Wendy. *The Rise of Intermarriage: Rates, Characteristics Vary by Race and Gender.* Washington, DC: Pew Research Center, 2012. www.pewresearch.org/wp-content/uploads/sites/3/2012/02/SDT-Intermarriage-II.pdf.

Waring, Chandra D. L. "'It's Like We Have an "In" Already': The Racial Capital of Black/White Biracial Americans." *Du Bois Review: Social Science Research on Race* 14, no. 1 (2017): 145–63.

———. "'They See Me as Exotic . . . That Intrigues Them': Gender, Sexuality and the Racially Ambiguous Body." *Race, Gender and Class* 20, nos. 3–4 (2013): 299–317. www.jstor.org/stable/43496947.

Waters, Mary C. *Ethnic Options: Choosing Identities in America.* Berkeley: University of California Press, 1990.

Webb, Amy. *Data, a Love Story: How I Cracked the Online Dating Code to Meet My Match.* New York: Penguin, 2014.

Weigel, Moira. *Labor of Love: The Invention of Dating.* New York: Farrar, Straus and Giroux, 2016

Weiss, Suzannah. "What Is Nice Guy Syndrome? 5 Signs That a Self-Proclaimed 'Nice Guy' Isn't All That Nice." *Bustle,* March 12, 2016.

Wells, Ida B. *Southern Horrors.* New York: New York Age, 1892.

White, Deborah Gray. *Ar'n't I a Woman? Female Slaves in the Plantation South.* New York: Norton, 1985.

———. *Too Heavy a Load: Black Women in Defense of Themselves, 1894–1994.* New York: Norton, 1999.

Whitman, James Q. *Hitler's American Model: The United States and the Making of Nazi Race Law.* Princeton, NJ: Princeton University Press, 2017.

"Why Does It Seem Like Every Dating Site Is a Sausage Fest?" Reddit. May 10, 2015. https://www.reddit.com/r/dating/comments/35jzj5/why_does_it_seem_like_every_dating_site_is_a/.

Wilkins, Amy C. "Becoming Black Women: Intimate Stories and Intersectional Identities." *Social Psychology Quarterly* 75, no. 2 (2012): 173–96.

Wilkinson, Abi. "We Need to Talk about the Online Radicalisation of Young, White Men." *Guardian,* November 15, 2016. www.theguardian.com/commentisfree/2016/nov/15/alt-right-manosphere-mainstream-politics-breitbart.

Williams, Kim M. *Mark One or More: Civil Rights in Multiracial America.* Ann Arbor: University of Michigan Press, 2008.

Wilson, Midge, and Kathy Russell. *Divided Sisters: Bridging the Gap between Black Women and White Women.* New York: Doubleday, 1996

Wolfe, Brendan. "Racial Integrity Laws (1924–1930)." *Encyclopedia Virginia.* Virginia Foundation for the Humanities. 2015. www.encyclopediavirginia.org/racial_integrity_laws_of_the_1920s.

Woodley, Emma. "91% of Surveyed College Students Use Dating Apps for More Than Just Hookups." Global Dating Insights. April 10, 2017. www.globaldatinginsights.com/news/91-of-surveyed-college-students-use-dating-apps-for-more-than-just-hookups/.

Wylie, Kevan R., and Ian Eardley. "Penile Size and the 'Small Penis Syndrome.'" *BJU International* 99, no. 6 (2007): 1449–55.

Yancy, George. *Backlash: What Happens When We Talk Honestly about Racism in America*. Lanham, MD: Rowman and Littlefield, 2018.

Yancey, George A., and Michael O. Emerson. "An Analysis of Resistance to Racial Exogamy: The 1998 South Carolina Referendum." *Journal of Black Studies* 31, no. 5 (2001): 635–50.

Yang, Wesley. *The Souls of Yellow Folk*. New York: Norton, 2018.

Yang, Yi Edward, and Xinsheng Liu. "The 'China Threat' through the Lens of US Print Media: 1992–2006." *Journal of Contemporary China* 21, no. 76 (2012): 695–711.

"The Yellow Terror in All His Glory." Wikimedia Commons. 1899. https://commons.wikimedia.org/wiki/File:YellowTerror.jpg.

Yuh, Ji-Yeon. *Beyond the Shadow of Camptown: Korean Military Brides in America*. New York: New York University Press, 2002.

Zamora, Sylvia. "Racial Remittances: The Effect of Migration on Racial Ideologies in Mexico and the United States." *Sociology of Race and Ethnicity* 2, no. 4 (2016): 466–81.

Zavery, Mihir. "Black Women Now Hold Crowns in 5 Major Beauty Pageants." *New York Times*, December 15, 2019.

Zhang, Qin. "Asian Americans beyond the Model Minority Stereotype: The Nerdy and the Left Out." *Journal of International and Intercultural Communication* 3, no. 1 (2010): 20–37.

Zheng, Robin. "Why Yellow Fever Isn't Flattering: A Case against Racial Fetishes." *Journal of the American Philosophical Association* 2, no. 3 (2016): 400–419.

Zickuhr, Kathryn, and Aaron Smith. *Digital Differences*. Pew Internet and American Life Project. Pew Research Center. April 13, 2012. www.pewinternet.org/wp-content/uploads/sites/9/media/Files/Reports/2012/PIP_Digital_differences_041312.pdf.

Index

Note: Figures are indicated by page numbers in *italics*.

abortion, 58, 246n31

Addams, Jane, 48–49

advertisements: courtship in, 54; matrimonial, 50–52; multiracial persons in, 192, 196

Afrocentrism, 129–30

agency: marriage advertisements and, 51; power inequities and, 59; racial vetting and, 129–36

algorithms, 62, 67, 221–22, 266n7

amalgamation, racial, 16, 28

American Dilemma, An: The Negro Problem and Modern Democracy (Myrdal), 41

Anderson, Carol, 83

anonymity, 4–5, 44, 93

Ansari, Aziz, 78

anti-Blackness, 223; antimiscegenation laws and, 29–44; Asians and, 34; compounded racialized disadvantage and, 106; desirability and, 124–25; digital-sexual racism and, 120, 136, 189; European immigrants and, 38; gender and, 117–20, 257n22; immigration and, 38; LGBTQs and, 208–9, 216; multiracial persons and, 208–10; non-White, 127–29. *See also* Blackness

antimiscegenation laws: anti-Blackness and, 29–44; Asians and, 146; stereotypes of Black men and, 119; civil rights agenda and, 216; dating and, 57; early, 25; gender and, 69; legacy of, 11–12; proliferation of, 27; Whiteness and, 90, 103; women and, 26. *See also Loving v. Virginia*

apps. *See* online dating

Arbery, Ahmaud, 221

Asian Americans: as "acceptable," 145; anti-Blackness among, 128; antimiscegenation laws and, 31–35; Black Americans and, 166; colorism and, 152–53; controlling images of, 90–91, 147; educational attainment and, 148–49, 259n20; femininity and, 146, 158–66, 259n9; fetishization of, 160–61; immigration laws and, 39, 73, 146–48, 259n7; internment of, 40; interracial relationships and, 9, 11, 145; LGBTQ, 151–52, 162–63; likelihood of messaging by, by race, *156, 163;* masculinity and, 74, 78, 144–45, 147, 149–58, 258n2; as "model minority," 100, 145–46, 148, 150; multiracialism and, 195–96, 199–200, *200,* 265n37;

297

Asian Americans *(continued)*
    non-Asian likelihood of messaging, by
        race, *155, 162;* in online dating demo-
        graphics, *71;* segregation and, 148; sex-
        ual racism and, 145–46; stereotypes of, 9,
        88, 147, 150, 159; as unassimilable, 18;
        War Brides Act and, 39–40; Whiteness
        and, 145
Asiatic Barred Zone, 39, 259n7
attraction. *See* beauty; individual preferences

Bagell, Ilana, 63
Bailey, Beth, 55
Baldwin, James, 24
Banks, Ralph Richard, 134–35
beauty: and attractiveness ratings by race,
    117; height and, 73; in partner selection,
    71–74; racialization and, 106; Whiteness
    and, 11, 18, 56, 74. *See also* individual
    preferences
beauty industry, 56
Bedi, Sonu, 4, 220–21
"bed wench," 140
Benjamin, Ruha, 4, 221
bisexuals. *See* LGBTQs
Black Americans: agency of, 129–36; Asian
    Americans and, 166; controlling images
    of, 57, 101, 118–20, 126–27, 139, 143;
    courtship among, 49; "double conscious-
    ness" of, 123–24; experiences of, as dis-
    tinct from other minorities, 121–23; as
    hypervisible, 120–27; interracial relation-
    ships and, 136–39; as invisible, 120–27;
    Latino/as and, 188–89; multiracial per-
    sons and, 201–2, *202;* in online dating
    demographics, *71;* racial vetting and,
    129–36; rejection feelings on part of, in
    online dating, 115–16; stereotypes of, 9.
    See also men, Black; women, Black
Black Is Beautiful, 18
Black Lives Matter, 1, 129, 220–21, 223
Black Love, 18, 156
Blackness: criminalization and, 120; eugen-
    ics and, 32; European immigrants and,
    38; homophily and, 130; hypodescent
    and, 31; immigration and, 37; multiracial
    persons and, 192, 197, 199, 203, 209;
    one-drop rule and, 31; in Reconstruction,
    29. *See also* anti-Blackness
body weight, 106, *107, 109*
Bogardus, Emory, 245n10
Brown University, 61–62
Brown v. Board of Education, 41–42, 193

Broyles, Maude, 24
Buggs, Shantel, 129

"Calof, Abraham, 51
capitalism: colonization and, 25; emotional,
    64, 251n31; intimacy and, early-stage,
    64, 251n31; monogamy and, 58–59
Caste and Class in a Southern Town (Dol-
    lard), 28
caste system, triracial, 29
Chan, Jeffery Paul, 145
Chanda, Rajib, 62
Charleston church shooting, 26
chat rooms, 61
Children of Sánchez, The (Lewis), 170
Childs, Erica Chito, 138
Chin, Frank, 144–45
Chin, Vincent, 149
China Men (Kingston), 144
Chinese Exclusion Act, 39, 146
Chinese immigrants, 31–32, 34–35, 146–47,
    248n40. *See also* Asian Americans
choice. *See* individual preferences
citizenship: Asian immigrants and, 39, 146,
    249n66; intermarriage and, 34–35; Mex-
    ican immigrants and, 36–37; war brides
    and, 147
cisgender, 70
Civil Rights Act of 1964, 41–42
Cold Intimacies (Illouz), 64, 251n31
Collins, Patricia Hill, 4, 10, 74, 118
colonialism, 10, 24–25, 89, 147, 180
"color-blindness," 14, 42–43, 59, 166, 196,
    212, 217
colorism, 128, 138–39, 152–53, 169,
    180–83
compulsory heterosexuality, 103–4
consumerism, 18, 46
consumption: courtship and, 52–60; dating
    and, 64
contraception, 58–59
controlling images, 9–10; of Asian Ameri-
    cans, 90–91, 147; of Black Americans,
    57, 101, 118–20, 126–27, 139, 143;
    digital-sexual racism and, 172; of Latino/
    as, 169–74, 187; of multiracial women,
    191–92. *See also* fetishization
cosmetics, 56
courtship: in advertisements, 54; in age of
    consumption, 52–60; among Black
    Americans, 49; dating *vs.,* 56–58; eco-
    nomics and, 74; as family undertaking,
    46–47; gays and, 54–55; gender and,

69–70, 253n3; gendered racial oppression and, 45; home-calling model for, 45–49; labor and, 53–54; LGBTQs and, 54, 79; matrimonial advertisements and, 50–52; multiracial persons and, 192; normative roles and, 72; racial categories and, 45–46; as transactional, 64; urbanization and, 53–55

COVID-19 pandemic, 149

Crazy Blind Date (app), 221

Crenshaw, Kimberlé, 15

criminalization: anti-miscegenation laws and, 52, 246n33; of Black men, 120; of Mexican immigrants, 36

data, 22–23

date, as term, 55

dating: from courtship, to online, 60–68; courtship and, 55–58; as final frontier of race, 216–17; shopping metaphor in, 64; transactional nature of, 74. See also courtship; online dating

Davenport, Lauren, 264n17

Dávila, Arlene, 169

Dear White People (television program), 192

"deaths of despair," 82, 253n1

de Tocqueville, Alexis, 82

digital-sexual racism: anti-Blackness and, 120, 136, 189; antimiscegenation and, 113; Asian Americans and, 166–67; Black women and, 127; controlling images and, 172; corporate responsibility and, 220–21; defined, 4–5; hypervisibility and, 120–21; individual preferences and, 68, 206; intersectionality and, 215–16; invisibility and, 120–21; Latino/as and, 173–75; multiracial persons and, 198, 210; naturalization of, 206; normalization of, 116; stereotypes and, 171

Dollard, John, 28

"double consciousness," 123–24

Du Bois, W. E. B., 49

educational attainment, 72–73, 109–13, 111–12, 141–42, 148–49, 259n20

education segregation, 17, 41

eHarmony, 67, 70, 252n71

Eng, David, 146–47

entitlement, 83, 93–94, 96–97, 118–19

ethnicity, race vs., 196

eugenics, 27, 30, 32, 36, 43

European immigrants, 37–39. See also Irish immigrants

exoticization: of Asian women, 161; of multiracial persons, 203–6, 212. See also fetishization

Expatriation Act, 34, 39

Family Guy (television program), 170–71

fashion industry, 56, 197

Feagin, Joe, 88

femininity: Asian Americans and, 146, 158–66, 259n9; race and, 9; White, as privilege, 97–101, 98–99; Whiteness and, 56–57, 118. See also women

feminism, 15–16, 58, 100, 140, 144, 154

fetishization: of Asian men, 88; of Asian women, 20, 158–61; of Black men, 120, 125; of Black women, 99; combating, 222; endogamy and, 226; of Latina women, 173; of multiracial persons, 204. See also controlling images; exoticization

Floyd, George, 221

Frazier, E. Franklin, 251n43

From Front Porch to Back Seat (Bailey), 55

Garcia, Rocio, 141–42

gays. See LGBTQs

gender: anti-Blackness and, 117–20, 257n22; colorism and, 138–39; courtship and, 69–70; in dating site demographics, 70–71, 71; desired characteristics and, 106–9, 107–9; interracial relationships and, 9; Latino/as and, 183–85; LGBTQs and, 80–81; messaging in apps and, 75; race and, 69; racial boundary work and, 141–43; racial stereotypes and, 9; and Whiteness preference, 89–90

genocide, 246n31

"ghosting," 77, 94, 125, 134

Glenn, Evelyn Nakano, 53

Grant, Madison, 29–30

Grindr, 62, 88, 255n28

Guess Who's Coming to Dinner (film), 1

Hart Cellar Immigration Act of 1965, 148

hegemonic masculinity, 86, 161, 163–64, 185, 198

hegemonic White femininity, 56, 73, 119

hegemonic Whiteness, 40, 88, 93

height, of men, 73, 108, 110

Hill, Shirley A., 49, 143

Holland, Sharon, 1

homophily, 13, 66–68, 84–85, 102, 258n31, 261n37, 263n20

Hondagneu-Sotelo, Pierrette, 157

"hookup" culture: courtship and, 59–60; Latino/as and, 184; LGBTQs and, 92; online dating history and, 61–62
Hudson, George, 45
hypermasculinity, 9, 57, 120, 125, 259n5
hypervisibility, 120–27
hypodescent, 29–31, 40

Illouz, Eva, 64, 251n31
Imitation of Life (film), 191
Immigration Act of 1924, 30, 38–39
"incels," 96
indentured servitude, 250n2
individualism, 3, 80–81, 100, 196, 216
individual preferences: championing of, 18; civil rights *vs.*, 43; as conditioned, 226; as learned, 226; LGBTQs and neutral, 91–93; *Loving v. Virginia* and, 42; marriage as collective, 46–50; multiracial persons and, 207–8; as personal, 15; predictability of, 215; racialization and, 13, 43, 65; for racial match in partner, *135;* racial segregation and, 3–4; as racism, 14–15, 103, 224–25; sexual racism and, 13–15
intermarriage: Asians and, 147, 161, 196; in colonial Latin America, 169; demographic changes and, 194, 217; immigrants and, 202; increase in, 136, 222; intersectionality and, 9; social distance scale and, 245n10; soldiers and, 147; trends, 105; White approval of, 101
interracial intimate unions: in 21st century, 136–39; current state of, 5–8, *6–7;* demographics of, *10;* as due to lack of exposure to others, 8–11, *10;* intersectionality and, 9; Latino/as and, 169; online dating as biggest source of, 219; public opinion on, 5–6, *6;* as rare, 7; segregation and, 17; as threat to White privilege and power, 16–18; in White gaze, 137. *See also* intermarriage
intersectionality, 9, 101, 123, 169, 174, 215–16
invisibility, 120–27
Irish immigrants, 34, 37–38, 52, 57, 128
Italians, 37–38, 57, 115, 181

Japanese immigrants, 33, 40, 147, 248n40. *See also* Asian Americans
Japanese internment, 40
Jdate, 51
"Jezebel," 126–27

Jim Crow: antimiscegenation laws and, 12, 41; Black men and, 119; Black women and, 127; education and, 34; slavery and, 118; violence and, 28
Johnson, Jack, 251n37
Johnson-Reed Act of 1924, 146
Jones, William Henry, 55

Keith, Verna, 138
Kingston, Maxine Hong, 144
Klinenberg, Eric, 78
Knight, Mark, 119–20
Ku, Esther, 154, 157

Lane, David, 246n31
Latino/as: anti-Blackness among, 128–29; antimiscegenation laws and, 35–37; attractiveness of, by sexual orientation, gender, and race, *175,* 175–76; Black Americans and, 188–89; as "Brown," 169; in Census, 246n13; colorism and, 169, 180–83; controlling images of, 169–74, 187; demographics of, 169; as ethnicity, 196; exclusion of, as daters, 174–79, *175–76, 178–79;* gender and, 183–85; intermarriage with, 169; "Latin lover" image of, 170; LGBTQ, *179,* 188–89; likelihood of messaging by, by race, *178;* likelihood of messaging of, *176;* machismo and, 170; masculinity and, 176, 185; and *"mejorando la raza,"* 89, 180–81; multiracial persons and, 200–201, *201,* 264n26, 265n38; in online dating, 171–74; in online dating demographics, *71;* "outlaw" image of, 170; pan-cultural affinity among, 185–89; "passing," 168–69; stereotypes about, 86; as subservient, 170–71
Lee, Jennifer, 166
lesbians. *See* LGBTQs
Lewis, Oscar, 170
LGBTQs: anti-Blackness and, 208–9, 216; Asian Americans and, 151–52, 162–63; attractiveness ratings, *117;* Black, messaging behavior of, by race of recipient, *132;* Black men and, 125–27; courtship and, 54–55, 79; gender and, 80–81; Latino/a, *179,* 188–89; neutral preference and, 91–93; race and, 79–81; Whiteness and, 91–93
Liebler, Carolyn, 194
Lin, Jeremy, 150–51, 163
Lovegety, 62

Loving, Mildred, 195
Loving v. Virginia, 1, 12, 16, 42–43, 193, 195
Lowe, Lisa, 148
Luna, Joshua, 145
lynching, 27–28, 38, 119, 249n63

Make America Great Again hats, 129
mammy figure, 119, 257n10
marriage: as collective choice, 46–50; matrimonial advertisements and, 50–52; right to, 47; in slavery, 47–48. *See also* antimiscegenation laws; intermarriage; interracial intimate unions
Marriage Guide for Young Men, 45
Marx, Karl, 251n31
masculinity: Asian men and, 74, 78, 144–45, 147, 149–58, 258n2; hegemonic, 86, 161, 163–64, 185, 198; hyper, 9, 57, 120, 125, 259n5; Latinos and, 176, 185; race and, 9; White, 82–83; Whiteness and, 86, 118
mass marketization, 63–65
Match (dating website), 67, 70, 85
matrimonial advertisements, 50–52
McDade, Tony, 221
Meeks, Jeremy, 197
men: height of, 73; as overrepresented on dating sites, 70; prioritization of appearance by, 253n3. *See also* masculinity
men, Black: attractiveness ratings, *117;* criminalization of, 120; likelihood of being messaged in online dating, *122;* messaging of Black women by, *131;* messaging of non-Black women by, *131;* in pornography, 120; sexuality of, 118, 120, 125–27; stereotypes of, 119; White women and, 27. *See also* Black Americans
men, Latino, 170–72, 176, *178,* 183–85
men, White: angry dater archetype of, 93–97; Asian women and, 153–54, 157, 159; attractiveness ratings, *117;* "deaths of despair" among, 82, 253n1; entitlement of, 83, 96–97; masculinity and, 82–83; multiracials and, 198–99, *199,* 265n36; and nonwhite dating partners, 105; popularity of, 83–85, *84–85. See also* Whites
methodology, 22–23
Me Too movement, 28
Mexican immigrants, 36–37, 169–70. *See also* Latino/as
Mexico, 35–36

mixed-race persons. *See* multiracial persons
Modern Romance (Klinenberg and Ansari), 78
monogamy, 57–59
mortality crisis, 82, 253n1
mulatto, 29, 191–92, 195. *See also* multiracial persons
multiracial persons: in advertising, 192, 196; Asian heritage and, 195–96, 199–200, *200,* 265n37; Black Americans and, 201–2, *202;* Blackness and, 197, 203; controlling images of, 191–92; courtship and, 192; defined, 194–96; dissection of, 203–6; exoticization of, 203–6, 212; in fashion, 197; Latino/as and, 200–201, *201,* 264n26, 265n38; as majority, 193; positioning of, in cyberspace, *197–202,* 198–203; racialization and, 196–97, 203–7, 211–12; representation of, 196–97; White men and, 198–99, *199,* 265n36; Whiteness and, 191–92, 195, 211; White women and, 198, *199*
Myrdal, Gunnar, 41

Nagel, Joane, 10
Nemoto, Kumiko, 157, 161
neoliberalism, 4–5, 113
Newman, Alyssa, 203
Nobles, Melissa, 195
Nuremburg Laws, 246n33

Obama, Barack, 193
obesity, 106, *107, 109,* 119
octoroon, 29. *See also* multiracial persons
Ohanian, Alexis, 140
OkCupid, 67, 70, 221
"one-drop rule," 30–31, 40, 191–92
online dating: acceptance of, 62–63; from courtship to, 60–68; history of, 61–62; homophily and, 66–68; mass marketization and, 63–65; messaging in, 75–79; removal of race filters in, 220–21; social change and, 217. *See also* dating
online disinhibition effect, 93, 245n2
Origins Act of 1924, 39
Osaka, Naomi, 120
outmarriage. *See* interracial intimate unions
overweight, 106, *107, 109*

Page, Horace D., 33
Page Act, 33, 39, 146–47
Pascoe, Peggy, 26
"passing," 16, 168–69, 191

Passing of the Great Race, The (Grant), 29–30
patriarchy, 15, 26, 49, 89, 95, 97, 103–4, 157–58, 164
Perez v. Sharp, 40
Philadelphia Negro, The (Du Bois), 49
physical factors, 71–74
"picture brides," 248n40
pornography, 95, 120
"postracial," 193, 196–97, 215, 223, 225
preferences. *See* individual preferences
privilege. *See* White privilege
purity, racial, 25, 29–30, 137, 191, 215

quadroon, 29. *See also* multiracial persons

race: antimiscegenation laws and, 16; colonialism and, 24–25; desired characteristics and, 106–9, *107–9;* doing, 224–26; femininity and, 9; future of, 222–24; gender and, 69; "hookup" culture and, 59–60; interracial relationships and, 9; LGBTQs and, 79–81; masculinity a, 9; multiracialism and, 194–96; social construction of, 246n13
race dilution, 30, 137
racial amalgamation, 16, 28
racial boundary work, 141–43
racial categories, 45–46, 206–12
racial choice narratives, 13–15
racial classifications, 29, 194–95
racial consciousness, 133
Racial Integrity Act (Virginia), 38, 41–42, 195
racialization: after World War II, 40; beauty and, 106; color-blind racism and, 14; courtship and, 60; dating marketplace and, 83–88; expectations and, 172; family and, 17; femininity and, 120, 158–66; fetishization and, 125; homogeneity and, 158; hookup culture and, 92–93; immigrants and, 36–39; individual preference and, 13, 43, 65, 112, 177; labor and, 53; and miscegenation as term, 28; multiracial persons and, 196–97, 203–7, 211–12; pornography and, 120; "private racism" and, 4; slavery and, 26; stereotypes and, 90–91, 184
racial purity, 25, 29–30, 137, 191, 215
racial segregation: antimiscegenation laws and, 30, 41; Asian Americans and, 148; courtship and, 60; individual preference and, 3–4; interracial intimacy and, 17; and lack of exposure to others, 8; Madi-

son Grant and, 30; persistence of, 8; of schools, 17, 34, 41; self-, of Whites, 111; Whiteness and, 101. *See also Brown v. Board of Education*
racial vetting, 129–36
racism: color-blind, 14; "new," 4, 119–20; preferences and, 14–15, 224–25; "private," 4; structural, 16. *See also* anti-Blackness; digital-sexual racism; sexual racism
Ramos, Carlos, 120
rape, 26, 28, 118–19
Reconstruction, 12, 16, 27, 29, 118
Rich, Adrienne, 103–4
Roberts, Dorothy, 17
Robinson, Brandon, 4–5
Rodger, Elliot, 96
Roof, Dylan, 26
Roosevelt, Franklin, 40
Rudder, Christian, 67

Said, Edward, 259n9
school segregation, 17, 34, 41
segregation. *See* racial segregation
sexuality: antimiscegenation laws and, 25; Asian, 147; of Asian women, 159; of Black men, 118; Black parents and, 49; controlling images and, 10; courtship and, 46; poverty and, 48; urbanization and, 54
sexual racism: anonymity and, 4–5; Asian Americans and, 145–46, 153; origin of term, 15; preferences as, 103; racial choice narratives and, 13–15. *See also* digital-sexual racism
shopping metaphor, 64
Slater, Dan, 66
slavery: anti-Blackness and, 118; antimiscegenation laws and, 12; interracial marriage and, 26; interracial relations and, 26; mammy figure and, 119; marriage in, 47–48; sexual objectification and, 118; women and, 53, 127, 140
social-contact theory, 93, 218
social distance scale, 245n10
socioeconomic factors, 71–74, 117, 157. *See also* educational attainment
Souls of Yellow Folk, The (Yang), 157
status-exchange theory, 117
Stember, Charles, 15–16
stereotypes, 9, 145; Asian American, 147, 150, 159; Black women, 100–101, 119–20; digital-sexual racism and, 171; masculinity and, 86; multiracial persons, 191–92; racialization and, 90–91

Takaki, Ronald, 32
Taylor, Breonna, 221
Thompson, Maxine, 138
Tinder, 62, 70, 87, 116, 218
Torney, Jim, 24
"tragic mulatto," 191–92
Tran, J. T., 151
transgender identities, 70. See also LGBTQs
Treitler, Vilna Bashi, 34, 37
triracial caste system, 29
Trump, Donald, 149, 160

"Unite the Right" rally, 43–44
urbanization, 53–55
U.S.-Mexican War, 35–36

vetting, racial, 129–36
Voting Rights Act of 1965, 41–42

Waller, Willard, 64, 74
War Brides Act of 1945, 39–40
Waring, Chandra, 207
Weber, Max, 251n31
Wesleyan University, 62–63
"White bondage," 251n37
White gaze, 10–11, 137, 145–46, 191–92, 219, 246n23
White genocide, 246n31
Whiteness: Asian Americans and, 145; as baseline, 9, 118; colonialism and, 25; European immigrants and, 37–38; femininity and, 56–57; framing oneself against, 88–91; hegemonic, 86, 88, 93; homophily and, 84–85; LGBTQs and, 91–93; masculinity and, 86; Mexican immigrants and, 36–37; minority women and, 202–3; multiracial persons and, 191–92, 195, 211; "one-drop rule" and, 30–31; and racialized dating marketplace, 83–88; White preference for, 101–6, 102, 105
White privilege: "angry White males" and, 93; femininity and, 97–101, 98–99; gendered aspects of, 98; interracial intimacy as threat to, 16–18; racial classification and, 29
Whites: as American, 88; antimiscegenation laws and, 12; cultural norms among, 90–91; as minority, 193, 217; in online dating demographics, 71; stereotypes about, 90–91. See also men, White; women, White
"white shariah," 96–97
White Slave Traffic Act, 251n37
White supremacy, 31, 38, 96–97, 127–28, 134, 145–46, 165; anti-Blackness and, 34–35; antimiscegenation laws and, 17, 41–44; eugenics and, 30; gendered, 28
Williams, Serena, 120, 140
women: contraception and, 59; feminism and, 58; and men's height, 73; prioritization of economic status by, 253n3; as proportion of users, 70–71; Whiteness and minority, 202–3; in workforce, 53–54. See also femininity
women, Black: attractiveness ratings, 117; Chinese men and, 34; colorism and, 138; interracial unions and, 137; as "Jezebel," 126–27; likelihood of being messaged in online dating, 121; mammy figure and, 119, 257n10; message response likelihood among, by race, 131; in pornography, 120; rejection expectations of, 134–35; sexual exploitation of, in slavery, 26; sexuality of, 126–27; in slavery, 118; stereotypes about, 100–101, 119–20; "unrapeability" of, 118–19. See also Black Americans
women, Latina, 170–74, 178
women, multiracial: admiration of, 197; controlling images of, 191–92
women, White: Asian Americans and, 163–64; attractiveness ratings, 117; Black men and, 27; educational attainment and, 109–13, 111; homophily among, 87; multiracials and, 198, 199; policing sexuality of, 25–26; as privileged, 97–101, 98–99; racial preferences of, 107–8. See also Whites
World War II, 39–40, 147

Yang, Wesley, 157

Zheng, Robin, 161

Founded in 1893,
UNIVERSITY OF CALIFORNIA PRESS
publishes bold, progressive books and journals
on topics in the arts, humanities, social sciences,
and natural sciences—with a focus on social
justice issues—that inspire thought and action
among readers worldwide.

The UC PRESS FOUNDATION
raises funds to uphold the press's vital role
as an independent, nonprofit publisher, and
receives philanthropic support from a wide
range of individuals and institutions—and from
committed readers like you. To learn more, visit
ucpress.edu/supportus.